Penguin Handbooks
London Shopping Guide

Elsie Burch Donald is an American who grew
up in the 'deep South' and has lived in
Britain for seven years.

She went to Edinburgh University and has
worked as a journalist and in publishing, both in
London and New York. She has also worked in the
field of documentary films.

London Shopping Guide is her first book.

London
Shopping
Guide

Elsie Burch Donald

Third Edition

Penguin Books

Penguin Books Ltd, Harmondsworth,
Middlesex, England
Penguin Books, 625 Madison Avenue, New York,
New York 10022, U.S.A.
Penguin Books Australia Ltd, Ringwood,
Victoria, Australia
Penguin Books Canada Ltd, 2801 John Street,
Markham, Ontario, Canada L3R 1B4
Penguin Books (N.Z.) Ltd, 182–190 Wairau Road,
Auckland 10, New Zealand

First published 1975
Reprinted with revisions 1976
Second edition 1977
Third edition 1979

Made and printed in Great Britain by
Hazell Watson & Viney Ltd, Aylesbury, Bucks
Set in Monotype Baskerville

For my grandmother,
Sarah Polk Burch

Contents

Contents

Contents

Contents

Contents

Author's note

About prices: writing during inflationary times, I have on the whole tried to avoid mentioning prices since they quickly go out of date. Instead, there is a simple coding system based on the pound sign [£] and the plus sign [+]. To indicate whether a shop is up-market, middle market or cut rate, [£££], [££] and [£] are used respectively. These are often followed by a + to indicate an upward latitude.

Prices are compared *within* given categories only. If a category has no real variation in price, then the signs are omitted. Two exceptions to the rule of not mentioning prices exist: when the cost of an item or service may be of interest from the standpoint of general information, it is included. For example, few people may know whether a billiard table costs £50 or £1,500 so its price is an interesting fact, even if it is somewhat out of date. The second exception concerns hairdressers and beauty treatments and is fully explained in the text.

About locations: in choosing the entries for this book some consideration was given to locality. A centrally-located source of goods was chosen over a similar source located outside central London on the basis it is easier for more people to get to.

Locations of shops can change without much notice, especially when new leases mean sudden jumps in rent. Therefore, if you are going to an out-of-the way shop, ring up first and make certain of the shop's location and its hours.

About catalogues: catalogues, when available, are mentioned under the entry and it is reasonably safe to assume that, unless stated otherwise, the catalogue is free. But shops can only maintain this service if it makes good business sense. Catalogues are expensive to produce and to post and a deluge of requests that result in very few orders make free catalogues commercially unviable. Therefore, do not send off for a catalogue unless you are honestly interested in purchasing the items it covers. Catalogues are one good custom the world may well corrupt.

Your comments

If you have a shop or special service – or know of one – that you feel would be a useful addition to this book, then please fill out the form and send it to us so that the information can be considered for inclusion in a future edition.

Furthermore, if you find any information given in the book is no longer pertinent or correct your help in letting us know would be appreciated.

To: Elsie Burch Donald
London Shopping Guide
Penguin Books
Harmondsworth
Middlesex

Name of firm: ....

Address: ....

....

Telephone: ....

Comments: ....

....

....

....

....

....

....

....

....

....

Sender's Name: ....

Address: ....

Chart of clothing sizes

Dresses, coats, suits and blouses (*Women*)

British	10	12	14	16	18	20
American	8	10	12	14	16	18
Continental						
French	40	42	44	46	48	50
Italian	44	46	48	50	52	54

Suits and overcoats (*Men*)

British	34	36	38	40	42	44
American	same					
Continental	44	46	48	50	52	54

Shirts (*Men*)

British	14	14½	15	15½	16	16½	17	17½
American	same							
Continental	36	37	38	39	40	41	42	43

Hats

British	6⅝	6¾	6⅞	7	7⅛	7¼	7⅜	7½	7⅝
American	same								
Continental	54	55	56	57	58	59	60	61	62

Shoes (*Men*) for ½ sizes add ½ to preceding number

British	6	7	8	9	10	11
American	7	8	9	10	11	12
Continental	39½	40½	41½	42½	43½	44½

Shoes (*Women*) for ½ sizes add ½ to preceding number

British	3	4	5	6	7	8	9
American	4½	5½	6½	7½	8½	9½	10½
Continental	35	36	37	38	39	40	41

Chart of clothing sizes

Socks

British	$9\frac{1}{2}$	10	$10\frac{1}{2}$	11	$11\frac{1}{2}$	12	$12\frac{1}{2}$
American	same
Continental	38-39	39-40	40-41	41-42	42-43	43-44	44-45

Stockings

British	8	$8\frac{1}{2}$	9	$9\frac{1}{2}$	10	$10\frac{1}{2}$	11
American	same
Continental	0	1	2	3	4	5	6	(as well as British-American style)

Gloves   same in all countries

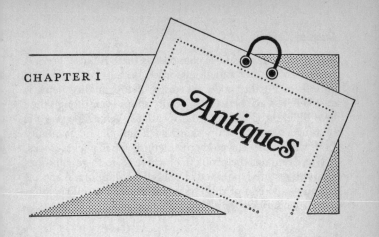

CHAPTER I

Antiques

London is the antique capital of the world and whether you are searching for a particular item or merely looking for something that strikes your fancy there is a better chance of finding it here than almost anywhere. There are four ways to go antique shopping in London and choosing the right one depends upon your motivation. Three of the methods are dealt with in this chapter and the fourth (auctions) in Chapter 2.

If you just want to look around the best thing to do is visit the antique streets or comb the antique supermarkets. There are six 'antique streets' in London and each has a distinctly different flavour created by the many little shops that cluster along it. The antique 'supermarkets' also have characters all their own. These are large indoor markets housing a variety of individually owned and operated stalls. Supermarkets are especially fine shopping places for all sorts of small objects like silver, bric-à-brac and china. They are, of course, ideal for rainy day shopping.

If, however, you know exactly what you want you can go straight to an antique specialty shop. Specialty shops are time savers. They make it easier to find a large selection of goods in one narrow field and for this reason they are useful to collectors, investors and house furnishers alike. *But they are rarely the source of big bargains.* Antique specialists know their stuff so there is little chance – as there is in the general market – of getting something for less because of the dealer's ignorance. Furthermore, the price of top quality items is less likely to vary between specialty shops even though they have different characters and locations. What does vary is the range. Some specialty shops stock only the finest quality goods while others try to keep something for all pocket-books.

There remains the problem of where to go to get antiques repaired, restored, polished or packed for shipping. A special section at the end of this chapter is devoted to information about such services for all types of antiques.

The antique streets

THE KING'S ROAD, SW3, SW6, and SW10. It takes a lot of stamina to really 'do' the King's Road since half a mile of it is devoted mainly to antique shops. Happily, they are divided into three fairly distinct blocs. The first begins at CHELSEA TOWN HALL (opposite Sydney Street) and continues west to MILMAN'S STREET. This is a good area for eighteenth- and early nineteenth-century English furniture. There are nearly twenty shops to choose from and the quality of most is good to excellent. Notable among them are **Jeremy** and **Heath-Bullock** for fine furniture and the **Chelsea Antique Market** for various small pieces and *objets d'art*. This is the most exclusive end of the King's Road. [££+] Further west between the junction of WORLD'S END and TETCOTT ROAD the ambiance changes dramatically. The emphasis is still on furniture but here it is stripped pine and bargain furniture. The line between 'antique' and 'secondhand' diminishes and prices are lower – particularly at the labyrinth **Furniture Cave** where profit is dependent on volume of turnover. [£] Across the viaduct past TETCOTT ROAD the scene changes again. The wares in these shops are mixed and as a result this end of the King's Road is more interesting for the general shopper who wants to browse around. Seventeenth-century oak coffers are cheek-by-jowl with ormolu commodes and stripped pine washstands. You can also find a lot more bric-à-brac and small decorative pieces here. A few of the shops are posh but on the whole the atmosphere is informal and relaxed. Prices are mixed. [££]

KENSINGTON CHURCH STREET, W8 is just the right size for shoppers who don't want to suffer from saturation or exhaustion. Start at the NOTTING HILL GATE end of the street and it is all down-hill. Kensington Church Street is an excellent source of good antique furniture, especially English period furniture, and it is the best street in London for porcelain. There are five specialists in Chinese porcelain alone. It is also a good street for continental furniture, chandeliers, pictures and collectors' glass. The quality of most of the goods tends to be high, and prices are medium to high. [££+] When you reach the bottom of the street, if you still want to see more turn left into Kensington High Street and visit the **Antique Hypermarket** whose stock is of the same quality and type (this market is treated in more detail under Supermarkets).

CAMDEN PASSAGE, N1. Located slightly off the beaten track in Islington, Camden Passage is a good source of reasonably-priced antiques of all kinds but particularly Victorian and Edwardian things. There is some furniture but most of the items in the shops and outdoor stands in this market tend to be small decorative objects like silver frames, cosmetic bottles, jewellery and assorted bric-à-brac. Three days a week there is a large open air market: on Wednesdays and Saturdays for general antiques and on Fridays for books. [£]+

PORTOBELLO ROAD and WESTBOURNE GROVE, W11. The Saturday antique market on the Portobello Road is world-famous. Hundreds of stalls and barrows selling all sorts of ornaments and *objets d'art* line the pavements and fill the arcades from CHEPSTOW VILLAS down to ELGIN CRESCENT. Prices are more or less standard so don't expect to find the same item much cheaper in one stall than another. It is perfectly acceptable to haggle but this has been over-emphasized in numerous guide books and has resulted in annoyance to dealers and customers, so if a dealer sticks to a price accept it or don't buy (usually dealers will reduce a price once). Most of the antiques in the Portobello Road are nineteenth-century decorative items of every conceivable kind: silver seems to predominate. There are also clocks, china, prints, brass, Victoriana and some furniture. During the week several of the permanent shops along the road are open for business and if you don't mind the reduced quantity it can be more agreeable to shop then and avoid the madding crowd.

Portobello Road intersects with WESTBOURNE GROVE and this street is a good area for late nineteenth-century furniture. There are also a couple of early English furniture shops and a smattering of junk shops but, generally, the character is Edwardian. [££]

FULHAM ROAD, SW3, SW10. There are several good eighteenth- and early nineteenth-century furniture shops along the Fulham Road between the intersections of REDCLIFFE ROAD and SYDNEY PLACE. Many of the dealers are members of the prestigious British Antique Dealers Association and the quality is therefore very high, while the overheads are not as steep as in similar shops in Mayfair or Belgravia. [££+]

Bermondsey Market, Long Lane, SE1. Once a week on Friday mornings at sunrise some 450 antique-laden stalls blossom forth on two vacant lots south of the river. Bermondsey market is a seed-bed of the English antique trade and much of the stock in London's many antique shops originates here. This is particularly true of late nineteenth-century decorative items. Officially the market opens at 7 a.m. but trading begins between dealers long before that. It is said that an item can be sold by a dealer at 5 a.m. and before the market closes at 1 p.m. it will have been traded four or five times and will eventually be sold the following day to an American in the Portobello Road.

This is a slight exaggeration but there is certainly a lot of trading between exhibiting dealers at Bermondsey and most of the visitors are dealers from elsewhere. Prices are lower, but not *significantly* lower, than in Portobello and Camden Passage. The main reason dealers get to the market so early is to get the pick of the crop and hear all the trade gossip. There is a good chance of getting a *real* bargain at Bermonsey if you know your antiques. Items often make their first London appearance here and sometimes they are much more valuable than the person selling them realizes. [£, ££]

Antique supermarkets

Antique Hypermarket, 26 Kensington High Street, w8 (937-8426). The sixty or seventy stands in this market sell a variety of antiques of good quality. There is a lot of furniture ranging from seventeenth-century oak and eighteenth- and nineteenth-century mahogany to selected pine and country furniture. There is a sizeable silver vault and a mass of decorative pieces: clocks, porcelain, pictures, dolls, jewellery and jade. Everything is guaranteed to be over 100 years old and if the period or description of any item is misrepresented the Hypermarket will refund the customer's money. Unlike many markets, this one is mostly a retail market and it is recommended for variety and quality rather than bargains. [££+]

Antique Supermarket, 3 Barrett Street, w1 (486-1439). While the wares in the Hypermarket mentioned above are akin to those in nearby Kensington Church Street, the wares in the sixty stalls of the Antique Supermarket resemble those on the Portobello Road. In fact, several dealers here have stalls in Portobello. The Antique Supermarket was one of the first indoor antique markets and it is often described as a dealers' market because all the resident dealers enjoy trading their wares among themselves. The stock is all mid-nineteenth century or later and although there is furniture in the basement the tendency is towards bric-à-brac which occupies less space and sells faster. There is quite a lot of silver and antique jewellery as well as some prints and art nouveau and art deco pieces. One stall specializes in antique fans and another in samplers. Prices tend to be slightly lower here than in the other supermarkets. [££]

Antiquarius, 15 Flood Street, sw 3 (351-1145), on the corner of the King's Road is the largest of the supermarkets (over 200 stalls) and the tone is trendy, in keeping with the Chelsea location. Antiquarius features art nouveau, art deco, clothes from the twenties and thirties and other items only recently christened 'antique'. It also houses silver, small pieces of furniture and some good antique jewellery. [££]

Furniture Cave, 533 King's Road, sw 10 (352-5373), is about the cheapest place in London to buy stripped pine tables, cupboards, dressers, kitchen chairs and large pieces of Edwardian furniture. There is plenty of secondhand furniture as well. The Cave occupies an old warehouse built around an open courtyard in which the stripping is done. The owners and staff are all jean-clad young people and are informal and pleasant if not always efficient. They rely on volume of business rather than getting the 'going' price and this system seems satisfactory from everybody's point of view. There is a small fee for deliveries. [£]

Chelsea Antique Market, 245A King's Road, sw 3 (352-9695), has stalls with small items of good quality – silver, brass, etc. – and some furniture. Buy here if you can't find it anywhere else, but you will certainly have to pay for it. [££ +]

Antique specialty shops

A note about specialty shops: remember that specialty shops almost by definition, tend to be up-market, so if you want something old but inexpensive, decorative but not 'important' try the markets and the auctions (Chapter 2) first.

Antique architectural items

Crowther of Syon Lodge, Busch Corner, Isleworth, Middx (560-7987), have the largest supply of architectural items in London: carved chimneypieces, grates, complete Georgian panelled rooms, wrought iron staircases, and entrance gates. Try them for anything. Large catalogue. Expensive. [£££]

Crowther and Son, 282 North End Road, Fulham, sw6 (385-1375), cousins of the Crowther listed above, are specialists in the same sort of thing: seventeenth- and eighteenth-century oak panelled rooms; elegant interior doors and frames and imposing entrance doors; and ornamental iron balconies and stairways. [£££]

Pratt and Burgess, 7 Old Brompton Road, sw7 (589-8501), and

H. W. Poulter and Sons, 279 Fulham Road, sw10 (352-7268), specialize in chimneypieces in carved wood or marble. They also sell antique grates, fenders and fire-backs and will replace hearths and cut any piece to size. [££+]

Thornhill Galleries, 76 New King's Road, sw6 (736-5830), and

J. Crotty, 74 New King's Road, sw6 (385-1789), sell period chimneypieces, grates and fire-backs. These shops are next to one another so between them there is a good selection to choose from. Also brass fire tools and lanterns. [££+]

Thornhill Galleries, 78 Deodar Road, sw15 (874-2101)

are another source of English and French panelling and
wood and marble chimneypieces. Thornhill have their own
craftsmen to install pieces and to adapt panelling to fit
rooms. [££+]

Antiquities (see also Oriental art, page 44,
   Ethnographic art, page 37, and Glass, page 40)

Charles Ede, 37 Brook Street, w1 (493-4944), has the
best range of classical, pre-classical and Coptic art in London. This gallery is especially geared to small collectors and
teaching collections and prices range from £10 to around
£2,000. Charles Ede publishes an illustrated catalogue
eight times a year. Four issues treat one special subject such
as Roman glass or Cypriot pottery and four are a general
stock list. The special subject catalogues have useful intro-
ductions to the subject covered. A catalogue subscription
fee is charged. [££+]

Bruce McAlpine, 15c Clifford Street, w1 (734-4202),
sells fine quality Greek, Roman and Egyptian antiquities to
museums, serious private collectors and the very rich. [£££]

Davies Antiques, Stall 37, 124 New Bond Street, w1
(493-5657). Pottery lamps, scarabs, Roman glass, terracottas, fossils and Cypriot and Greek pots line the walls and
fill the counter of this stall in the Bond Street Antique
Centre. These are not important pieces. Prices start at £2,
making it an excellent source for *anyone* who is fascinated by
the past. Mr and Mrs Davies make a point of keeping a
supply of very inexpensive pieces especially for children.
[££]

Jonathan Mankowitz, 49 Chiltern Street, w1 (486-
5168). Egyptian, Classical, pre-Columbian and African
works of art of quality. [££+]

Coins and Antiquities, 20–22 Maddox Street, w1
(629-9835). The atmosphere in these first-floor premises is
rather like a library and many books on antiquities and
coins are, in fact, for sale, but most of the cases and shelves

contain ancient artifacts ranging from lead seals and glass tear bottles (about £4) to fine Greek amphorae (at £1,000) and ancient coins of all kinds. An annual catalogue of antiquities and coins in stock is available for 50p and £1 respectively. [££]

Robin Symes, 3 Ormond Yard, Duke of York Street, sw1 (930-9856), is out of the reach of most people, including many collectors and dealers, but no list of antiquity dealers is complete without him. Some of the finest works of art of the ancient world pass through this gallery, usually *en route* to museums. [£££]

Arms and armour

E. Fairclough, 61 South Audley Street, w1 (493-3946). Antique arms of all kinds: arquebuses, crossbows, European and Japanese swords. Japanese sword furniture, pistols and full suits of armour. [££+]

Angel Armoury, 320 Upper Street, n1 (226-5155), have over 1,000 antique military items in stock. There are percussion, flintlock and matchlock guns, edged weapons from most countries, and full suits of European armour. [££+]

Peter Dale, 11 Royal Opera Arcade, Pall Mall, sw1 (930-3695). A small shop full of excellent specimens of antique arms and armour. [££+]

Art nouveau and art deco (see also Glass, page 40, and Pottery and porcelain, page 46)

Editions Graphiques, 3 Clifford Street, w1 (734-3944), **John Jesse**, 164 Kensington Church Street, w8 (229-1978), and

Chiu, 10 Charlton Place, Camden Passage, n1 (359-1055). These three galleries exhibit the finest designs of the art nouveau and art deco periods. The art glass, ceramics, sculpture, furniture and jewellery are by Mackintosh,

Hoffman, Gallé, Daum and others, or from the workshops of Liberty and Tiffany. **Chiu** is almost entirely art deco while **John Jesse** is half deco and half nouveau. **Editions Graphiques** has the largest stock and also functions as an art gallery with regular exhibitions of quality posters and prints from the period between the 1880s and 1930s. All three galleries are expensive. [£££]

Giselle Menhenett, 198 Westbourne Grove, W11 (707-8708). Flower-shaped lamps and colourful hanging lamps give this shop the air of a strange and fanciful garden. Dotted among beaded curtains and palms are wicker furniture, umbrella stands and bric-à-brac typical of turn-of-the-century fashion. [££]

Autographs (see also Secondhand, rare and antique books, page 75)

Winifred Myers, Suite 52, 91 St Martin's Lane, WC2 (836-1940), is London's most important dealer in autographs. The boxes that line the walls of her office contain the private and public correspondence of major literary, political, military, musical and scientific figures of the past 500 years. With perhaps the understandable exception of Napoleon, the letters and documents are all English. A catalogue is available. All prices.

Books (see Books, Chapter 3)

Boxes

H. A. Osborne, Stall 29, Hildreth's Arcade, 139–49 Portobello Road, W11. Wooden boxes of all sorts: writing slopes, tea caddies, jewellery and vanity cases and humidors. The average price is around £35. Open Saturdays only. No phone. [£+]

S. J. Phillips, 139 Bond Street, W1 (629-6261), have a

good selection of fine quality eighteenth- and nineteenth-century gold, silver and enamel boxes originally designed for spice, snuff, money and smelling salts. All are delicately-wrought and all are expensive. [£££]

Keith Harding, 93 Hornsey Road, N7 (607-6181), are specialists in musical boxes. They have a four-storey building full of them. Harding's are the biggest restorers of musical boxes in the world and publish a spare parts catalogue. They also stock all books in print about musical boxes, clocks and mechanical musical instruments. [££]

Brass (see Metalware, page 43)

Carpets and rugs (see also Auctions, Chapter 2, and Carpets and rugs, page 204)

Vigo-Sternberg, 6A Vigo Street, W1 (493-1228). Despite its imposing appearance, not all the stock in this Mayfair gallery is expensive and every kind of old and antique rug from Persian and Caucasian (including tribal rugs) to Chinese, European and Indian carpets can be found here. The staff are helpful and responsive to serious customers. In fact, only serious customers should visit carpet galleries because the stock must be laboriously unrolled for viewing. Prices at Vigo-Sternberg start at about £50 and go up to £20,000, but £200 is more the norm. [££+]

David Black, 96 Portland Road, W11 (727-2566), specializes in village and tribal rugs from Persia, Turkey, the Caucasus and Russian Turkestan. There is a large stock of kelims. This gallery is informal and rugs are often displayed out on the pavement in true souk style. The proprietor is a young man who tries to keep a good number of less expensive rugs on hand as well as fine collectors' items. Open afternoons only. [££]

Benardout and Benardout, 7 Thurloe Place, SW7 (584-7658). Selling Oriental carpets has been the Benardout family's business since 1908. They have a good selection of secondhand and antique rugs and carpets from £50. [££]

C. John, 70 South Audley Street, w1 (493-5288), is the doyen of London's antique rug business. The two floors of his gallery carry fine quality rugs of all kinds. There is an especially good stock of Savonnerie and Aubusson carpets and it is said that Mr John will give you a very reasonable price if he has a mind to. [£££]

Bond Street Carpets, 31 New Bond Street, w1 (629-7825), is operated by Mrs Madga Shapiro, a Hungarian, who keeps a good stock of Oriental carpets at fair prices and twice a year (in January and July) holds a big sale with many substantial reductions. [££]

Caroline Bosly, 13 Princess Road, nw1 (722-7608). Oriental carpet broker with access to a vast warehouse of secondhand and antique rugs as well as new ones. (For details see under Carpets and rugs, page 206.) [££]

Chandeliers and lighting fixtures

Crick, 166 Kensington Church Street, w8 (229-1338), has London's largest stock of antique cut-glass and ormolu chandeliers. Only a small percentage of the store's total stock is on display in the Kensington Church Street shop (a tiny bit more can be seen at Mrs Crick's sister's shop, 87 Marylebone High Street). Be warned that Crick's is an eccentric establishment and anyone coming in off the street is likely to find his queries unanswered. It is therefore advisable to make an appointment with Mrs Crick beforehand. Those who are listed in Debrett may then find the going fairly smooth but others, particularly Americans, had better tread carefully. [££+]

Christopher Wray, 600 King's Road, sw6 (736-8008). About 80 per cent of the enormous stock of Victorian and Edwardian fixtures at Christopher Wray's are of the period. The rest are quality reproductions. Literally hundreds of hanging lamps, bracket lamps and student lamps in brass and steel with colourful glass shades cover the walls and ceiling. All old lamps have been restored to mint condition and most have been electrified. Although it is possible to get the odd Victorian light fixture for less elsewhere you won't find the selection you get here. Prices range from £5 to around £200. The shop also sells replacement parts for oil and gas lamps and electrical parts for their conversion and you can get reproduction glass shades, globes and chimneys in a variety of shapes and sizes. [££]

W. G. T. Burne, 11 Elystan Street, SW3 (589-6074), specializes in eighteenth- and early nineteenth-century crystal chandeliers of the finest quality. They cost, on average, about £2,500 and can run much higher. The store also carries antique English and Irish table glass. Mr Burne is a man of the highest reputation. He is also helpful and willing to talk about antique glass to those who are interested. [£££]

Woodall and Emery, Haywards Heath Road, Balcombe, W. Sussex (044-483-608), has been a family business since 1884 and is now operated by Mr Emery and his daughter. Recently the firm moved from the central London premises which had been Mr Emery's grandfather's house. The new address comprises a huge showroom and two large storage sheds. They are all chock-a-block with period and second-hand chandeliers and bracket fixtures, the majority of which are ormolu. Most of the firm's business is with the trade, especially decorators, since Mr Emery specializes in providing lighting fixtures for rooms or entire houses. He will visit you free of charge to give advice and estimates for chandeliers and other fixtures. [££+]

Pratt and Burgess, 7 Old Brompton Road, SW7 (589-8501), and

H. W. Poulter and Sons, 279 Fulham Road, SW10 (352-7268). Although both of these firms deal primarily in chimneypieces, they also stock fine seventeenth- and eighteenth-century brass chandeliers and lanterns. These are very expensive. [£££]

China (see under Pottery and porcelain, page 46)

Clocks, watches, barometers and scientific instruments

Aubrey Brocklehurst, 124 Cromwell Road, SW7 (373-0319),

Camerer Cuss, 54–6 New Oxford Street, WC1 (636-8968), and

E. Hollander, 80 Fulham Road, SW3 (589-7239), are all specialists in eighteenth- and early nineteenth-century English longcase and bracket clocks. All three sell barometers and have workshops on the premises to repair and restore clocks. Repairs, unfortunately, can take from three to six months. Unlike many antique dealers these men are not just merchants but craftsmen who understand the intricacies of their wares. They are helpful, reputable and willing to talk about their speciality. **Camerer Cuss** has an occasional seventeenth-century clock and some watches while **Brocklehurst** stocks scientific instruments. [££+]

Strike One, 1A Camden Walk, N1 (226-9709), deal in English eighteenth- and nineteenth-century clocks and although they have clocks of fine quality they carry some items in a moderate range. Usually about fifty clocks in stock. First-class repairs. [££]

Philip and Bernard Dombey, 174 Kensington Church Street, W8 (229-7100), specialize in French clocks from the seventeenth to the nineteenth century. Normally there are some 700 clocks in stock: Sèvres porcelain, bronze, ormolu and buhl. The shop keeps a colour photo album of about sixty clocks which it will send out on loan for a deposit of £10. [££+]

Huggins and Horsey, 26 Beauchamp Place, SW3 (788-4641), deal exclusively in French clocks, particularly the period Napoleon I to III. They have carriage clocks too. A huge amount of their business is in exports (£65,000 in 1972 alone) and prices are not exorbitant since Huggins and Horsey depend upon volume for their profit. They estimate that their entire stock changes every fortnight. [££+]

A. E. Gould, 193 King's Road, sw3 (352-8739), usually has as many as thirty early nineteenth-century barometers in stock and sometimes an earlier piece. Nearly all are the banjo variety. [££+]

Graus, 125 New Bond Street, w1 (629-6680), is a Mecca for antique watch collectors. There are pocket and chatelaine watches from the sixteenth-century and diamond Cartier wrist watches from the thirties but the main emphasis is on antique enamel watches and watches with unusual movements. Graus also sells antique fans. [£££]

Harriet Wynter, 352 King's Road, sw3 (352-6494), is London's most important dealer in medical, navigational, astronomical, mathematic and measuring instruments and devices. All are quality pieces. A catalogue is available. [££+]

Ronald A. Lee, 1 Bruton Place, w1 (629-5600), have seventeenth- and eighteenth-century English clocks of museum quality. Early barometers on occasion. [£££]

Clothes (see Vintage clothes and exotica, page 98,
and Textiles, tapestries, needlework and lace, page 58)

Coins and medals (see also Antiquities, page 28,
and Auctions, Chapter 2)

Spink, 5 King Street, sw1 (930-7888), London's leading coin and medal dealers, have been in business since 1666 and believe they have the largest and finest selection of antique and modern coins and medals in the country. Medals date from 1793 and include campaign medals, civil orders and decorations from all countries. Coins range from Greek and Roman coins and English hammered gold and silver coins to modern collectors' items. [££+]

A. H. Baldwin, 11 Adelphi Terrace, wc2 (930-6879). Numismatists specializing in English, Greek and Roman coins and old medals. Baldwin's stock ranges from the curious to the very rare. [££+]

Dolls and toys (see also under Models and model-making, page 123, and Toys, Chapter 20)

Kaye Desmonde, 17 Kensington Church Walk, w8 (937-2602). Mrs Desmonde may well have the largest collection of pre-1920 dolls in the world. There are about 200 on display in her shop and an additional 2,000 in reserve. Most are German and French makes like Jumeau and Handwerck but she usually has a few pedlar dolls, English wax dolls and sometimes the collector's *pièce de résistance*, a Bru. All have authentic bodies and costumes. Here there is also a selection of doll's houses and a large stock of doll's house furniture. Mrs Desmonde is the author of a book entitled *Dolls and Doll's Houses* (Letts, £1·50). [££+]

The Doll Shop, 18 Richmond Hill, Richmond, Surrey (940-6774), is run by two sisters, Misses Amie and Muriel Bailey, who specialize in antique dolls dressed in either their original costumes or in careful reproductions of period costumes. The sisters get their dress patterns by taking old doll clothes apart and they use old fabrics and lace in their reconstructions. They also make wigs, hats and even shoes for dolls. They will not, however, dress other people's dolls. Ring for an appointment. [££+]

Carol Ann Stanton, 109 Portobello Road, w11, is open on Saturdays only, but it is another good source of old dolls; also doll's houses, doll's furniture, some old toys and tinplate. [££+]

Pat Walker, Antiquarius Market, 139 King's Road, sw3 (352-3315). Stall and front window filled from floor to ceiling with pretty turn-of-the-century French and German dolls in authentic dress. [££+]

Marée, Hypermarket, 26 Kensington High Street, w8 (937-1842). Good selection of antique dolls of all types. [££+]

Ethnographic art (see also Textiles, tapestries, needle-work and lace, page 49, and Antiquities, page 28)

Herbert Rieser, 20 New Quebec Street, W1 (723-9695), has been selling primitive art for over thirty years. Most of the tribal figures, masks and jewellery on display are from the Ivory Coast, Nigeria and West Africa. All are good quality and in the medium price range. Most of Mr Rieser's customers are, in fact, other dealers. [££]

Ian Auld, 1 Gateway Arcade, Camden Passage, N1 (359-1440). Primarily West African pieces. Mr Auld has lived in Nigeria and has an extensive knowledge of West African cultures, especially the Yoruba. Many who live in the area frequent the gallery and Mr Auld makes a point of keeping some quite inexpensive items as well as more important pieces. Open afternoons during the week and all day Saturday. [££]

Gallery 43, 28 Davies Street, W1 (499-6486). An impressive Mayfair gallery dealing in important works of primitive art from the Pacific (especially Melanesia), Africa and pre-Columbian South America. Once a year there is a special exhibition of one aspect of ethnographic art. Prices start at £50 but go to thousands of pounds. [£££]

Berkeley Galleries, 20 Davies Street, W1 (629-2450). Primitive art is one of three specialities at this gallery – classical and Far Eastern antiquities are the other two – and African masks hang side by side with Wayang puppets and Roman terracottas. Mr Ohly, the director, has been in business a long time and is much respected by his competitors. His pieces are geared to collecting and academic interests. [££+]

Turak, 5 St Christopher's Place, W1 (486-5380), is a relatively new gallery with ambitions to become the leading dealer in ethnographic jewellery. Pieces come from Ethiopia, Yemen and other Middle Eastern countries; also India, Pakistan and Nepal. Regular exhibitions on special subjects. Helpful staff. [££]

Antiques

Anthropos, 67 Monmouth Street, w c2 (836-8162). The only gallery in Europe specializing in Eskimo art. [££]

Furniture

Sixteenth and seventeenth century

William Job, 86 Pimlico Road, sw1 (730-7374), specializes in seventeenth-century English oak, but he usually has a few early Spanish pieces and occasionally a primitive French piece. [££+]

Tobias Jellinek, 66b Kensington Church Street, w8 (727-5980). Quality early English oak furniture. [££+]

Talavera, 62 Pimlico Road, sw1 (730-3390). Exclusively sixteenth- and seventeenth-century Spanish furniture and a few ceramics and sculpture of the same period. [££+]

Rendlesham and Dark, 498 King's Road, sw10 (351-1442), deal mainly in Jacobean oak furniture concentrating on the more rustic, country-made pieces. Also some continental pieces, particularly chairs, from this period. [££+]

Geoffrey Van, 107 Portobello Road, w11 (229-5577). Continental Gothic and Renaissance furniture, and some early English oak. Van also have a fine stock of continental wood carvings from these periods. [££+]

Mike Mallinson, 10 Davies Street, w1 (620-3739), deals in seventeenth-century English and continental furniture and paintings and in sixteenth-century pieces when he can get them. [££+]

Louis Stanton, 299 Westbourne Grove, w11 (727-9336). Fine selection of early oak furniture of quality. [££+]

Eighteenth and early nineteenth century (see also Antique supermarkets, page 25, and Antique streets, page 22, especially the Hypermarket and the Fulham Road and King's Road sections)

Pelham Galleries, 163 and 165 Fulham Road, sw3 (589-2686), have the biggest selection of eighteenth- and early nineteenth-century furniture in London. Everything is guaranteed 'of the period' and the stock tends to be 'representative' rather than 'important' pieces. The Galleries are a good place for big items like dining-room tables, sideboards, desks, bookcases and sets of chairs. [££]

Hotspur, 14 Lowndes Street, sw1 (235-1918). Eighteenth-century English furniture which is the workmanship of the very finest cabinet-makers. Hotspur has been owned by four generations of the Kern family and has the highest possible reputation. Museums and collectors buy from the shop seeing only photographs. Hotspure deals in rare and unusual pieces and its accent is on academic interest. [£££]

Edwin H. Herzog, 49 Brook Street, w1 (629-5460). Finest examples of eighteenth-century English cabinet-making. Three small showrooms of museum-quality furniture. [£££]

Mallett, 40 New Bond Street, w1 (499-7411). Of London's three top eighteenth-century furniture dealers – Hotspur, Herzog and Mallett – Mallett is the largest and the flashiest. The store has two huge floors designed as several elegantly-furnished rooms with lamps and other decorative objects for sale as well as English and continental furniture. [£££]

Church Street Galleries, 77 Kensington Church Street, w8 (937-2461), have a good selection of quality eighteenth-century English furniture and are especially known for their Queen Anne walnut. [££+]

William Redford, 9 Mount Street, w1 (629-1165). This elegant gallery sells fine quality continental furniture, mostly French, and concentrates on the unusual. [£££]

Troll, 27 Beauchamp Place, sw3 (589-5870), is the only Scandinavian antique shop outside Scandinavia. Troll specialize in eighteenth-century Scandinavian country furniture and most of the rose-painted coffers, pine tables, chairs, plate racks and cupboards are of Norwegian origin. They also have early lighting fixtures. [££]

Philip and Richard Parker, 98 Fulham Road, sw3 (589-7327). Five floors of English antiques with prices clearly marked. A written guarantee accompanies every purchase. [££+]

Late nineteenth century (see also Antique supermarkets, page 25, and Antique streets, page 22)

Just Desks, 20 Church Street, nw8 (723-7976). Desks from Victorian era to the forties, mostly leather-topped pedestal models. Not just desks – desk chairs too. [££]

Bamboo ~ rosperity, 91 Lots Road, sw10 (352-0763). Late nineteenth- and early twentieth-century bamboo furniture in excellent condition. [££]

Pelham Antiques, 14 Crawford Street, w1 (935-7627), always have a plentiful supply of stripped pine cupboards, desks, settles and Welsh dressers expertly re-finished and waxed by staff who care about what they are doing. This is an excellent place to buy pine. [££]

John Creed, 5A Camden Passage, n1 (226-8867). Quality pine furniture which has been carefully refinished. [££]

And So to Bed, 7 New King's Road, sw6 (731-3593). Old brass beds and continental and other nineteenth-century English styles. A few are even earlier. They also have patchwork quilts. [££]

Through the Looking Glass, 563 King's Road, sw6 (736-7799). Nineteenth-century mirrors in all sizes, some made from carved picture frames, others original. [££]

Glass

Howard Phillips, 11A Henrietta Place, w1 (580-9844), is the leading name in ~ne antique glass. Mr Phillips sells glass from all periods and all countries and ancient Egyptian, Roman and Persian pieces are on display with continental, English and Irish ones. Collectors' pieces predominate but there are sets of pre-1830 table glass and many fine decanters, including ship's decanters. All are expensive. [£££]

Delomosne, 4 Campden Hill Road, w8 (937-1804). Fine quality English and Irish eighteenth-century table glass and nineteenth-century French paperweights. [£££]

Traub, Gray's Antique Market, 58 Davies Street, w1 (629-7034). Victorian art glass: Burmese glass, satin glass, French and English cameo glass, peachblow, amberina and Moser. According to the shop most of the demand is from America, especially the mid-West. [££]

J. F. Poore, 5 Wellington Terrace, Bayswater Road, w2 (229-4166). This is a good place to find the odd piece of Georgian or Victorian glass at a bargain price. There are usually several antique decanters and claret jugs for sale as well as occasional specimen Georgian glasses and salt cellars. [£+]

Maureen Thompson, 34 Kensington Church Street, w8 (937-9919). Eighteenth-century English tableware glass and nineteenth-century Bristol coloured glass. [££+]

Richard Dennis, 144 Kensington Church Street, w8 (727-2061). Late nineteenth-century glass is just beginning to develop as a speciality and many pieces of fair quality can still be picked up in the antique markets but designer pieces are both costly and hard to find. Richard Dennis specializes in signed pieces by Gallé, Daum and other designers of the art nouveau period. (See also Art nouveau and art deco, page 29.) [££+]

Alan Tillman, 9 Halkin Arcade, Motcomb Street, sw1 (235-8235). Eighteenth-century English glasses and nineteenth-century paperweights. Mr Tillman stocks many sets of wine glasses and decanters which he says are competitively priced with fine quality contemporary glass. A set of Georgian wine glasses or a pair of antique decanters are, he maintains, in reach of anyone who can afford fine reproduction or contemporary glass. Georgian wine glasses begin around £60 for six. Pairs of decanters at about the same price. Both go up to £400 or £500. [££+]

Icons (see Pictures, prints and maps, Chapter 15)

Ivory and jade (see also Oriental art, page 44)

Tortoise Shell and Ivory House, 24 Chiltern Street, W1 (935-8031). Specialists in eighteenth- and nineteenth-century ivory and jade carvings. [££+]

Jewellery (see also Ethnographic art, page 37, and Antique supermarkets, page 25)

Cameo Corner, 22 New Bond Street, W1 (629-0071), Victorian and Georgian jewellery and, of course, cameos. Some ancient pieces: Egyptian scarabs, gold Roman earrings, etc. Once a year there is a special exhibition of antique jewellery and one of contemporary designs. [££+]

Sac Frères, 45 Old Bond Street, W1 (493-2333), are amber merchants. This is an inscrutable, old-fashioned firm and new customers often get the feeling they are an unwelcome disturbance. Sac Frères never seem to have much stock but for good antique pieces you can be sure about, this is the place to go. Ruby red Burmese amber, dark translucent Rumanian amber and green Sicilian amber mounted in rings, brooches and earrings, or conventional amber-coloured amber from the Baltic made into pipe stems and bead necklaces. [££+]

Robin Symes, 3 Ormond Yard, Duke of York Street, SW1 (930-9856). Ancient Etruscan, Greek, Roman and Egyptian gold jewellery of the finest quality. They occasionally have an unusual medieval or Renaissance piece. [£££]

Purple Shop, Antiquarius Market, 15 Flood Street, SW3 (352-1127), is one of the many jewellery stalls in this market, but Purple has established a special reputation in art nouveau and art deco jewellery, and, to a lesser extent, Victorian jewellery. [££]

Lace (see Textiles, tapestries, needlework and lace, page 49)

Maps (see Prints and maps, page 244)

Metalware (see also Silver, page 48)

Old Pewter Shop, 142 Brompton Road, sw3 (589-7370). During his forty years in business more pewter has passed through the hands of Charles Casimir, the proprietor of this shop, than any dealer's in the country. Many pieces are now in museum collections like the Rockefeller collection in Williamsburg, Virginia. Finding fine quality pewter is increasingly difficult. However, there are a number of eighteenth-century tankards, plates and candlesticks in this shop as well as a few earlier pieces. Mr Casimir warns buyers of pewter that there are many fakes on the market and urges everyone, no matter where they buy, to get a guarantee of the period. [£££]

Jack Casimir, 23 Pembroke Road, w11 (727-8643), and Stall 61, Antique Hypermarket, 26 Kensington High Street, w8. Like pewter, seventeenth- and eighteenth-century brass and copper are difficult to get and most of the scuttles, fenders, trivets, fire-tools, candlesticks and horse-brasses in this Notting Hill shop are late nineteenth century or are new. But everything in Mr Casimir's stand at the Hypermarket is guaranteed over 100 years old. (Mr Jack Casimir is the brother of Charles Casimir mentioned above.) [££]

Gordon Hand, 18 Chepstow Mansions, Chepstow Place, w2 (229-0322), carries seventeenth- and eighteenth-century brass and usually has a good supply of Georgian candlesticks. (A pair costs from £250.) Mr Hand also has a few iron cooking utensils and implements, and a small amount of pewter and tin Betty lamps. [££+]

Peter Place, 156 Walton Street, sw3 (584-2568). Specialists in seventeenth- and eighteenth-century brass. Mr Place believes he has the largest stock of fine antique brassware in England. [££+]

Robert Preston, 121 Kensington Church Street, w8 (727-4872). Mr Preston can be a little difficult to deal with but there is usually a good supply of nineteenth-century copper and brass in his shop: kettles, hearth fenders, trivets and some lighting fixtures. [££]

Richard Mundey, 19 Chiltern Street, w1 (935-5613). Pewter from the eighteenth century and earlier. Mr Mundey has a private collection which he will sometimes show to those who are interested. He does not welcome browsing and it is wise to ring first for an appointment. [£££]

Troll, 27 Beauchamp Place, sw3 (589-5870). Eighteenth-century brass candlesticks and early metal lighting fixtures. Occasionally they even have medieval things. [£££]

Coppermine, 17 Halkin Arcade, sw1 (235-0128). Copper kettles, pots, pans and decorative pieces: most are nineteenth century, some are reproductions. Large stock includes some brass. [££]

Oriental art (see also Pottery and porcelain, page 46, and Textiles, tapestries, needlework and lace, page 49)

A note to novices: Oriental works of art are extremely costly but if you are interested in collecting them you will do well to visit a top gallery or two and introduce yourself. Most Oriental art is sold through getting to know a client and his needs. Sometimes a moderately valuable piece can be got for less at a top gallery because they value it less highly than a shop which rarely gets anything truly fine and overprices when it does. Although Mayfair Oriental galleries look forbidding they are normally pleasant and helpful to anyone who is really interested in Oriental art.

Bluett, 48 Davies Street, w1 (629-4018). Fine quality Chinese works of art from 1500 B.C. to 1850, including porcelain, archaic bronzes, jade and lacquerware. Bluett's are specially known for their porcelain designed for Chinese taste. They are highly respected and, although very expensive, are a must for collectors and scholars. [£££]

Sparks, 128 Mount Street, w1 (499-2265), deal, like Bluett's, in Chinese art, but unlike Bluett's, Sparks sell antique Chinese furniture, screens and pictures. Each room in this gallery is furnished with works of art from one particular dynasty. [£££]

Hugh Moss, 12 Bruton Street, w1 (499-5625). Sung, Ming and Chi'ng are the special periods at Hugh Moss, but all dynasties are well represented not just in porcelain but in lacquerware, enamel and hardstones. Snuff bottles are another speciality. Hugh Moss also have Japanese and Korean antiques and Chinese paintings. This is a young company and it is a lot more informal than similar galleries. It is also a public company. [£££]

Eskenazi, Foxglove House, 166 Piccadilly, w1 (493-5464). Chinese art up to the fifteenth century, notably Tang and Sung but also early bronzes. Each summer Eskenazi have a special exhibition of early Chinese art. Catalogue available on request. [£££]

Nihon To Ken, 23 Museum Street, wc2 (580-6511). Japanese works of art from £20: lacquer, swords and sword furniture, armour, pottery, paintings, inro and netsuke. [££]

Douglas Wright, 34 Curzon Street, w1 (629-9993). Chinese and Japanese pieces from the seventeenth and eighteenth centuries; also Tibetan and Indian bronzes and occasionally Persian items. [££+]

Spink, 5 King Street, sw1 (930-7888). Fine Chinese, Japanese and South-east Asian works of art dating from neolithic times to the eighteenth century. Spinks have especially fine Indian pieces. [£££]

Pewter (see Metalware, page 43)

Pictures and prints (see Pictures, prints and maps, Chapter 15)

Pottery and porcelain (see also Oriental art, page 44)

The prices antique pottery and porcelain fetch today place it outside the reach of many people who buy antiques for personal use. Increasingly, ceramics are a collectors' and investors' market and most of what is sold in London shops goes overseas. Some dealers estimate that as much as 90 per cent of continental and Oriental pieces are sold to overseas buyers.

As well as the specialty shops listed below, there are three streets in London that are full of small shops selling antique ceramics. The largest of these is Kensington Church Street, w8, but York Street, w1, and Harcourt Street (a continuation of York Street) have several antique pottery and porcelain shops and are worth a visit.

Vandekar, 138 Brompton Road, sw3 (589-8481). Mr Vandekar believes he has the largest stock of pre-1830 pottery and porcelain in Europe. Collectors' plates, whole services, ceramic figures of Chinese export, Sèvres, Meissen, Chelsea blue and white, Derby and other fine makes are displayed on the two floors of this Knightsbridge gallery. If you want a particular piece of antique porcelain this is the place to start looking for it. [£££]

Jellinek and Sampson, 156 Brompton Road, sw3 (589-5272), is London's foremost dealer in early English pottery: English Delft, slipware, saltglaze, Whieldon, Creamware, Prattware and Staffordshire up to 1830. Some medieval pottery. [£££]

Oliver-Sutton, 34c Kensington Church Street, w8 (937-0633), specialize in Staffordshire figures. Mr Oliver is the author of a book called *The Victorian Staffordshire Figure*

(Heinemann, £6). Portrait figures, decorative groups, animals and pastille burners of Staffordshire line the walls. Oliver-Sutton also have pot-lids. [££+]

Heirloom and Howard, 1 Hay Hill, sw 1 (493-5868), are specialists in armorial antiques of all kinds, but porcelain is the mainstay of their business. They will do searches for free and can, with luck, slowly reassemble sets of family china which have been broken up in the course of time. Single pieces and complete sets with heraldic devices are on display in the Hay Hill shop. [££+]

Haslam and Whiteway, 105 Kensington Church Street, w8 (229-1145). Victorian Parian porcelain and studio pottery from 1851 to 1920. De Morgan, lustreware, Pilkington, Doulton, Ruskinware, Linthorp can be found here. [££+] (See also Art nouveau and art deco, page 29.)

J. and J. May, 40 Kensington Church Street, w8 (937-3575). Specialists in historical and commemorative pottery and porcelain. [££]

John Creed, 5A Camden Passage, n 1 (226-8867). Blue and white Staffordshire is displayed on the pine dressers and chests that are the shop's other speciality. [££]

David B. Newbon, 56 Beauchamp Place, sw3 (589-1369). Antique English and Oriental ceramics. The basement and half the ground floor are devoted entirely to Oriental export porcelain while the other half of the ground floor and the whole of the first floor are exclusively early English pottery. English porcelain occupies the second floor. Newbon is also London's leading Wedgwood specialist. [£££]

Richard Dennis, 144 Kensington Church Street, w8 (727-2061), is a glass expert who switched to English Studio Pottery (*circa* 1870–1930). This field, a new one in the 'antique' world, includes among other things Martinware, De Morgan, Doulton and Minton ware. Mr Dennis puts out a detailed and highly informative catalogue about each kind of studio pottery. These are available at the shop and cost £2·50. He also has some collectors' glass from the same era. [££+]

Michael Hogg, 172 Brompton Road, sw3 (589-8629), dealer in eighteenth-century export porcelain: *famille rose*, tobacco leaf, Nanking blue and white and pure export. Like most Oriental porcelain dealers, the greater part of his stock is sold to buyers and dealers from overseas. [£££]

Winifred Williams, 3 Bury Street, sw1 (930-4732), is well known for fine eighteenth-century English and continental china, especially Meissen. [£££]

Mansour Gallery, 46 Davies Street, w1 (491-7444), are specialists in fine Islamic pottery. [£££]

Sculpture (see also Antiquities, page 28, and Oriental art, page 44)

Sladmore Gallery, 32 Bruton Place, w1 (499-0365). Animal bronzes dating from 1820 to the present day. [££+]

Joanna Booth, 247 King's Road, sw3 (352-8998). German, Flemish and Italian wood carvings from the sixteenth and seventeenth centuries. This gallery usually has a few carved continental doors too. [££+]

Dumez-Onof, 109 Mount Street, w1 (499-6648). Greek and Roman sculpture and Gothic and Renaissance carvings. Most of these are large pieces and they are costly. [£££]

Silver

S. J. Phillips, 139 New Bond Street, w1 (629-6261), have the largest stock of pre-1800 English and continental silver in London. The firm has been in business since 1869 and customers include private collectors and dealers from all over the world. Phillips concentrate on very important pieces but they are a good place to look for the small item of quality. They say such pieces are likely to be cheaper than in a shop where they would be thought one of the best things in stock and priced accordingly. [££+]

How, 2–3 Pickering Place, St James's Street, sw1

(930-7140), occupies the ground-floor premises of Mrs How's London home, a Georgian town-house hidden away in a close. In it are the very finest examples of early English, Scottish and Irish silver. Mrs How is London's most important dealer in provincial silver. Telephone first for an appointment. [£££]

Bond Street Silver Galleries, 111, New Bond Street, w1 (493-6180), are by no means as familiar to the public as the big silver vaults in Chancery Lane, yet they are a better place to buy antique silver. Most of the customers in the Galleries' first- and second-floor premises are dealers, and the little shops are brimming with trays, candelabras, serving dishes, cutlery and decorative pieces of all sorts. [££+]

T. Lumley, 2 Old Bond Street, w1 (629-2493). Important English and continental silver, including some Victorian and art nouveau pieces. Lumley's are noted for decorative items and for gilt. They tend to go in for the unusual; they sold the famous Walpole salver to the Victoria and Albert museum, for example. But, like Phillips, Lumley's feel they have less important items of quality at a somewhat lower cost than the general market. Ring first for an appointment. [£££]

N. Bloom, 153 New Bond Street, w1 (499-3502). Large stock of big, unusual pieces. [£££]

Shrubsole, 43 Museum Street, wc1 (405-2712). Fine reputation as dealers in Sheffield plate and eighteenth-century and Victorian British silver by makers like the Foxes and Garrards. [££+]

Note: Antique markets and Antique streets (see page 22) are the best places to look for late nineteenth-century silver, especially picture frames, candlesticks, miscellaneous cutlery and small decorative pieces.

Textiles, tapestries, needlework and lace

Vigo-Sternberg, 37 South Audley Street, w1 (493-1228) may well have the largest stock of fine tapestries in the world. There are normally about 500 in stock, early Gothic to contemporary. Only a fraction is on display but the gallery has a colour photo album with pictures of every item in stock and will gladly show you any piece that interests you. (Don't ask unless you're seriously thinking of buying.) [£££]

Mayorcas, 38 Jermyn Street, sw1 (629-4195). Antique European textiles of all descriptions fill this small shop in the Princes Arcade; there are woven fabrics, printed fabrics, painted fabrics and embroidered fabrics. Damasks, velvets and brocades, tapestry and needlework. Mayorcas also sell church vestments, early costumes of museum quality and covered pillows made up from tapestry fragments and trimmed with antique trimmings. They also have needlework pictures. [£££]

Arditti, 12b Berkeley Street, w1 (629-0885), sell European textiles, tapestries and needlework of superior quality. Arditti have the largest selection of brocades in Europe. They also have a number of church vestments and a few early costumes. [£££]

Catherine Buckley, 302 Westbourne Grove, w11 (229-8786). A wealth of old, lace-trimmed tablecloths, cutwork cloths, lace cushions and collars and some old clothes. [£+]

Mrs Field, Alfie's Antique Market, 13 Church Street, nw8 (723-0564), specializes in collectors' and costume lace; also hand-decorated household linen. [££]

Hindu Kush, 231 Portobello Road, w11 (no phone), and 49 Kensington High Street, w8. Central Asian textiles, especially from Afghanistan: tribal dress, donkey bags, tent hangings. [£+]

Note: Auctions are a particularly good source of lace and tapestries; also costumes and embroidered textiles. **Phillips'** galleries have regular sales of lace and costumes, as, to a lesser extent, do **Christie's**, South Kensington. **Sotheby's** is probably the best auction room for fine tapestries. For addresses, see Chapter 2. See also Vintage clothes, page 98.

Antique repairs and restoration

Nearly all repair shops are overloaded with work, and because antique repairs often require painstaking handcraft, getting something restored can take a very long time. So be prepared to wait, sometimes for months, for the results. If the piece is a good one it is worth it.

It is advisable to always telephone first and either discuss your problem with the workshop or make an appointment to bring the piece in.

Architectural and ornamental restoration (see also Household decoration, Chapter 11)

G. Jackson and Sons, Rathbone Works, Rainville Road, w6 (385-6616), restore and replace ornamental plasterwork.

J. E. Lucas and Sons, 3 Swanscombe Road, w11 (603-7543), repair and refinish oak and pine panelling. They will strip off old paint or varnish, repair splits and missing pieces, bleach (if required) and apply any desired finish.

H. W. Poulter, 279 Fulham Road, sw10 (352-7268), clean and restore marble, particularly fireplaces, but also sculpture and tables.

Ornamental Ironworks, 1A Netherwood Place, w14 (603-2857), will repair antique ironwork of all kinds: railings, gates, staircases, whatever.

Plaster Decoration, 30 Stannary Street, se11 (735-8167), have plaster moulds from all periods and can adapt these to individual rooms or do plasterwork to order.

Books (see Books, Chapter 3)

Carpets

A. Rezai, 117 Middlesex Street, E1 (247-9316), cleans and restores Oriental and European carpets and rugs. He is highly recommended and used by many leading dealers.

Benardout and Benardout, 7 Thurloe Place, SW7 (584-7658), handle minor restorations on all types of rugs (as do many carpet galleries).

Chandeliers and lighting fixtures

N. Davighi, 117 Shepherd's Bush Road, W6 (603-5357), are specialists in the restoration and repair of chandeliers and lighting fixtures in both glass and metal. Anything from re-wiring to gilding, brass casting, re-stringing and, when possible, replacing missing prisms can be done here. They also make chandeliers to order.

Woodall and Emery, Haywards Heath Road, Balcombe, W. Sussex (044-483-608), repair metal and glass lighting fixtures in a workroom in the basement of their shop.

Clocks, watches and barometers

Aubrey Brocklehurst, 124 Cromwell Road, SW7 (373-0319),

Camerer Cuss, 54–6 New Oxford Street, WC1 (636-8968),

E. Hollander, 80 Fulham Road, SW3 (589-7239), and **Strike One**, 1A Camden Walk, N1 (226-9709), have size-able workshops on their premises and do expert repairs on clocks, and clock cases. It takes a long time, though – sometimes six months.

Huggins and Horsey, 26 Beauchamp Place, SW3 (584-1685), repair clocks, especially continental ones whose cases often need re-gilding or re-plating. Mr Masterson, the proprietor, does all buhl repair work himself.

Garner and Marney, 41–3 Southgate Road, N1 (226-1535), are specialists in barometer restoration. There are twenty craftsmen on hand to do re-building, polishing and re-silvering of dials and glass blowing as well as mechanical repairs and replacements. Careful hand-work like this can, of course, take months to complete.

A. Lee, 122 St John Street, EC1 (253-6901), restores and repairs antique watches of all kinds.

Obsolete and Modern Watch Materials, 38 Caledonian Road, N1 (837-3838). Specialize in repairing and replacing parts in old watches and, to a lesser extent, in clocks. They believe they have the biggest stock of old watch parts in the country and if they don't have a part a watch needs they will make it.

China (see Pottery and porcelain, page 57)

Dolls and toys

Edward Callow, Two Steps, 45 Tranquil Vale, SE3 (852-4732), restores mechanical toys and makes new parts.

Kersey Craft Workshops, The Forge, Kersey Uplands, Ipswich, Suffolk (047-338-3344). James Bosworthick, who runs this workshop, will restore and repair antique wooden toys and some tinplate. His speciality is rocking horses.

Ray Marston, Flat 10, 20/21 Marylebone High Street, W1 (486-5960), restores wax dolls. He cleans them, fuses facial cracks, remodels melted parts and can even make new limbs, and affix wigs. Mr Marston also makes wax portrait dolls.

Doll's Hospital, 16 Dawes Road, SW6 (385-2081). Complete restoration of bisque dolls, also soft toy restoration.

Furniture

Antique Restorations Ltd, 212 Cricklewood Broadway, NW2 (452-4239). This firm has expert restorers specializing in all kinds of repairs to fine English and French furniture. They replace missing pieces, do custom carving, remove old finishes, gild, lacquer, upholster, polish – anything, in fact that needs doing. Sotheby's and Christie's are among their customers. Collection and delivery.

M. J. Baker, 114 Landor Road, sw9 (274-5200), does highly accomplished furniture restoration of all kinds, but his speciality is gilt and gesso work and Buckingham Palace is one of his clients.

H. J. Hatfield, 42 St Michael's Street, w2 (723-8265), restores all kinds of antique furniture but specializes in inlaid pieces of marquetry and buhl and also painted furniture.

K. J. Trayler, 67 Palmerston Road, e17 (520-3485), does caning, sea-grassing and rush seating. He will collect and deliver to you free of charge.

Trap, 48 Bell Street, nw1 (262-2036), specialize in stripping wood, especially pine. Doors, panelling, fire surrounds and furniture. There is no collection or delivery service, unfortunately.

Kem-Strip, 112 Greyhound Road, sw6 (381-2155), operate a huge stripping factory for furniture, architectural items and metal. They use special products which are also on sale to customers. An average job takes two to three days but same-day service is available for a 25 per cent surcharge.

Careful handstripping can be arranged for fine furniture.

Glass (see also Chandeliers and lighting fixtures, page 52, and Mirrors, page 56)

R. Wilkinson, 45 Wastdale, se23 (699-4420), repair glassware and are recommended by leading London glass dealers. The firm also does hand engraving to order.

W. G. T. Burne, 11 Elystan Street, sw3 (589-6074), will undertake repairs on fine glassware when they feel adequate repair is possible.

William Lowe, 75 Randolph Avenue, w9 (286-5018), repairs stained glass.

J. Preedy, Ashland Place, Paddington Street, w1 (935-3988), repairs and restores mirrors: re-silvering of antique mirrors, fitting to frames, bevelling and 'anti-quing'.

Andrew Glass Engraving, 25 Motcomb Street, sw1 (235-8777), cut monograms and pictures in lead crystal.

Ivory

Baumkotter, 63A Kensington Church Street, w8 (937-5171), will repair ivory and replace carving.

Lacquer

Vilmo Gibello, 40 Homer Street, w1 (262-7463). Chinese lacquer restoration.

Leather

Antique Leathers, 4 Park End, South Hill Park, nw3 (435-8582), are specialists in dyeing leather to match worn-out antique leather or to give an 'antique' appearance. Each piece must be dyed several times to achieve this effect. The firm re-covers everything from tables to chessboards, pony traps, chairs and sofas. All upholstery is done with horsehair. Nicest of all, the craftsmen are enthusiastic about their work and very proud of it.

Murga Candler, 57 Bayham Place, nw1 (387-7830), will gild leather and hand-polish it to any desired colour. They line desks, repair screens, do leather upholstery and make dummy book-backs for cabinets.

Woolnough, 23 Phipp Street, ec2 (739-6603), will send leather table tops by post anywhere. They also do custom leather work and gold tooling. The Houses of Parliament are customers.

Metalware (see also Sculpture, page 58, Silver, page 58, Chandeliers and lighting fixtures, page 52, and Iron and metalwork, Chapter 11)

Watts and Co., 7 Tufton Street, sw1 (222-7169), repair most small metalwork – brass, pewter, bronze, silver. By 'small metalwork' they mean anything that can be carried. Watts also re-plate silver.

J. J. Contracts, 787 Wandsworth Road, sw8 (622-9604). All metal restoration and polishing that 'shows a profit'.

Kem-Strip, 112 Greyhound Road, sw6 (381-2155), will strip most metals.

Mirrors (see also Glass, page 54)

Clifford Wright, 171 Dawes Road, sw6 (385-9175), specialize in restoring carving and gilt on antique mirrors.

Chelsea Glassworks, 105 Fulham Road, sw3 (581-2501), re-silver mirrors. Cost is per square foot.

Monuments

Jorgen Sedgwick, 330 Upland Road, East Dulwich, se22 (693-3646), restores tombs and ancient monuments. He cleans, replaces carving and missing stones and does whatever else needs doing.

Musical boxes

Keith Harding, 93 Hornsey Road, n7 (607-6181), are the biggest restorers of music boxes in the world. They also publish a catalogue of spare parts.

Music Box Gallery, 81 George Street, W1 (935-4700), mends music boxes as well as singing birds and other automata. Repairs are confined to working parts only, not exteriors.

Objets d'art (see also Sculpture, page 58, and Pottery and porcelain, below)

G. Garbe, 23 Charlotte Street, W1 (636-1268). Established in the eighteenth century, Garbe still do fine repairs on jade, fans, inlay, jewellery etc.

Paper (see also Books, services, page 76)

Drescher, 17 Alverstone Road, NW2 (459-5543), are invisible menders of all kinds of paper. They specialize in repairing old master drawings, prints, antique maps and documents. They also restore vellum.

Pictures, prints and maps (see Pictures, prints and maps, Chapter 15)

Pottery and porcelain

Sutcliffe's of Croydon, 23 Brighton Road, South Croydon (688-1907). The very finest restoration of quality pottery and porcelain. If you have a valuable piece of china that needs mending, this is the place to go. Sutcliffe's is patronized by London's leading porcelain dealers and if you live in the West End, the firm will collect and deliver.

Chinamend, 54 Walton Street, SW3 (589-1182). There are various ways and degrees of mending china, and what you choose should depend on how much attention the piece merits. Coldset gluing is less dear than hotset gluing, for example. Cracks can be left in or painted out. Sometimes missing pieces must be re-made. Chinamend repairs all kinds of china and will give you the type of service that suits the quality of the piece.

Sculpture (see also Monuments, page 56)

Morris Singer Foundry, 18 South Parade, sw3 (352-6452). 'Provided it's metal, we can repair it,' say Morris Singer's. The Renaissance fountain in the Victoria and Albert museum and the 'Copper Horse' in Windsor Great Park are two examples of their restoration work, which also extends to delicate sculptures in gold and silver.

Silver

For economy and consistency in quality it is best to get silver repaired or re-plated by a dealer of the same calibre as the piece.

S. J. Phillips, 139 New Bond Street, w1 (629-6261), will repair fine quality antique silver.

Mappin and Webb, 170 Regent Street, w1 and 63 Brompton Road, sw3 (734-0906), restore silver and silver plate. They won't tackle everything: some repairs they feel are too expensive to be worthwhile and others are too special for their workshop; but what they do, they do well.

Watts and Co., 7 Tufton Street, sw1 (222-7169), repair, recast and re-plate silver.

Textiles, tapestries, needlework and lace

Royal School of Needlework, 25 Prince's Gate, sw7 (589-0077), restore and re-mount all kinds of embroidery and tapestry and will copy any needlework design. They also clean and repair lace. These services can take a week or a few months, depending on the extent of the damage.

Special services

Davies Turner, 326 Queenstown Road, sw8 (622-4393), will collect, pack and ship any antiques anywhere. They also supply finders. That is to say, if you want a special item, they will search it out and send it to you.

Harris and Frank, 53 Holland Park, w11 (727-4769), give expert valuations on antique jewellery and silver. They also undertake research. By appointment only.

The widest range of decorative and household goods imaginable is for sale in London auction rooms. Not only are the world's most important works of art sold in them, but also old fridges, used carpets and curtains and antique and secondhand furniture of every description. Whether you are a multi-millionaire or a penniless student, if you have the time to spare auctions are the most sensible place to get furnishings for your home. When, for example, you buy antiques from a shop, you are paying – and rightly so – for the time the dealer has spent combing the auction rooms, and for the money he has invested in his stock and spent on premises and staff. In an auction you can buy exactly what a dealer buys before expenses and profit are added on to the price. (Over half the clientele at London auctions are dealers.) So whether you want fine art, antiques or second-hand furnishings, you are going to get them for considerably less at an auction.

A lot of people are afraid of auctions. Some are not sure how to behave in them and fear scratching their nose might land them with a Rubens. Others steer clear of posh auction rooms like Sotheby's and Christie's because they think nothing less than old masters and Ming vases ever go on the block. In fact, two thirds of the items sold at Christie's go for under £100. It's the other third we read about in the newspapers.

Details of forthcoming London auctions are published every Monday in the *Daily Telegraph* and every Tuesday in *The Times*.

A note to novices on how to bid: every auction gallery has a viewing period before each sale when you may go in and examine what is to be sold. Printed catalogues are available describing each item. These cost from 10p to a couple of pounds, depending on the importance of the sale and whether they are illustrated. This is often the only expense to the customer (and you don't have to buy a catalogue unless you want to). Most auction galleries make their money by charging the seller a percentage (10 to 15 per cent) of what an object fetches.

All auction rooms will tell you the price each item is *expected* to fetch in the sale, so always ask for the estimated price of any piece you are interested in. If you decide to place a bid it is not necessary to actually attend the auction but *it is advisable to do so if possible*. If you cannot, ask for a bidding slip, fill it out and leave it with the auctioneer or another employee (preferably the auctioneer as porters expect to be tipped.) If your written bid is £20, this does not mean the auctioneer is going to open the bidding by saying he has £20. He will only say this when the bidding has reached £18. Bidding usually goes up a pound at a time up to £10, then £2 to £20 and so on – the jumps getting bigger and bigger as the price gets higher. If you have left a £20 bid and the open bidding stops at £12, then the auctioneer or clerk will bid £14 on your behalf. If your bid is successful the gallery will notify you. Should you attend the auction in person, however, remember that the main thing is to make sure the auctioneer sees your bid. So raise your hand or your catalogue even though everyone else appears to be communicating by ESP. (Dealers and others who attend auctions regularly are known to the auctioneer and he usually knows when they are likely to bid and sees what is to others an imperceptible nod.) If you get the item you bid on, a sales clerk will come over and hand you a slip to fill out with your name and address. You may then go straight to the cashier and make your payment or wait until the auction is over. All auction galleries will arrange a delivery service.

Sotheby and Co., 34–5 New Bond Street, w 1 (493-8080), are the world's oldest and largest art auctioneers. Sotheby's have over 500 sales yearly covering a vast range of art and antiques. There is a one-week viewing period before each sale and this is open to everyone. Even if you don't want to buy it is worth going in for a look. As Sotheby's point out, it's just like going to a museum except that the exhibitions are constantly changing. Viewing hours are 9.30 to 4.30. Catalogues are available about one month before the sale and can be ordered by post or bought on the premises.

From September to July Sotheby's have the following regular sales:

Monday: *books, objects of Vertu* (snuff-boxes, etc.) and *glass*.

Tuesday: *books* and *porcelain*.

Wednesday: *pictures*.

Thursday: *silver* and *jewellery*.

Friday: *furniture* and *works of art*.

Sotheby's also have special sales of *wine, vintage cars, textiles, arms and armour, contemporary pictures, prints,* and *engravings.* The firm will give you a free appraisal on any item, and if you do want to sell it, commissions are normally 10 per cent. Ten per cent is also charged to buyers at Sotheby.

A special note about absentee bidding: bidding slips can be left with the sales clerk or telephoned in and then confirmed by letter to the sales clerk. No other employee is authorized to accept a bid and in this Sotheby's appears to be unique. Other galleries allow porters and other employees to act on behalf of the customers and many employees are on regular commissions from dealers to be on the look-out and bid for them if certain items appear to be going for less then expected. This means that for the private customer the chances of getting a bargain are not as good as they may seem at most auctions. (Important book sales are held at 115 Chancery Lane, w c2.) [£££]

Sotheby's Belgravia, 19 Motcomb Street, SW1 (235-4311), is a branch of Sotheby's which is devoted entirely to Victoriana, art nouveau and art deco. Sales are held at 11 a.m. Viewing is for three days before each sale. On Tuesdays Sotheby's Belgravia usually sell *pictures*, on Wednesdays, *furniture*, on Thursdays, *silver* and *porcelain*, and on Fridays there is an occasional special sale. Sotheby's Belgravia publish in their catalogues estimates of what each item is expected to fetch. A fee of 10 per cent is charged to buyers. [££+]

Christie's, 8 King Street, SW1 (839-9060), are similar to Sotheby's in most respects. Both the buyer and the seller are charged 10 per cent fees. Christie's have regular sales of quality antiques and works of art five days a week except during August and September. They are as follows:

Monday: *pottery*, *porcelain* and *jade*.

Tuesday: *drawings*, *watercolours*, *prints*, *coins*, *antiquities* and *glass*.

Wednesday: either *jewellery*, *silver*, *books* or *armour*.

Thursday: *furniture*, and usually *wine*.

Friday: *pictures*.

Most sales take place at 11 a.m. and viewing is for two days preceding each sale, and sometimes for a bit longer. Occasionally there are special sales of *musical instruments*, *clocks*, *toys*, *costumes*, *textiles* and *photos*. Remember that two thirds of all the items sold at Christie's go for under £100. [£££]

Christie's South Kensington, 85 Old Brompton Road, SW7 (589-2422) is a new annexe of Christie's in St James's and an outlet for old and antique goods not up to the standards of the main gallery. Turnover is quick and if you have something to sell you can probably get it into a sale here in four or five weeks. There is a 15 per cent commission on sales but no fee to buyers. Sales are as follows:

Mondays at 10.30 a.m.: *jewellery* and sometimes *silver* (view Fridays).

Wednesdays at 10.30 a.m.: *furniture*; at 2 p.m., *watercolours* and *pictures* (view for two days before the sale).

Thursdays at 2 p.m.: *ceramics* (view for two days before the sale). Special sales of *textiles*, *costumes*, *dolls* and *toys* are also held on Thursdays.

Fridays at 10.30 a.m.: *fur*, once a month (view Thursday) and *wine*, once a month at 11 a.m. [££]

Phillips, 7 Blenheim Street, w1 (629-6602), is London's third largest auction gallery. Phillips is in the medium range of the art and antique market and is a source of good but not important antiques and decorative pieces. Phillips is open all the year round and is the only gallery which is open Saturday mornings. Regular sales are as follows:

Monday at 11 a.m.: *antique furniture*, *watercolours*, *rugs*, *ceramics*, *glass* and *objets d'art* (view Friday, Saturday morning and day of sale). At 2 p.m.: *pictures* (view as above).

Tuesday at 11 a.m.: antique *English and continental furniture*, *Eastern rugs*, *clocks*, *bronzes* and *objets d'art* (view Friday, Saturday morning and Monday 9 a.m. to 4 p.m.).

Wednesday at 11 a.m.: antique *porcelain*, *pottery* and *glass* (view Monday and Tuesday).

Friday at 11 a.m.: antique *silver* and *plated ware* (view Wednesday and Thursday).

Phillips have a reputation as promoters of new kinds of collector's items like *pot-lids* and *fairings* and they have many special sales throughout the year of *books*, *jewellery*, *Oriental works of art*, *lace*, *costumes*, *lead soldiers*, *furs* and *ethnographica*. They also have monthly *wine* sales. [££]

Marylebone Auction Rooms, Hayes Place, NW1 (723-1118), is Phillips' outlet for *secondhand furnishings*. This is a fine place to get upholstered *chairs*, *bric-à-brac*, odd *tables* and *chairs*, *prints*, *pianos* and *curiosities*. There are also a few antiques on sale, probably as appetizers. Sales are held on Thursdays at 10 a.m. Viewing, 9 a.m. to 5 p.m. on Wednesdays. [£]

Phillips West 2, 10 Salem Road, w2 (221-5303), another Phillips outlet for household furnishings. Sales: Thursdays 10 a.m. View Wednesdays.

Glendining, 7 Blenheim Street, w1 (493-2445), auction *coins*, *military* and *naval medals* and some *Oriental works of art*.

They are housed in the same premises as Phillips and have about twenty sales a year at regular intervals. The majority of these are coin sales. Two days for viewing precede each sale. [££]

Bonham's Montpelier Galleries, Montpelier Street, SW7 (584-9161), are another art and antique gallery in the medium price range. Bonham's are probably best-known for pictures (though not important ones) but they have plenty of antique furniture, mostly nineteenth-century, as well as carpets, silver and books. The gallery estimates that about 80 per cent of the clientele are dealers. Sales are as follows:

Tuesday at 11 a.m.: *antique* and *modern silver* fortnightly. Sales of *wine* once a month and *jewellery* every two months.

Wednesday at 11 a.m.: *watercolours*, *drawings* and *prints* fortnightly; *modern pictures* and *sculpture*, including the work of young artists, bi-monthly. During the winter there are *fur* sales once a month.

Thursday at 11 a.m.: *English and continental furniture*, also *oil paintings*. On the first Thursday of every month there is a special sale of *better oil paintings*.

Friday at 11 a.m.: *ceramics* and *works of art*.

Periodically there are sales of *arms and armour*, *antiquities* and *models*. Viewing is possible for two days before each sale. [££]

Bonham's Chelsea Galleries, 75 Burnaby Street, SW10 (352-0466), or 'Junk Bonham's' as they are popularly known, are one of the best places in London to get home furnishings cheaply. *Appliances, curtains, carpets, reproduction furniture, upholstered chairs* and *tables* of all kinds are auctioned every Tuesday at 11 a.m. Pictures and very 'minor *works of art*' are sold every other Tuesday, at the same time. According to the gallery you can buy an entire set of ancestors for £10. Much of these goods come from estate settlements and many of the *televisions* and *home appliances* on the block are almost new. [£]

Persian Carpet Galleries, 152 Brompton Road, SW3 (584-5516), are *antique Oriental rug* auctioneers. They hold seven sales yearly at seven-week intervals. Many dealers sell carpets through this gallery and all items are top quality. Viewing is for one week before each sale and a catalogue will be mailed to you on request. [££+]

Harrods Auction Galleries, Arundel Terrace, sw13 (748-2739), is another fine source of home furnishings. Located in Barnes, just over the Hammersmith Bridge, Harrods is popular with people in the Home Counties as well as London since there is a huge free car park. The Galleries have sales every other week on Wednesdays, Thursdays and Fridays and much of the goods sold at that time are from estates which Harrods (Knightsbridge) have bought. There are a few antiques on sale, both furniture and bric-à-brac, but the majority of items are *reproduction furniture, upholstered sofas* and *chairs* (usually several sets on sale), *mirrors, kitchen appliances, carpets, beds, curtains, linen* and occasionally *books, pictures* and *jewellery*. Viewing is on Mondays and Tuesdays before the sale. *Carpets* are sold on Wednesday at 10 a.m. followed by *furniture*. *Objets d'art* are auctioned on Thursday at 10 a.m. *Household effects* are sold on Fridays at 10 a.m. [£+]

A. Stewart McCracken, 69 Dean Street, w1 (437-8374), are auction rooms specializing in *used catering* and *restaurant equipment*. Although much of their stock is too large for private use there is always plenty that is suitable for normal kitchens: things like *steel sinks, used cookers* and *electrical toasters, cutlery, china, kitchen tables, chairs* and *gadgets* of all kinds. Auctions are held every Wednesday at 2 p.m. and viewing is all day Tuesday and on Wednesday morning. This is a place to keep popping into since sooner or later every kind of kitchen device gets sold here. [£+]

Harveys, 22 Long Acre, wc2 (240-1464) is a new auction gallery which is still getting its footing and building up its reputation. It sells 'general goods and chattels' – which means general *household furnishings* and some *antiques* – on Wednesdays at 10.30 a.m. Viewing is on Tuesday. There are also *wine* sales about every six weeks at 6 p.m. A vendor's commission of 10 per cent is charged on all goods sold. [££]

*see also
Auctions,
Chapter 2, and
under relevant
subject headings*

BOOKS

More books are in print in Britain than anywhere in the world and the numbers continue to rise. If you read a book a day from the age of seven until you were seventy you would not get through the output of a single year. This is a mind-boggling prospect, but it shows the huge variety available to buy or order from London bookshops. Several booksellers specialize in one subject and many have a large postal trade. All the bookshops mentioned in this chapter will send books anywhere in the world and nearly all produce catalogues which they will gladly send you on request.

Books are practically the only goods that have 'fixed' prices in Britain. These are fixed by the publisher and booksellers must sell each title at its set price. Once a year, however, a book sale is held throughout Britain (it is called the National Book Sale) and during this time booksellers can reduce the price of books to get rid of overstock. The sale lasts ten days. Afterwards, any unsold books revert to their original price. Publishers also have a method of getting rid of unsold stock and this gives the public one other way to get new books at reduced prices. From time to time publishers sell their remaining stock of a title or titles to special 'remainders' dealers, and in doing so remove the fixed conditions of sale. The dealer then disposes of the books at any price he chooses and this usually means a reduction of 50 per cent or more. Many bookshops sell a few remainders and a few shops specialize in them.

Books make popular gifts and all bookshops sell Book Tokens which can be given to friends who can then choose their own books. Book Tokens are redeemable for new, un-remaindered books at any bookshop in Britain.

General bookshops

Dillon's, 1 Malet Street, WC1 (636-1577), is London's most scholastic general bookshop. There are over 80,000 titles covering a vast range of subjects which are of interest to the educated general reader as well as the academic. Dillon's is partly owned by London University and feels it has the best selection of educational and scientific books available in London. The foreign language, African and Oriental sections are also outstanding; but readers of history, biography, political science, fiction and many other topics will find their interests well represented in both hard-cover and paperback on the four floors of this large shop. There is a secondhand department, an antiquarian book section and a special Penguin section. In the basement is a small coffee shop where browsers can put their feet up, and there is a record shop that specializes in the spoken word but carries good music too. The shop's staff are knowledge-able and helpful. (Disabled persons will find that ramps and lifts between all the departments make it easy for wheel-chairs to move about the store.)

Hatchards, 187 Piccadilly, W1 (734-3201), is London's oldest bookshop. Since 1767 it has occupied the same site and been London's leading bookseller to the carriage trade. Hatchards stock newly-published general books and have strong sections on art, nature and *belles-lettres*. There is a paperback section in the basement and an antiquarian section specializing in fine bindings on the second floor. The shop publishes free lists of new books in stock and gardening books. More than one third of the firm's business is, in fact, by post. The staff at Hatchards know their books and although the shop seems a bit crowded because of the many tables stacked with volumes and the narrow spaces between them, the atmosphere is pleasant.

Harrods, Knightsbridge, sw1 (730-1234), lacks the dusty, cluttered atmosphere that many people love in bookshops but its efficient organization makes it the easiest big bookshop in London to find your way around. There are three very large rooms with wide aisles between the shelves and display tables, and every subject area is clearly marked and can be seen from a distance. The paperback section occupies one entire room and the books jut out at an angle so you can see the whole cover and not just a bewildering array of titles. Harrods' emphasis is on recent books: history, biography, fiction, travel and art. They also have sections devoted to military subjects, sports, gardening, cooking, even railways. One room is given over entirely to children's books.

The Government Bookshop, 49 High Holborn, wc1 (928-6977), sell the publications of Britain's biggest publishers, Her Majesty's Stationery Office. H.M.S.O. publish over fifty items every day and nearly all are available in the High Holborn shop. These are not just Hansards and parliamentary papers but include books on cooking, industrial management, growing strawberries, embroidery technique and regional geology – to name a few. H.M.S.O. publish no fiction (knowingly) but there is almost every other kind of book among the 2,000 titles on display. A further 30,000 are actually available. There is also a guide to hotels and restaurants in Britain, a big series on careers and a fine paperback series on antiques published in conjunction with the Victoria and Albert museum. Books tend to cost less here than those on the same subjects published commercially. H.M.S.O. are also the outlet in Britain for the publications of the United Nations.

Foyles, 119 Charing Cross Road, wc2 (437-5660), is the

leviathan of the book world with over four million volumes housed in two buildings. The store suffers from its sheer size. It is difficult to get around and you have to go through two processes to buy a book, first getting a slip and then queuing at the cashier. But whether it is general, technical, medical, in paperback or hardcover, they will probably have it if it's in print and maybe even if it isn't since there is both an antiquarian and a secondhand department. There is also a Penguin bookshop.

A shortlist of good general bookshops:

Compendium, 240 Camden High Street, NW1 (485-8944).

High Hill, 6 Hampstead High Street, NW3 (435-2218).

Truslove and Hanson, 205 Sloane Street, SW1 (235-2128).

Collet's Penguin Bookshop, 52 Charing Cross Road, WC2 (836-2315).

Special subjects

Turret Bookshop, 43 Floral Street, WC2 (837-9473). This bookshop was located for years in a sort of greenhouse and had the most distinctive atmosphere of any bookshop in London. But the lease expired and at the time of going to press the proprietor, Bernard Stone, had just found new premises in Floral Street where he intends to keep the flavour of the original shop. The Turret specializes in poetry and stocks all English poetry in print from the works of well-known poets published by established houses to that of struggling poets printed by equally struggling *avant-garde* presses. But poetry books are not the only attraction, there are lots of poetry magazines, poetry criticism and there are *poets* (who always find a free glass of wine waiting for them). There is a good secondhand stock.

Children's Book Centre, 229 Kensington High Street, w8 (937-6314), specializes entirely in books for boys and girls up to about thirteen years of age. The books are arranged according to subject – fiction, geography, arts and crafts – and not according to age as the management rightly feel that what a child wants to read is not always a matter of how old he or she is. There are over 5,000 titles in stock and parents are encouraged to bring their children in to choose for themselves. Every Saturday afternoon at 3.00 p.m. there is a story-telling session, often with film-strips, and sometimes authors and artists come in and give talks or answer questions. A newsletter is published quarterly about new books for children and includes discussions of topics like 'children's sex books'. The store is conveniently located next to a toy shop.

Foyles (Educational) Ltd, 36 Upper Berkeley Street, w1 (262-5310) (no connection with Foyles in Charing Cross Road), is the nation's largest school-book contractor. Most of the textbook business is handled from Sussex, however, and the purpose of the London shop is to stock fiction and non-fiction books for children from pre-school to O-level age. Teachers and librarians, as well as parents, come here from all over Britain and from overseas to buy books for schoolchildren. There is a general book department too.

Robinson and Watkins, 19 and 21 Cecil Court, Charing Cross Road, wc2 (836-2182), has been called the most magical bookshop in the world. Tucked away in Cecil Court, this firm has a world-wide reputation as a bookseller of the occult, the mystical and the exotic. There are books on magic, Oriental philosophy, astrology, Masonry, meditation, herbal medicine and acupuncture; in fact, almost anything dealing with that intriguing netherworld just beyond the grasp of both science and conventional religion.

St George's Gallery, 8 Duke Street, sw1 (930-0935). The best bookshop for the fine art trade and for art libraries. The Gallery specializes in exhibition catalogues from all over the world and keeps a large stock of foreign art books. They publish a catalogue quarterly.

Zwemmer, 76–80 Charing Cross Road, wc2 (836-4710). Britain's biggest specialist, if not the world's, on art and architecture books. Zwemmer's stock includes foreign language art books as well as English ones and there are usually a few 'remaindered' books on sale at greatly reduced prices.

Dance Books Ltd, 9 Cecil Court, wc2 (836-2314), have 99 per cent of what is published in Britain about dance plus a lot of books from America. These cover all forms of dance except ballroom dancing.

Luzac, 46 Great Russell Street, wc1 (636-1462), specialist booksellers on the Middle and Far East: books on the history, geography, travel, politics and religion of these areas, including a few books in French, Arabic and Indian languages. Luzac ship to all parts of the world and 90 per cent of their business is mail order. The firm publishes a list of books on special subjects about six times a year.

Cinema Bookshop, 13 Great Russell Street, wc1 (637-0206). Books for film-makers and film-goers: cinema history, cinema technique, television, animation, biographies of stars and directors, and film magazines from America as well as Britain. The owner-operator, Fred Zentner, also keeps a big supply of photographs of stars, directors and stills from movies.

Collet's Chinese Gallery and Bookshop, 40 Great Russell Street, wc1 (580-7538), specialize in books about China and books for learning to speak Chinese. They also sell folkcrafts from mainland China, and some prints and quality reproductions of Tang horses. The shop publishes a catalogue of paint brushes and a catalogue of books in stock. They also sell kites.

Economists Bookshop, Clare Market, Portugal Street, wc2 (405-5531), is owned jointly by the London School of Economics and the *Economist* newspaper and specializes in the social sciences. There are about 8,000 titles in stock plus a separate secondhand shop.

Samuel French, 26 Southampton Street, Strand, wc2 (836-7513), have a world-wide reputation as play publishers.

They also operate a theatrical bookshop in the house where actor David Garrick lived and sell books about the theatre and theatrical personalities as well as plays.

London Music Shop, 218 Great Portland Street, w1 (387-0851), carry about 700 titles on music history, theory, and instruction. They also sell sheet music and musical instruments.

H. K. Lewis, 136 Gower Street, wc1 (387-4282), is London's leading medical and scientific bookshop. Lewis's also run a lending library which includes many out-of-print and hard-to-get books as well as recently-published volumes. The yearly library subscription is from £3 and the service is indispensable to students and valuable to doctors, scientists and others with a serious interest in medicine and science.

Collet's International Bookshop, 129 Charing Cross Road, wc2 (734-0782). Russian language books, books about Russia and Russian works in translation. Free catalogue four times a year of books in stock. These include American publications and many paperbacks.

Hachette Librairie Française, 4 Regent Place, w1 (734-5259). Books in French and books about France, French newspapers and French magazines.

Kegan Paul, Trench, Trubner and Co., 39 Store Street, wc1 (636-1252), are specialists in Oriental and African culture, religion, history and politics. There is a secondhand department and a small art gallery selling Japanese prints.

Wholefood Bookshop, 112 Baker Street, w1 (935-3924). Books on health foods, nature cures, vegetarian diets, organic gardening and ecology – many are American publications.

Motor Books, 33 St Martin's Court, wc2 (836-5376). Books about the history, design and mechanics of cars, motorcycles and aircraft.

Stobart and Son, 67 Worship Street, ec2 (247-8671). Specialists in books on woodworking, metalworking and handicrafts, also building techniques and forestry. History as well as technique is covered. Catalogue can be supplied. (See also under specific craft subject in Chapter 5.)

A. Moroni and Son, 68 Old Compton Street, w1 (437-2847). Though not strictly speaking a bookshop, Moroni's is an important centre in the world of print. Their speciality is foreign newspapers and magazines. So whether you want to see the morning news from Ankara, find out the stock market quotations in the *Wall Street Journal* or read up on what the continental press is saying about the private life of British royalty, Moroni's is the place to go.

Discount books

The Booksmith, 148 Charing Cross Road, wc2 (836-3032), 36 St Martin's Lane, wc2 (836-5110) and 33 Maiden Lane, wc2 (836-3341), specialize in remaindered books. These are new books but all are reduced from their original price by at least one third and sometimes by considerably more. Apart from the volumes on the shelves The Booksmith have some three quarters of a million books on reserve in their warehouse. Discount shops like these are good places to buy gifts: expensively illustrated books sell at a fraction of their original cost – a fact your friends won't know unless, of course, they're doing the same thing.

Notting Hill Books, 132 Palace Gardens Terrace, w8 (727-5988). About 75 per cent of the stock in this pleasant little shop is remaindered and priced at 50 per cent or more below retail price. The rest is secondhand. There is a good section on art and literary criticism plus a selection of fiction, biography, history and political science.

Secondhand, rare and antique books

Quaritch, 5 Lower John Street, Golden Square, W1 (734-0562), are leading dealers in old and rare books, including *incunabula* (books printed before 1500), manuscripts, English literature, medicine and science, but are best-known for natural history books. Quaritch's books can cost £15 or £50,000, but the bread-and-butter trade is between £50 and £150. [£££]

Maggs, 50 Berkeley Square, W1 (499-2051), sell private press books, travel books of all countries, *incunabula*, fine bindings, illustrated manuscripts and military books. Housed in a handsome Georgian building, the firm publish several catalogues of books in stock and are always happy to advise young collectors. [£££]

Francis Edwards, 83 Marylebone High Street, W1 (935-9221). Best-known for their books on voyages and travels and for their maps, Francis Edwards also specialize in naval and military books and books on the history of transport and technology. But you can find something on almost any subject on the five floors of this building. If you want an out-of-print book which is not in stock, the firm will find it for you. [££+]

Bell, Book and Radmell, 80 Long Acre, WC2 (240-2161), is the place to go for first editions of early twentieth-century and contemporary literature. [££]

E. Joseph, 48A Charing Cross Road, WC2 (836-4111). Secondhand books on history, literature, art, natural history, military and naval history and travel. [££]

Albert Jackson, 68 Charing Cross Road, WC2 (836-9144). Secondhand books on general topics, with literary criticism and biography as specialities. Closed Mondays. [££]

Peter Eaton, 80 Holland Park Avenue, W11 (727-5211), deals in secondhand, antiquarian and rare books. General topics. [££]

Note: If you are looking for a particular out-of-print or rare book, ask your local bookdealer to place an ad for you in *Clique*, the trade magazine of antiquarian booksellers. Ads cannot be placed direct by customers but most booksellers are eligible, even though they don't have many secondhand books. In fact, the less their business is dependent on old books the more likely they are not to take a commission or finder's fee.

Cecil Court, wc2, is the home of several secondhand and antiquarian booksellers and additional addresses can be obtained from the Annual Directory of Booksellers published by *Clique* or the antiquarian directory published by the *Shepherd Press*.

Book services

Whitaker's, 13 Bedford Square, wc1 (636-4748), will tell you whether a book you want is in print or not and if so who publishes it and what other books are available by the same author. They are the publishers of *Books in Print*. Telephone them and ask for 'Booklist'.

Drescher, 17 Alverstone Road, nw2 (459-5543), are expert menders of paper and of vellum. They can repair tears and remove discoloration in fine books, maps and prints.

Sangorski and Sutcliffe, 1 Poland Street, w1 (437-2252), re-sew and hand-bind books in leather or cloth and leather. This can take a long time as there are thirty-six operations involved and the firm has a lot of work in hand.

Bernard Middleton, 3 Gauden Road, Clapham, sw4 (622-5388). If you have a really fine book in need of restoration or rebinding, take it to Mr Middleton as do London's leading rare book dealers. He not only does fine handbindings in leather and (when appropriate) in cloth, but he bleaches and re-sizes pages and can replace a page if necessary by printing a facsimile on comparable paper.

E. A. Weeks and Son, 168 North Gower Street, NW 1 (387-4674), bind books in cloth, buckram and leather. They will bind a thesis for around £6. This takes five days. Other binding jobs can take considerably longer.

A. Holt, 115 Whitecross Street, EC1 (606-5676), sells bookcloth of various types and spine materials for do-it, yourself binders. Mail orders accepted, but if you visit the shop yourself, call before 4 p.m. and avoid lunch hour. *Note:* Those wishing to learn the art of bookbinding should contact the **Camberwell School of Arts and Crafts**, Peckham Road, SE5 (703-0987).

John T. Marshall, Canonbury Works, Dove Road, N1 (226-9757), bookbinders' engraving tools, rolls and fillets and gold leaf.

Security Microfilm Systems, 10 Caledonia Street, N1 (837-0784), do all forms of microfilming as well as microfiche. They will microfilm out-of-print books and produce a bound Xerographic copy. This costs about £5 per 100 microfiche exposures, plus £3 per 100 pages of Xerography.

Harrods Lending Library, Knightsbridge, SW1 (730-1234). For those who like to read the latest books but don't want to buy them or wait for them to become available in local libraries, Harrods is the solution. Their lending library specializes in recent books for the general reader. A subscription costs about £12 and allows you one book at a time. (You can borrow more for a somewhat larger fee.) Harrods will deliver by van if you live in London (small fee) or post books to you in the country (you pay postage).

London Library, 14 St James's Square, SW1 (930-7705), is the world's largest private library and has provided the research facilities for a vast number of the histories, biographies, books of literary criticism etc., written in this country. The library does not stock *recent* fiction but every other non-professional subject for the educated reader is fully represented. Membership costs £30 a year and members can take out ten books at a time if they live in London and fifteen if they live in the country. They may keep the books until someone else asks for them provided they re-register them at regular intervals. The London Library also sends books to members who live abroad.

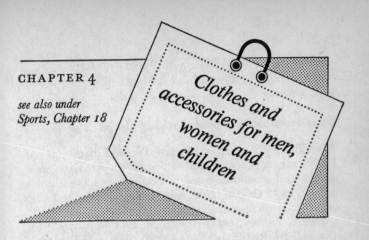

CHAPTER 4

see also under
Sports, Chapter 18

Clothes and accessories for men, women and children

Londoners usually know where they like to shop, but may not know about many specialist shops and services in London that are useful for finding a particular item, be it a hat, shirt, umbrella or an odd size, and this guide seeks to provide such information. It is worth remembering, however, that because specialty shops concentrate on the unusual they tend to be up-market, this is especially true where custom-made services are involved. Bargain hunters are advised to check the list of secondhand shops: these are often a source of well-made clothes in fine condition at highly reasonable prices. A model dress or Savile Row suit bought in a secondhand shop is probably going to look better and wear longer than a cheap, new outfit at the same price.

London visitors who want to browse around but are not looking for anything in particular will find the sections on boutiques and general clothing shops a help. These have brief listings of a range of shops for a variety of tastes and budgets. Visitors looking for a definite item will find the speciality sections of interest, too. A clothing chart giving British equivalents of European and American sizes can be found on pages 19 and 20.

Women's clothes

Boutiques and general clothing shops

The following is a brief summary of several shops that normally carry a general range of women's wear: coats, suits, dresses and separates. Some are expensive, some are not; some cater to elegant tastes, some to trend-lovers and a few to unswerving conservatives.

Laura Ashley, 9 Harriet Street, sw1 (235-9796), and 157 Fulham Road, sw3 (584-6939). Inexpensive and very popular with the young. Laura Ashley clothes are made in Wales and are mostly cotton prints in demure, *circa* 1890 styles. On the whole they are badly made but cheap and pretty. [£+]

Bazaar, 24 Brook Street, w1 (408-1673), and **Hampstead Bazaar**, 30 Heath Street, nw3 (794-6862). The Brook Street shop is a welcome off-shoot of the Hampstead one: both stock fashionable ethnic dress, including second-hand Afghan tribal garments; also smart new fashions. [££+]

Bellville-Sassoon, 73 Pavilion Road, sw1 (235-5801). English couture. Belinda Bellville shows a collection twice a year and clothes are made-to-measure. There is also a boutique with ready-to-wear, and a few things in it are part of the collection. Wedding dresses a speciality. [£££]

Brown's, 25 South Molton Street, w1 (499-5630) are an elegant and expensive boutique featuring many imports – Missoni knits for one – plus clothes by top English designers like Jean Muir. Lots of separates. [£££]

Bus Stop, 3 Kensington Church Street, w8 (937-4081). Fashionable clothes at moderate prices. Their styles are young, but not way out. [££]

C and A, 505 Oxford Street, w1 (629-7272) and branches. Very inexpensive clothes, some surprisingly smart. [£+]

Chic of Hampstead, 100 Heath Street, NW3 (435-5454).
One of the most elegant shops in London: worth a trip to
Hampstead. Clothes by top British designers and others.
[£££]

Crocodile, 58 Beauchamp Place, SW3 (589-4455) and
176 Kensington High Street, W8. Smart boutique with many
pretty knitted garments by Ulla Heathcote. [££, ££+]

Mary Davies, 12 Queen Street, W1 (499-1696). Clothes
by Donald Davies: checked wool shirts and shirt-dresses
and sweaters in shades that evoke Irish moors. There is a
branch at 79A Elizabeth Street, SW1. [££+]

Feathers, 40 Hans Crescent, SW1 (589-0356). As in most
fashionable London boutiques, most of the stock in Feathers
is imported from Italy and France. Pretty dresses, lots of
separates. This is a favourite spot for the young and well-to-
do. [££+]

Fenwicks, 63 New Bond Street, W1 (629-9161). A
moderately-priced department store with an emphasis on
women under forty, Fenwicks have clothes for all occasions;
also hats, handbags, shoes and accessories. [££]

Harrods, Knightsbridge, SW1 (730-1234). Huge first
floor devoted to women's wear, including designer rooms,
Jaeger shop, Cacherel corner, sweater section and fur shop.
There is a special youth wing on the fourth floor. Harrods
is more trad than fad, fourth floor excepted. [££, ££+]

Harvey Nichols, Knightsbridge, SW1 (235-5000), have
reorganized their women's clothing departments and the
result is two floors of exceptionally fashionable clothes in the
upper middle price range. Some of the older clientele are
disgruntled but other shoppers are delighted. Among many
agreeable aspects is the fact that clothes sold here tend to be
less expensive than the same garment sold in other shops.
Environment is pleasant, though lighting is perhaps a bit
too subdued. [££+]

Just Looking, 5 Brompton Road, SW3 (589-9329), plus
branches at 88 King's Road, SW3 and 464 Oxford Street,
W1. Fashionable dresses and separates priced somewhere
between moderate and expensive. [££, ££+]

Kensington Market, 49 Kensington High Street, w8 (no central telephone), is a large clothes market with three floors of individually operated stalls. The market is full of jeans, jazzy clothes, shoes and 'nostalgia' clothes made from old and pseudo-old fabrics. Some tribal dress and exotica. Lots of imagination, a Mecca for the young. [£+]

Lucienne Phillips, 89 Knightsbridge, sw1 (235-2134). Some people feel this is the best dress shop in London. Mrs Lucienne Phillips runs the shop and keeps a good selection of model dresses by Jean Muir, Bill Gibb and others. Separates are in the basement. [£££]

Marks and Spencer, 458 Oxford Street, w1 (486-6151) and branches. It is said that many Europeans come to London just to buy their clothes at Marks and Spencer and certainly there is no better value for money anywhere. M & S clothes are long-wearing, straightforward, washable styles designed for slender pocketbooks; but often just as popular with fat ones. Especially good for blouses and sweaters. [£+]

Parkers, 13A Heath Street, nw3 (435-8629) and 31 Brook Street, w1, small expensive boutiques noted for delicate gossamer designs. [£££]

Plaza 9, 33 Brompton Road, sw3 (581-1818). Very expensive, very smart, and very French. [£££]

Thea Porter, 8 Greek Street, w1 (437-0781). Miss Porter's one-of-a-kind designs are inspired by caftans and other Near Eastern styles. She has a fine sense of colour and mixes her fabrics with fascinating results. [£££]

Rahvis Couture, 50 Grosvenor Street, w1 (629-8301). The Rahvis sisters are among the few couturiers of the old style still in existence. They do two collections a year and each order is made-to-measure with the finest workmanship and painstaking attention. And they are moneysavers if you were planning to get the same service in Paris. By appointment only. [£££]

Zandra Rhodes, 14A Grafton Street, w1 (499-3596), one of England's top designers, sells her floating, feminine chiffons and other splendid creations from this address and from a boutique in Harrods. [£££]

Yves St Laurent Rive Gauche, 113 and 73 New Bond Street, w1 (493-1800), and in Knightsbridge, sell St Laurent's ready-to-wear. [££+]

Spectrum, 72 Gloucester Road, sw7 (584-7327), 151 Fulham Road, sw3 and 6 Kensington Church Street, w8. Excellent source of pretty clothes for comparatively little money. Young, rather romantic. [££]

Top Shop, Oxford Circus, w1 (636-7700), is in fact in a basement underneath Peter Robinson. It purports to be the largest fashion floor in Europe and certainly it is the best place to sample trendy styles. There are masses of boutique stalls, some of which are independently operated. Goods vary from inexpensive to up-market and include Kickers, Inca and Jeff Banks. [££]

Wallis, 490 Oxford Street, w1 (629-2171) and several branches. Moderately priced clothes that are well made and in good taste. Their designs lean towards the traditional but some styles are based on up-market designs. These are somewhat more expensive than the other stock. [££]

Blouses and shirts

James Drew, 3 Burlington Arcade, w1 (493-0714), is the female counterpart of the top men's shirtmaker Turnbull and Asser. All shirts are silk and all the fabrics are designed by the firm's own designers. Needless to say, they are pretty expensive. Prices start at £20. [£££]

Marks and Spencer, 458 Oxford Street, w1 (486-6151). All shirts and blouses bear the St Michael label, exclusive to Marks and Spencer, and most are not only below the price of similar goods elsewhere but are better made. Marks and Spencer try to keep abreast of fashion but within the limits of most people's pocketbooks. The firm tries out new lines in West End branches, especially the above (their largest store), so there is a good chance of getting the latest here. [£+]

Deborah and Clare, 29 Beauchamp Place, sw3 (584-2875), make custom-made shirts for men and women in specially imported silks and cottons. Delivery takes about three weeks. They also sell ready-made shirts in their own designs and unless you want something different or are an odd size it makes sense to buy these. They are a couple of pounds cheaper than the made-to-measure version. [££+]

Do-it-yourself clothes (see also Dress and suit fabrics, Chapter 6 and Sewing accessories, trimmings and related services, page 136)

Quintessence, 51 Chelsea Manor Street, sw3 (352-7403). Mrs Weisz designs, cuts and fits dresses and suits. The customer gets a kit which includes the lining, cut and fitted fabric, and trimming. All you have to do is sew it up. Each design is exclusive and only quality fabrics are used. Since many home sewers make muck-ups by not cutting a fabric correctly or fitting themselves properly, Mrs Weisz is worth knowing about. [££+]

Leslie Fogel, 5 South Molton Street, w1 (493-2541), will design, cut, fit and tack a garment which you then sew up. You provide the material and, if you like, the pattern too. If you need additional aid in hemming, fitting, etc., Fogels will assist you. If you give up altogether, they will make the whole garment. [££]

Clothkits, 24 High Street, Lewes, Sussex (Lewes 3487), do a business by catalogue and mail order. Long skirts, pinafores, blouses and other simple designs. The pattern is drawn on the cloth. You cut it out and sew it up. Ideal for young people. Clothkits include any haberdashery required and have a ten-day approve-or-return service. The firm also sells yarn and knitting patterns. [£+]

Furs (see also Auctions, Chapter 2)

Reputable furriers agree on one thing: it is not worth buying poor quality furs. Their advice is to decide just what kind of fur you can afford and then, whether it is rabbit or sable, get the best quality. Fur is, after all, a luxury item, so it is possible to wait.

Calman Links, 149 Brompton Road, sw3 (581-1927), are Britain's leading furriers. They believe this is because the best craftsmen work for them. Customers can, in fact, go upstairs to the workrooms and see what goes into the making of a fur coat. You can see mink pelts being 'let out' or 'stranded' (as they always are in better coats). Each pelt is slit practically to shreds and then patiently sewed up again. Calman Links use only female skins since these have a more furry texture than male pelts which tend to be hairy. Mink coats start at £1,000 but the average price for a 'stranded' coat is around £1,800. A 'stranded', female, *wild* mink coat – the best – costs at least £2,400. Calman Links sell more mink than all other furs combined but they also stock considerably less expensive furs (and more expensive ones). They make rabbit coats, for instance, but they use the best rabbit. Most designs are fairly classic. Mr Links believes a fur coat ought to outlast a fashion trend. Calman Links also clean, store and remodel quality furs. They have a sale in January and July of quality secondhand coats and model furs. [£££]

Frank Cooney, 23 Avery Row, w1 (629-4664), aims at smart but youthful tastes. Like most furriers he deals largely in mink but he also makes fashionable – even trendy – styles in fox, monkey, musquash, etc. Cooney's styles are stylish. Many of his mink coats are in unusual herringbone or flecked patterns. All are quality furs but are not in the highest price range. Mr Cooney also remodels coats and will let you trade your old coat in on a new one. [££+]

Maxwell Croft, 105 New Bond Street, w1 (629-6226), Elegant, highly-styled, sophisticated furs of top quality. [£££]

C. Sparrow, 273–87 Regent Street, w1 (493-1196), deal in quality secondhand furs of all kinds. These are greatly below current prices though many are like new. It is wise to ring first since the better furs are in cold storage and must be got out. All can be altered and remodelled. [£+]

M. Bennett, 19 South Molton Street, w1 (629-2757). Secondhand and remodelled furs of quality. This is a good place to sell your old coat if it is in good condition. [££]

Moss Bros., Bedford Street, wc2 (240-0567). Illusions of grandeur are fulfilled here: Moss Bros. rent fur coats and stoles. A mink coat for an evening costs about £25.

Antiquarius, 15 Flood Street, sw3 (351-1145). Several stalls in this market sell secondhand furs.

Hats

Frederick Fox, 26 Brook Street, w1 (629-5706), is the hat king. His boutique and model hats are available in fashionable stores all over the world but he still maintains a tiny salon in Brook Street which you enter through the back of a flower shop. Here, by appointment only, Mr Fox will personally show you his model hats and advise you on what style becomes you. All models can be made-to-measure, if necessary, and all can be adapted in style and fabric to individual needs. This takes about two weeks. Model hats average around £35 or £40. [£££]

Selfridges, Oxford Street, w1 (629-1234), have a large supply of medium-priced hats in many styles and colours and are reputed to do a bigger business in hats than any other department store. [££]

Simone Mirman, 9 Chesham Place, sw1 (235-5656), well-known couture milliners with a new collection every season. [£££]

Herbert Johnson, 13 Old Burlington Street, w1 (439-7397), somewhat better known as a man's hatter, but famous among both sexes for his casual floppy-brimmed felts and sporting hats. [££+]

George Malyard, 3 Kingly Street, w1 (437-1848), designs casual headgear which he sells in his showroom as well as in department stores. He will make up hats in your own design or fabric. [££+]

Miss Sanders, 83 George Street, W I (935-9014), re-models old hats. Now in her seventies, Miss Sanders has been a milliner since she was fourteen years old and she still makes a few creations of her own. [££]

Bourne and Hollingsworth, Oxford Street, W I (636-1515), have a variety of trimmings for do-it-yourself milliners and madcaps. There are pom-poms, feathers, veiling, ribbons, hat pins and stiffened hat shapes. [£]

Knitwear

Marks and Spencer, 458 Oxford Street, W I (486-6151). If you want to get value for money, Marks and Spencer have the best sweaters in the country. They are well-made yet inexpensive and come in a variety of traditional and trend-setting styles. Another advantage of Marks and Spencer is that you can return merchandise if you get home and change your mind. [£+]

Beatrice Bellini, 11 West Halkin Street, SW I (235-3027), designs and sells beautiful couture knitwear, nearly all of which is hand-knitted. There are sweaters (ski to evening-wear), shawls, dresses, suits and hats. A custom service is available and takes about five weeks. [£££]

Scotch House, 2 Brompton Road, SW I (589-4421), is, as every tourist knows, synonymous with sweaters and tartans. It has the widest choice of Scottish knitwear in cashmere, Shetland and lambswool that can be found. Well-known lines like Ballantyne, Pringle and Barrie are fully stocked; also Aran and Fair Isle pullovers and cardigans. Many styles are dyed to match Scottish tartans. Foreign customers save on V.A.T. However, you must pay the full price and fill out a form, and the store will send a refund when you get home. [££]

Scottish Merchant, 16 New Row, WC2 (836-2207). Splendid collection of casual sweaters. Styles tend to be more imaginative than most and colour abounds. Sweaters are attractively displayed on hangers with outstretched 'arms'. [££]

Homebound Craftsmen, 25A Holland Street, w8 (937-3924), is an outlet for the handiwork of old age pensioners and the disabled. Homebound Craftsmen will knit any sweater or garment, provided you supply the pattern and the yarn. Prices are calculated according to amount and weight of yarn needed, but, generally speaking, prices start around £3. An Aran sweater costs about £8. The store has some reasonably-priced hand-knit baby clothes on display as well as men's socks and a variety of stuffed animals. [££]

Ritva, 8 Hollywood Road, sw10 (352-2533). Mike and Ritva Ross – he's American, she's Finnish – design and make most of the knitwear in their shop but they also have 'limited editions' of sweaters designed by David Hockney and other artists. The Hockney edition, for example, is limited to 150 plus twenty 'artists' proofs'. Each costs £65. Others are less expensive. [££+]

Leather, suede and sheepskin garments

Leather, like fur, is a luxury material. Even the cheapest leather garments cost a lot of money, yet they are often badly cured and badly stitched and really not worth the price you pay for them. To get your money's worth wait until you can afford a reasonable standard of workmanship.

Janet Ibbotson, 7 Pond Place, sw3 (584-2856), is a remarkable young woman who personally designs and cuts the patterns for all the suede and leather garments in her shop. Everything is made downstairs and she believes she is the only designer in London who can come in early in the morning with an idea and have it in the window that afternoon. These are couture designs but not wildly expensive for leather. Many are trimmed with Eastern embroidery and Miss Ibbotson makes knit trim herself on a knitting machine and also hand-screens prints on leather. There are several styles in stock and the shop will make a style to measure if you are an odd size. This costs 20 per cent more since a special pattern must be made. [££+]

Miller and Bernstein, 224 Edgware Road, w2 (723-5058), will make your own designs up in leather or suede. Their first-floor premises are really the workrooms for their shops in Brighton but they have some things you can buy off-the-peg too. [££+]

Antartex, 143 Knightsbridge, sw3 (584-8410) and 6 Vigo Street, w1 (734-5906), is by far the best place for men, women and children's sheepskin coats and jackets. This is a Scottish family firm and most of the business is mail order. (Members of the family model all the styles illustrated in the catalogue.) There is a good selection on sale in their London showrooms and because they cut out the 'middle man' prices are better than elsewhere. A sheepskin jacket self-lined in wool costs about £50. [££]

Skincraft, 100 New Bond Street, w1 (629-5454). Quality leather garments, often by top designers. Good prices because Skincraft own several shops selling less expensive goods, so get buying advantage on fine quality too. [££+]

Loewe, 25 Old Bond Street, w1 (499-0787). Coats and suits, as well as shoes, bags and luggage of the finest quality, for women and men. Loewe have been Spain's leading leather merchants since the nineteenth century. All goods are proofed against spotting in the rain. Expensive, but worth it if you can afford it. Coats cost around £150 and upwards. [£££]

Lingerie

Bradley's 83 Knightsbridge, sw1 (235-2902), is London's largest lingerie specialty shop. Foundation garments, negligées and housecoats in English, continental and American designs. Bradley's try to stock things that are not generally available in department stores. They have their own factory and if your size is not in stock they will make it up for you in twenty-four hours. (All outsizes cost 10 per cent extra.) [££]

Rigby and Peller, 12 South Molton Street, w1 (629-6708), make the Queen's foundation garments. All Rigby and Peller foundations are made to measure and customers can use their own fabrics if they wish. Every design is individually adapted from basic patterns. The shop will also copy a favourite style which is no longer available elsewhere. Foundation garments take from two to six weeks to make. Bras cost from £15 to £25. Rigby and Peller are *corsetiers* and do not make slips and nightgowns but they do make some beachwear and housecoats. [£££]

Marks and Spencer, 458 Oxford Street, w1 (486-6151), can't be beaten for underwear at modest prices. [£+]

Courtenay, 22 Brook Street, w1 (629-0543). Some of the most exquisite ready-made lingerie in London. Courtenay specializes in small sizes, and all the delicate hand-finished nightgowns, slips and bedjackets are continental imports. Courtenay also sell towelling robes and turbans. [££+]

Rose Lewis, 40 Knightsbridge, sw1 (235-6885), guarantees to make a woman feel 'desired and desirable, whatever her age, whatever her size'. Most of the girdles, bras, suspender belts and knickers in this shop are Rose Lewis's own design (Dior also does some designs exclusively for her), and she will design lingerie especially for you or make up your own designs. If you have a rich imagination *and* pocketbook, anything is possible. [££+]

S. & S. Underwear, 38 Church Street, nw8 (723-7730). Most women's lingerie seems designed to give warmth by provoking some man to buy mink. S. & S.'s actually does the job itself. All kinds of old-fashioned things such as longjohns, cotton bloomers, long wool vests, side-zip corsets and sturdy brassieres are sold in this unpretentious little shop which has substantially ignored the whims of fad and fashion. Many garments are sold at discount prices and large sizes are a speciality. [£]

The White House, 51 New Bond Street, w1 (629-3521),

specializes in hand-made silk lingerie: slips, nightgowns and dressing-gowns are all made in the shop's own workrooms and are beautifully hand-stitched, and trimmed with lace, Slips start around £50. Nightgowns are slightly more. Orders take at least a week depending on the amount of hand work involved. The White House also sells hand-knitted bedjackets and bedsocks and carries a line of elegant ready-to-wear lingerie. [£££]

S. Weiss, 59 Shaftesbury Avenue, W1 (437-1821), cater to the realms of fantasy and anyone who is interested in the underpinnings of the British mind or body should pay a visit here. They stock colourful, beribboned silk stays (waspies), frilly garters and suspender belts, fishnet stockings, and sheer black stockings with seams. There are G strings in triangles and in lacy rosettes, zip-front briefs, even crotchless briefs and cupless brassieres, open tights and loose legged knickers. The clientele look quite ordinary on the outside. [££]

Janet Reger, 33 Brook Street, W1 (629-6504) and 2 Beauchamp Place, SW3 (584-9360). Boutiques filled with Miss Reger's delightful designs which combine the romantic and the provocative. Satiny nightgowns and peignoirs, slips and bras in matching ice-cream colours. [££+]

Secondhand and discount clothes (see also

Vintage clothes, page 98)

Mme Crisp, 61 Praed Street, W2 (723-4640), London's oldest dress agency, sells secondhand model dresses and suits as well as less expensive garments. The stock is somewhat conservative but there is the occasional Jean Muir or Bill Gibb to be had at less than half the original price. Sometimes bargains like these are not on display and customers should try and gain access to hidden stocks in the basement. Mme Crisp has many outsize garments and some hats and shoes. Those who wish to sell clothes can get cash outright here (other agencies take clothes on sale or return only), but garments must be in first-class condition. [£+]

Jenny, 40 Gordon Place, w8 (937-8493). 95 per cent of the clothes for sale in this cheerful boutique are secondhand; the rest are manufacturers' samples. Jenny also sells used handbags, jewellery and other odds and ends. Youthful emphasis. If you want to sell, not buy, the shop accepts clothes on a commission basis. After two months they are reduced and if they remain unsold they go to charity unless you collect them. [£+]

Just A Second, 10 Queensway, w2 (229-9422) and 19A Craven Road, w2 (402-5693), sell seconds, not secondhands. All stock is new: either end-of-line or reject. Especially recommended for separates. [£+]

The Frock Exchange, 450 Fulham Road, sw6 (381-2937). A fashionable dress agency for young women. The Exchange takes only the latest styles and these must be in good condition. There are many models by Ossie Clark, Jean Muir and Thea Porter. These can cost anywhere from £20 to £50 depending on style and condition but there are plenty of very inexpensive 'boutique' separates too. [££]

Mary Leigh, 47 South Molton Street, w1 (629-0750), is a dress agency for model gowns and a good place to get well-turned-out on a budget. People like Julie Andrews once bought their clothes here – now they sell them – and Dior, Givenchy and similar labels are not unusual. Furs and handbags are sold as well as dresses and suits. Models cost from £10 to £100 and sizes go up to 18. [££]

Panache, 70 High Street, Wimbledon, sw19 (947-4200), deals in top-quality clothes 'for women over twenty-five'. Lanvin, Pucci and other classics. If you have clothes of this type to sell, Panache will come to your house to collect them. [££]

Dress Pound, 125 Notting Hill Gate, w11 (229-3311), sell a variety of clothes including designer secondhands by Bill Gibb, Jean Muir, Zandra Rhodes. They also stock jewellery, shoes, handbags, belts. Customers wishing to dispose of old clothes must be prepared to collect unsaleables at the end of two months, otherwise garments are sent to charities. [££]

A shortlist of dress agencies

Daphne's, 66 Lower Sloane Street, SW1 (730-1416).
Dinah Lee, 275 Kensington High Street, W8 (602-6030).
Phyllis Kay, 158 Marylebone Road, NW1 (486-2638).
Pamela, 93 Walton Street, SW3 (589-6852).
Note: on Saturdays in the Portobello Road there are two open-air markets selling youthful secondhand clothes (jeans, etc.). One is called **The Good Fairy**, and the other has no name but is located under and around the bridge near the Tavistock Road intersection.

Every week *Time Out* magazine publishes a list of forthcoming Jumble Sales.

Shoes (see also Sports and games, Chapter 18)

Lilley and Skinner, 358 Oxford Street, W1 (629-6381), have a vast stock of moderately-priced shoes in traditional and trendy styles. Branches all over London, but their Oxford Street store has some unique departments. The 'Tall and Small' department stocks sizes 2 and 3 and sizes 9 to 12. There is a department for wide feet as well. Lilley and Skinner sell Clark's walking shoes and boots and their own famous Hush Puppies. [££]

Rayne, 15 Bond Street, W1 (493-3241), are the Queen's shoemaker and Britain's leading manufacturer of fine quality shoes. Some styles come in AAA to C widths and if they don't have your fitting they will make it for you for £5 extra. This takes about five weeks. 80 per cent of the shoes at Rayne are the firm's own designs. There are branches in Regent Street and the Brompton Road. [£££]

Deliss, 41 Beauchamp Place, SW3 (584-3321). Mr Deliss will make any style to measure (your design or his). Custom shoes start at around £45. Boots are more. If you are hard to shoe, Mr Deliss will sculpt a last for you. Then, he points out, you can have shoes made at Deliss or in Spain, where it's cheaper. Custom shoes take less than a week to make; lasts cost £35 and take a few days longer. Mr Deliss has his own line of fashion shoes for sale too. [£££]

Small and Tall Shoe Shop, 71 York Street, w1 (723-5321), specializes in English sizes 13 to 3 and 8½ to 11. Widths are from AA to D in some styles. The shoes are conservative and are not expensive. Illustrated mail-order brochure available. The shop is closed on Mondays. [££]

Lillywhites, Piccadilly Circus, sw1 (930-3081), famous for sportswear and sport wares, sell classic country walking shoes as well as special sporting shoes. [££]

T. Elliott, 184 Regent Street, w1 (734-9004), and branches, specialize in narrow fittings, one of the hardest things to find in Britain. AA and AAA widths. [££+]

Andy's, 61 Goldhawk Road, Shepherd's Bush, w12 (743-4978). Bespoke shoes at non-exorbitant prices. Andy has a few trendy designs of his own but most of his business is copying customers' shoes or making up shoes of their design. He has a wide selection of materials and delivery takes about two and a half weeks. [££+]

Scholl's, 59 Brompton Road, sw3 (589-1887), foot doctor to the nation, sell exercise sandals and clogs plus support hose, arch supports and corn plasters: everything to ease the aching foot. They also give foot treatments and pedicures (see Hairdressers, health and beauty treatments, Chapter 9). [££]

Orthopaedic Footwear Co., 4 Paddington Street, w1 (935-4149), fill orders for the Ministry of Health and for private customers. All orthopaedic shoes are made entirely by hand and take about four months to finish. [£££]

Anello and Davide, 33–5 Oxford Street, w1 (437-4042), are famous as dance and theatrical shoemakers. Students' dance shoes are sold at 96 Charing Cross Road, wc2, while professional dance shoes and theatrical shoes can be found at 30 Drury Lane. This store will make shoes from any period: Egyptian sandals to Empire pumps. Anello and

Davide also make boots to measure and anyone attached to an out-of-date style will find special 'end of line' annexes in north Oxford Street and Drury Lane shops: winkle pickers, stilettos, platforms – all at a fraction of what they cost when they were the rage. [££+]

Roots, 4 Conduit Street, w1 (493-5555), sell shoes for men and women which are based on a new principle of footwear. The shoe not only fits the contour of the foot but, more importantly, the heel is recessed. This distributes the body's weight more evenly, making it easier to be on one's feet for long periods. Roots shoes are almost a must in jobs which require standing up all day. Three widths. [££+]

Special occasions

Pro Nuptia, 19 Conduit Street, w1 (629-0424). A French firm specializing in wedding dress for brides, brides-maids and page boys. Most designs are exclusive to the firm. Bridal gowns cost from £25. They also sell special bridal underwear: slips designed to hold the train in place, blue garters, etc. [££]

Young's 178 Wardour Street, w1 (437-4422), rent wedding and party dresses. Since weddings are a one-time affair (in white anyway) this service makes a lot of sense. Rentals start at £16 and include price of alterations, veil, shoes and headdress. They also hire bridesmaid and pageboy outfits. Party-goers with 'nothing to wear' can rent an evening gown and matching shoes from Young's. Also a velvet cloak or fur stole. [££]

Berman and Nathan, 18 Irving Street, wc2 (839-1651), very old-established providers of wigs and theatrical cos-tumes. Particularly varied selection of ladies' period dress up to 1950, mostly from theatrical and film productions. Fancy dress, including national dress and fanciful character dress, is available even at short notice. You can also hire an evening dress if you want a jazzy, cabaret style. [££]

Elegance Maternelle, 101 Marylebone High Street, w1

(486-1176), and 199 Sloane Street, SW1 (235-6140). Everything for the expectant mother: separates, coats, dresses, slacks and lingerie. Styles tend to be conservative and in the medium price range but there is an expensive made-to-measure service too. The firm points out that specially-cut clothes can prevent pregnancies from showing for a long time. A catalogue is available showing some fifty styles in stock plus underwear and accessories. They also do large sizes, have a twenty-four-hour alteration service and, when possible, will alter styles 'back to normal' after pregnancy. [££+]

Just Jane, 6 and 8 Sloane Street, SW1 (235-6639), 60 Baker Street, W1 and 187 Brompton Road, SW3, sell model and boutique maternity wear. Youthful and attractive: many can be worn as ordinary clothes. Catalogue. [££+]

Moss Bros., Bedford Street, WC2 (240-4567), hire full-length maternity evening gowns. [££+]

Special sizes

There are several shops devoted exclusively to the needs of large people but tiny people must generally resort to children's shops. One advantage here, however, is the absence of V.A.T. Children's clothes are dealt with in some detail on pages 111-13, but everyone with special sizing problems should refer to other sections in this chapter since many contain information about made-to-measure clothes, shoes and accessories.

Evans, 538 Oxford Street, W1 (499-5372) and 204 Kensington High Street, W8. Separates, coats, suits, dresses and lingerie for women whose size is between 40 and 60. Clothes are moderately priced, traditional but not dowdy. Garments above size 48 are slightly more expensive. There are two large floors of stock and the staff appreciate customers' special problems. Evans have shops throughout the country. They publish a mail-order catalogue twice a year and any order that is unsatisfactory can be returned within seven days for a refund. [£+]

Tall Girl Shop, 17 Woodstock Street, w1 (499-8748). Most tall girls are not fat and the emphasis in this shop is definitely on the vertical. Everything for women between 5 foot 8 inches and 6 foot 2 inches high including special size gloves, shoes, tights and swimsuits. Prices are reasonable. A winter coat costs between £25 and £35. [££]

Long Tall Sally, 40 Chiltern Street, w1 (487-3370), is another shop catering for tall women. Stock includes extra-long jeans.

Martha Hill, 39 Marylebone High Street, w1 (935-4050), are not really an outsize shop but they carry large sizes in most of their styles and will make any design to measure. Their clothes are youthful, bright and not at all expensive. [££]

Buy and Large, 4 Holbein Place, sw1 (730-6534), is a boutique for women size 16 to 24 (hips 40 to 48). Quality dresses, coats and suits. Exclusive stockists of large size Donald Davies shirt-dresses. [££+]

Swan and Edgar, 49 Regent Street, w1 (730-1616) have a special 'Forty Four Room', stocking sizes 20 to 44. Traditional styles. [£+]

Sportswear (see Sports and games, Chapter 18)

Tailors

S. Cavalieri, 6 South Molton Street, w1 (629-5950), is a ladies' tailor who will make coats, suits and dresses. You bring in the material and lining. Two to three fittings are required. A trouser suit costs around £50. [££+]

Ladies' Habits, 5 Cale Street, sw3 (351-3281), is a new venture by an ex-fashion editor. She makes trousers, suits and long skirts in fine woollens and smart designs. A suit costs around £230 and a pair of trousers about £80. [£££]

Vintage clothes and exotica (see also under Textiles, tapestries, needlework and lace, page 49, and Auctions, Chapter 2)

Essenses, 410 King's Road, sw10 (352-0192), sell clothes dating from the late nineteenth century to the forties. Victorian nightgowns and chemises, embroidered shawls, Chinese robes and dresses of the thirties and forties. Essenses also have beautiful old fabrics – silks, velvet, lace – which they will only sell made into a garment for you by their dressmaker. The quality of the old clothes is usually above average (as are the prices) and there are a few old textiles for sale too. [££+]

Us, 51 Pembroke Road, w11 (727-8760). Men and women's clothes from the twenties, thirties and forties, including old fur coats; also lots of velvet curtains for rehanging or, like Scarlett O'Hara, wearing. Scruffy but fun. [£+]

Antiquarius, 15 Flood Street, sw3 (351-1145). The entire front of this indoor antique market on the corner of the King's Road is devoted to stalls specializing in vintage clothes; Chinese and paisley shawls, spangled dresses from the twenties, fox capes and trilbys from the thirties, padded-shouldered suits from the forties. Even the cartwheel skirts from the fifties are beginning to arrive. There is exotica from the Middle and Far East; some new costumes made with old fabrics and some old-fashioned costumes made with new fabrics. The stock is constantly changing. [££+]

Hindu Kush, 231 Portobello Road, w11 and 49 Kensington High Street, w8 (no phone), sell central Asian tribal dress, mostly from Afghanistan and embroidered with buttons, beads and needlework. [££+]

Forbidden Fruit, 325 King's Road, sw3 (351-1157) Afghan tribal dress and variations thereon. Some new, some secondhand. [££]

Rumak, 109 Walton Street, sw3 (584-2357). Rumak is a tiny world all its own. The long, flowing gowns are by the house designer and most have a romantic Eastern flavour. Fabrics range from chiffon to cotton and nearly all designs are trimmed with colourful ribands. [££+]

Tatters, 152A Fulham Road, SW10 (373-2084), sell fashion clothes from the 1850s through the 1940s, mainly for wearing rather than collecting. [££+]

Capricorn, 118 Kensington Park Road, W11 (727-6985). Clothes from the 1890s to 1930s; also dresses made from old lace and vintage fabrics. Special stock in the basement can be seen on request. [££+]

Bianca Buscaglia, 3 Halkin Arcade, SW1 (235-5552). Luxuriously embroidered garments from Yugoslavia – old and new – all have folkloric character. [£££]

Note: the Portobello Road and Camden Passage Market are good sources of vintage clothes. For details see Chapter 1.

Men's clothes

(See also Sports and games, Chapter 18)

Bespoke tailors

The English language and the English suit have spread throughout the world and of the two the suit has probably made the deeper impression. In far-flung places tailors cut British cloth into British-styled suits for customers who may never see an Englishman or learn a word of English. Yet despite the ubiquity of so-called 'western dress', the best tailoring in the world remains where it has been for over a hundred years: in London's Savile Row. The reputation of Savile Row's tailors, however, has spread almost as far as the dress they made famous. In Japan the word for suit is *seb-i-ro*.

Huntsman 11 Savile Row, W1 (734-7441), is the undisputed king of Savile Row. In 1800 the firm expanded from leather gloves into making leather riding breeches. They became, and still are, the world's premier maker of riding clothes for men and women. But they have built an equally unassailable reputation as tailors of ordinary clothes and today 180 employees are at work on the premises making town suits, sports jackets, trousers, evening dress and topcoats as well as riding habits. Classicists by reputation, Huntsman also adapt themselves to individual tastes and changing times. They make denim suits and jeans for underground moguls as well as three-piece worsteds for dukes and City folk. Everything is expensive. Suits start around £250, even in denim, take six weeks to make and require as many fittings as Huntsman feel are necessary for a perfect fit. Compensation: a Huntsman suit will last twenty years or more and many are altered to fit a second generation. [£££]

Nutters, 35A Savile Row, W1 (437-6850). A new and off-beat addition to Savile Row, Tommy Nutter is a designer first and a tailor second. He uses traditional fabrics in improbable ways, often combining two different tweeds or checks in one suit and trimming one cloth with another or with braid. Expertly made and very highly styled. Nutter suits costs about £160 and take eight weeks to make. Bespoke ladies' suits cost a lot more. Another speciality is frock coats. Clients include the Duke of Bedford and Mr and Mrs Mick Jagger. [£££]

Blades, 8 Burlington Gardens, W1 (734-8911). A youngish man's tailors with an eye on fashion. Suits cost between £130 and £275 depending on style and fabric. Blades make velvet suits, silk suits, whatever, and have an informal atmosphere. Two fittings are required, and delivery takes three to four weeks. Blades also sell ready-to-wear clothes. [£££]

Douglas Hayward, 95 Mount Street, W1 (499-5574). A very fashionable tailor, with very fashionable clientele, and top quality workmanship. Suits average around £150. Disregard rumours that Mr Hayward won't see you without an introduction. These have been spread around by snob customers to emphasize their own importance. [£££]

Anderson and Sheppard, 30 Savile Row, W1 (734-1420). Established Establishment tailors who have separate cutters for their older and their younger clientele. A boon for foreign visitors, Anderson and Sheppard will make a suit in three days, if necessary. Cost, around £140. [£££]

Regent and Gordon, 180 New Bond Street, w1 (493-7180). Those who want a Savile Row suit but can't afford it can get one at Regent and Gordon for less than half price. Regent and Gordon sell uncollected suits from top tailors, including Huntsman. If a client dies between fittings, changes his mind or won't pay his bill (apparently some people still don't pay their tailor) then the order goes for sale to Regent and Gordon, who usually have more than 100 suits in stock. Alterations available. [££]

Burtons, 114 Regent Street, w1 (734-1951), and over sixty London branches. One *Which* consumer survey recommended that to get value for money men should either go to an established Savile Row tailor or to an inexpensive tailoring chain like Burtons. Burtons sell made-to-measure suits from only £25. Each suit is cut to individual needs but there are no fittings. Measurements are made by trying on a sample style and size. If the final product doesn't fit, however, alterations are free. Burtons will also copy your old suit. Delivery takes five to seven weeks. [£+]

Tom Gilbey, 36 Sackville Street, w1 (734-4877), is a men's couturier. Gilbey's ready-made line is on sale in department stores like Harrods but he also does a made-to-measure collection of suits and knits available only in Sackville Street. Suits are ready in one week, and there is a 50 per cent deposit on orders. Ring first for an appointment. [£££]

Cyril Grimes, 48 Bishops Mansions, Bishops Park Road, sw6 (736-7976), comes to see the client. The ideal busy man's tailor, Mr Grimes will call at a customer's home in the evenings and fit him at his firm during lunch or working hours. What's more, Mr Grimes's prices are reasonable since he has few overheads: suits and topcoats are about £85. Good quality and highly recommended. [££]

General men's wear shops

Aquascutum, 100 Regent Street, w1 (734-6090), are world-famous for raincoats and tweed jackets. They also have everything else for men (except shoes, hats and umbrellas). Traditional styles. Suits average around £70. Their 'Club 92' boutique is more fashion-conscious. [££+]

Austin Reed, 103 Regent Street, w1 (734-6789), believe they are the largest men's wear store in Europe. Nearly 5,000 suits are in stock in Regent Street and there are over fifty branches. Austin Reed clothes are fashionable but not way-out. Masses of shirts, ties and casual clothes – all of good quality. The shoe department carries Church's shoes. other English styles and several trendy imports. Knightsbridge branch at 163 Brompton Road, sw3. [££, ££+]

Browns, 27 South Molton Street, w1 (629-4049), is thought by some to be the smartest men's boutique in London. A small, elegant and expensive selection of men's wear including Walter Albini, Missoni, Quasar and Derek Morton designs. (There is a women's section next door.) [£££]

Burberry's, 18 Haymarket, sw1 (930-3343), is another big name in raincoats but carries lots of other clothes in traditional styles. [££+]

Burtons, 114 Regent Street, w1 (734-1951). This is the showcase address for this large chain. Everything for men at modest prices. Styles get younger all the time. [£+]

Emperor of Wyoming, 404 King's Road, sw10 (351-0504) and 22 Pembridge Road, w11 (229-6600). Western-styled clothes: jeans, denim jackets, sheepskin, cowboy hats and boots and embroidered shirts. Also Navaho blankets and jewellery. Whatever you want from the West, the Emperor will get it. [£+]

Harry Fenton, 62 Shaftesbury Avenue, wc2 (734-3140), and other addresses. Fashionably-styled men's wear at budget to moderate prices. Youthful emphasis. Suits cost between £30 and £60. [££]

Gieves and Hawkes, 1 Savile Row, w1 (734-0186),

made their reputation as naval and military tailors respectively and have retained it, but they now sell everything for civilian wear too. They provide low-key fashion, and have lots of Chester Barrie clothes. Ready-made suits from £80. Also bespoke wear. [££+]

Harrods, Knightsbridge, sw1 (730-1234), has the best men's shop of any general department store. They stock everything and lots of it. [££+]

Marks and Spencer, 458 Oxford Street, w1 (486-6151), are a byword for good things at low prices. Their shirts and sweaters are first-class and many men swear by their suits too. Marks and Spencer have copied expensive suits with considerable success. £[+]

John Michael, 16 Savile Row, w1 (734-0831), and branches. Fashion minded businessmen and advertising executives dress here. Good selection, fairly pricey, and a chrome and maroon atmosphere. [££+]

Piero de Monzi, 68 Fulham Road, sw3 (589-8765), is a chi-chi boutique adjoining a women's shop. It sells Nino Cerruti suits, and is expensive. [£££]

Moss Bros., Bedford Street, wc2 (240-4567), has absolutely everything for men. Moss Bros. has made its name as a hire shop (see Special occasions, page 109) but it is equally worthwhile as a place to buy clothes. [££, ££+]

Simpsons, 203 Piccadilly, w1 (734-2002), is the home of Daks clothing. Four floors of merchandise for men. Hats to shoes plus sizes for every build: 36 inch to 50 inch in short, medium, long, portly and stout fittings. Trousers have 36 inch to 46 inch waists and lengths from 29 inches to 36 inches. There is a Trend boutique with a separate entrance on the corner specializing in *dernier cri* fashions. Simpsons has an interpreter service available in twenty-five languages including Japanese. [££+]

John Stephen, 36 Carnaby Street, w1 (734-5164) and other addresses. John Stephen is the Carnaby king. He sells everything for men but casual clothes are a speciality. Best-known for trousers, Denim suits from £15. [£+]

Wallers, 21 Newport Court, w1 (437-2057), is an old

family-run business which has developed from secondhand clothes to well-made 'ends of ranges'. The labels have been removed but the makes are clearly in the more up-market end of the trade. [££]

Hats

James Lock, 6 St James's Street, sw1 (930-8874), have been in St James's over 200 years and, as most people know, made the first bowler, which they still call a Coke hat after the man they made it for. Customers are fitted for Coke hats and top hats by trying on a turn-of-the-century device that looks like a circle of typewriter keys and gives the correct head shape. The hat is then heated and moulded to the shape. This takes about fifteen minutes. Known for formal headgear, Lock's have casual hats and caps too. Old English atmosphere, polite service. Unbeatable label. [££+]

Herbert Johnson, 13 Old Burlington Street, w1 (439-7397), stock the widest variety of hats in town: felt, straw, fur, tweed, bowlers, top hats, crash helmets, welding helmets, riding caps, topees and yachting caps, but are best known for wide-brimmed felts. [££+]

Knitwear (see under Women's clothes, page 87)

Leather and suede garments (see under
Women's clothes, page 88)

Paraphernalia

James Smith, 53 New Oxford Street, wc1 (836-4731), have been making umbrellas and walking sticks for 150 years. Available in silk, nylon and plastic, Smith's umbrellas include ladies' parasols and golf umbrellas. Prices start around £2 and go to £30 for an ivory-handled silk model. Smith's do very little custom work today but they have a good selection of canes and shooting sticks in stock. [££]

Kingsway Trunks, 3 Sicilian Avenue, wc1 (405-7500). Cut-rate umbrellas. Many shops claim to deal in 'lost property' but don't. Kingsway are the exception and usually have some fifty or sixty umbrellas lost on British Rail, costing from 80p to £2. They also have new, inexpensive luggage and briefcases. [£]

E. H. Rann, 21 Sicilian Avenue, wc1 (405-4759), specializes in old school ties, regimental ties and university and college ties and badges. [£+]

Finnigans, 198 Sloane Street, sw1 (245-9141), are leather merchants with a big selection of briefcases, attaché cases and luggage. Mostly English makes. [££+]

Maxwells, 177 New Bond Street, w1 (493-1097). Famous bootmakers, also make briefcases and wallets to any size or specification. Top quality but expensive. [£££]

Clements, 125 Regent Street, w1 (734-4910), sell real bristle shaving brushes and hairbrushes in ivory, wood, silver or imitation tortoise-shell. Brand names include Mason Pearson and Kent. [££+]

United Services Supply, 17 Terminus Place, sw1 (834-5929), and 58 Charing Cross Road, wc2 (836-7392), is a good place to get inexpensive luggage, knapsacks, sleeping bags and camping equipment (see also Sports and games Chapter 18). [£]

Inderwick's, 45 Carnaby Street, w1 (734-6574), England's oldest pipemakers, sell every kind of pipe at their old-fashioned premises in swinging Carnaby Street: briars, meerschaums, clay pipes, even hookahs. Pipe repairs a speciality. Free catalogue. [££]

Astleys, 109 Jermyn Street, sw1 (930-1687), are famous for their meerschaum and briar pipes. Astleys also repair pipes. They have a private collection of antique pipes and sell some antique meerschaums but not from their collection. [££+]

Fribourg and Treyer, 31 Haymarket, sw1 (930-1305).

Quintessentially English, this bow-windowed shop is thought to be the oldest shop in the West End. Fribourg and Treyer have been selling snuff since the early eighteenth century and anyone wishing to sniff snuff will find snuff boxes, spoons and handkerchiefs there too. Those who prefer to inhale tobacco through their mouths rather than their noses will find a fine selection of cigars and cigarettes. [££+]

Secondhand clothes (see also Vintage clothes and exotica, page 98)

Barry Gee, 82 Wilton Road, sw1 (828-1081). Men's secondhand town suits and dress suits. Some 'ends of line' and tailors' rejects. All in good condition. Suits and top-coats cost from £5 to £40; alterations are available. For those with clothes to sell, Mr Gee will usually give cash on the spot if he's convinced the goods aren't stolen. [£+]

Axfords, 306 Vauxhall Bridge Road, sw1 (834-1934), have been selling secondhand men's wear for years but are finding it harder to get quality merchandise and have branched out into selling colourful women's underwear, although they still keep a sizeable suit stock. [£+]

Lipman's, 37 Oxford Street, w1 (437-5711), sell formal dress from their hire department: dinner suits, morning suits and tail suits that originally cost £75 are priced around £25. [££]

Marks, 75-7 Praed Street, w2 (723-7447), and

A. Alexander, 79 Praed Street, w2 (no phone), next door to one another, are excellent sources of leather, suede and tweed jackets at unbeatable prices. Suits, too. [£]

George Salvidge, 51 Praed Street, w2 (723-0632), have mostly secondhand suits from £4 to £30. [£]

Note to secondhand shoppers: on Saturdays in the Portobello Road there are two open-air markets selling secondhand clothes (jeans, etc.). One is called **The Good Fairy** and the other has no name but is located under and around the bridge near the Tavistock Road intersection.

Every week *Time Out* magazine publishes a list of forth-coming Jumble Sales.

Shirts

Turnbull and Asser, 71 Jermyn Street, w1 (930-0502), are London's leading shirtmakers. They sell ready-made and bespoke shirts in their own English cottons and silks. Expensive: cotton shirts from £10 and silk around £30. Turnbull and Asser will make or copy any style, and ready-made white shirts can be bought with extra collars and cuffs that can be replaced when needed. Bespoke work takes six weeks. [£££]

Marks and Spencer, 458 Oxford Street, w1 (486-6151), and other branches. Not a large selection but Marks and Spencer shirts are well-made and durable and cost £4 and under. [£+]

Millions of Shirts, 18 Beauchamp Place, sw1 (584-1100). Ready-made shirts in a variety of colourful prints, some with matching ties. [££+]

Deborah and Clare, 29 Beauchamp Place, sw3 (584-2875), make custom-made shirts in imported silks and cotton. Delivery takes about three weeks. They also sell ready-made shirts in their own designs and unless you want something special or are an odd size it makes sense to buy these. They are a couple of pounds cheaper than the made-to-measure versions. [££+]

Erich Weiner, 93 Mortimer Street, w1 (636-3030), is a shirtmaker specializing in theatrical and unusual styles. Most of his clientele are in show business and need period styles for films or flashy extravaganzas to mesmerize pop audiences, but Mr Weiner will and can make up whatever you want. Special seven-day service for tourists. [££+]

Shoes (see also General men's wear shops, page 102, and Sports and games, Chapter 18)

John Lobb, 9 St James's Street, (930-3664). World-famous bespoke shoemaker with congenial, old-fashioned premises in St James's where you can see shoes being made. There are several styles to choose from but Lobb's will make anything. All shoes are entirely hand-made and each customer's lasts are cut in wood. Be prepared to wait several months, however, and to fork out £115 or more. Trees are £23 extra. (A special rush service can be arranged.) Lobb's say their shoes will last ten years or more with proper care. This means never wearing them two days running and sending them to the firm for all repairs: (a complete resoling costs £22). [£££]

Derber, 79 Wardour Street, w1 (437-2125), and branches, sell way-out, jazzy styles for men and women. [££]

Gucci, 172 New Bond Street, w1 (629-2716). The top international name in leather, Gucci shoes have a look which other Gucci wearers and jet-setters recognize. *The* shoe for those who feel it is important to look well-heeled, they also wear extremely well and are really not as expensive as some other top makes of shoe. (For men and women.) [££+]

Maxwell's, 177 New Bond Street, w1 (493-1097), make the world's finest riding boots but are expert shoemakers too. Most shoes are bespoke but they also have some ready-made styles. Like Lobb's, Maxwell shoes are entirely hand-made and individually lasted. It takes an estimated forty hours of work to make a pair of lasts and shoes by hand. Orders take considerably longer to fill, however. Boots now take a year and bespoke shoes three months. Maxwell's were spurriers in the eighteenth century and still carry over fifty kinds in stock. (See also Riding, page 284) [£££]

New Form, 4 Denbigh Street, sw1 (834-6988), specialize in discount shoes direct from the factory, also ends of lines and odd lots. They are good value for leather shoes, desert boots, sneakers and bedroom slippers. [£+]

Blackman's, 28A Cheshire Street, E2 (739-3902). Some people think this shop gives the best value for money in men's shoes to be found in London. A good deal of the stock consists of brand-name shoes at well below West End prices. [£+]

Trickers, 67 Jermyn Street, SW1 (930-6395), sell hand-made, hand-lasted shoes at half the price of Lobb's and Maxwell's. They claim this is because they have their own works in Northampton. Bespoke shoes take five months to get but half of Trickers' business is selling ready-made, hand-made shoes. Trickers make velvet monogrammed slippers and make up slippers from customers' own needle-work (get details about this before you start). [££+]

Note: the following entries under Shoes, Women's clothes, page 93 make or sell men's shoes too: **Anello and Davide, Andy's, Deliss, Lilley and Skinner, Ortho-paedic Footwear Co., Roots.**

Special occasions (see also Sports and games, Chapter 18)

Alkit, Cambridge Circus, WC2 (836-1814), are specialists in tropical kits: they have lots of washable, light-weight clothing including drip-dry shirts, khaki shorts, cotton socks, safari suits and some camping equipment. They also do be-spoke tailoring and have a boutique for trendy tropicals. [££]

Berman and Nathan's, 18 Irving Street, WC2 (839-1651), and other addresses, hire costumes. Their stock includes men's period dress, military uniforms and fanciful dress. Each category is located at a different address, so ring first and find out where to go. [££]

Moss Bros., Bedford Street, WC2 (240-4567), is synony-mous with clothes hire. Morning suits, dinner clothes and evening dress, livery, diplomatic or military dress, can all be hired here or, if you prefer, purchased. No deposit is re-quired and every suit is altered to fit the customer. For those who can't come in personally Moss Bros. also have a postal hire service with a special self-measurement form. Complete outfits cost between £4 and £8 to hire. [££]

Ede and Ravenscroft, 93 Chancery Lane, WC2 (405-0602), make, sell and hire legal, academic and peers' robes; also powdered wigs. [££]

Special sizes (see also under other sections in Men's clothes since many include made-to-measure services)

High and Mighty, 145 Edgware Road, W2 (723-8754), also in High Holborn and the Brompton Road, have clothes for tall men and broad men. High and Mighty sell suits, jeans, shoes, coats, shirts and underwear. Tall sizes come in 30 inch to 44 inch waists with a 36 inch or 37 inch inside leg measurement; portly sizes go from a 42 inch to a 60 inch waist. Medium prices. [££]

Cooper's All Size, 72 and 74 Edgware Road, W2 (402-8635). Ready-to-wear clothes for men from 5 foot 1 inch to 7 foot 5 inches high. Coopers can fit a man with a chest measurement of 34 inches or 65 inches and inside leg goes to 42 inches. Alterations are available and can often be done in only two hours if required. Prices are low to medium. [£+]

Children's clothes

(see also Sports and games, Chapter 18, Toys, Chapter 20, Crafts, Chapter 5, and Children's parties, page 269. for babysitters see Domestic services, page 261).

General children's wear

C and A, 505 Oxford Street, w1 (629-7272), and many branches, have first-class inexpensive children's wear; usually well-made, nicely styled and easy to clean. [£+]

Children's Bazaar, 162 Sloane Street, sw1 (730-8901). Secondhand children's clothes that were outgrown before they were outworn. There is a good stock of coats, jackets and dresses, and these are on the whole top quality items: velvet party dresses between £2 and £5. The shop accepts children's clothes for sale on a sale or return basis. [££]

Clothkits, 24 High Street, Lewes, Sussex (Lewes 3487). supply do-it-yourself children's wear which can save money for any mother who likes to sew. Clothkits are ordered by post through their illustrated catalogue. Each item has the pattern drawn on the fabric and the kit includes all the sewing materials and trimmings required. You just cut it out and sew it up. Most patterns are easy: pinafores, simple dresses, T-shirts and trousers. If you don't like your choice when you get it you can get your money back by returning the kit within ten days. Free catalogue. [£+]

Colts of Hampstead, 5 Hampstead High Street, nw3 (435-7387), are well known for their knock-about clothes for boys aged four to sixteen. [££]

Greens of Kensington, 168 Kensington High Street, w8 (937-4465), have an excellent selection of children's clothes at moderate prices. Greens have several branches in the London area and stock clothes for boys and girls from day of birth to teens. [££]

Homebound Craftsmen, 25A Holland Street, w8

(937-3924), is an outlet for the work of the elderly and disabled. They will knit any children's garments provided you bring in the pattern and the wool. There is always a supply of handknitted infants' wear on sale at low prices and a selection of stuffed animals. [£+]

Kids in Gear, 49 Carnaby Street, w1 (437-6009), sell denims and trendy styles for Carnaby kids aged one to fourteen. [££]

Marks and Spencer, 458 Oxford Street, w1 (486-6151), and branches. More children's clothes are probably bought in Marks and Spencer than anywhere; if not, they ought to be. Marks and Spencer children's wear is well-made, inexpensive and hard-wearing. [£+]

Mothercare, 461 Oxford Street, w1 (629-6621), and suburban addresses, is a children's department store – everything from clothes to prams, baby linen, bottles and toys for children up to five. The utilitarian appearance of the store is a bit off-putting but prices are low and emphasis is on the practical. If you don't want to go there, send for their illustrated mail-order catalogue. Mothercare also supply disposable nappies monthly by post. [££]

Tigermoth, 166 Portobello Road, w11 (727-7564) and 425 Richmond Road, Twickenham, is the favourite of many mothers. Tigermoth clothes boys and girls from cradle to college but infants' wear is the real speciality. Send a stamp for mail-order catalogue. [££]

Rowes of Bond Street, 120 New Bond Street, w1 (734-9711), is England's most exclusive children's shop. 200 years ago when they were sailors' outfitters they made a few sailor suits for sailors' children. The idea caught the fancy of the Royal family who brought the Royal children to Rowe's to be outfitted in mini-sailor suits. As a result all well-to-do Victorian children and their descendants were decked out in sailor suits. Not surprisingly, Rowes have the Royal warrant for children's clothes. They do bespoke tailoring for boys and girls, including riding wear, and they have recently added a trendy department on the ground floor. Rowe's shoe department is full of old-fashioned styles:

buckled Cromwells, patent Oxfords, button bars, girls' opera shoes and ankle strap shoes. There is a mail-order catalogue and Rowe tailors go to America twice a year to take orders. [£££]

Valerie Goad, 48 Beauchamp Place, sw3 (584-7270). Delightfully romantic dresses for children from 6 months to 15 years. All are Miss Goad's own designs. [££+]

Zero Four, 53 South Molton Street, w1 (493-4920). This is the best of the boutiques for rich kids. Pretty imports and fine knitwear which is exclusive to the shop. Infants to twelve-year-olds. Gifts vouchers. [£££]

Special occasions and accessories

Berman and Nathan, 18 Irving Street, wc2 (839-1651), hire children's fancy dress; mostly period costumes which have been used in film and theatrical productions.

Theatre Zoo, 28 New Row, wc2 (836-3150), rents animal costumes – camels, gorillas, bears, etc. for children who are 3 foot 9 inches or over.

Boots Chemists, Criterion Building, Piccadilly, w1 (930-4761), and branches everywhere, stock perhaps more baby accessories than anyone – baby foods, medicines, soaps and lotions, and nappies with disposable liners – all at reasonable prices.

Hire Service Shops, 192 Campden Hill Road, w8 (727-0897) and other branches, rent high chairs, push chairs, safety gates, carrying cots, playpens, scales and prams by the day or week. Collection and delivery service.

Clothing repairs and services

Since clothes and shoes need constant attention and cleaners, laundries and repair shops are part of any neighbourhood, the following list concentrates on the more off-beat, special services.

Jeeves, 8 Pont Street, sw 1 (235-1101) and 6 Heath Street, nw 3 (794-4100), are a complete clothes care service. They do fine dry-cleaning and laundering and, although expensive, are recommended for difficult fabrics, furs and leather (cleaning leather gloves is a speciality). Jeeves also do alterations, re-weaving, even shoe mending, and will professionally pack your clothes for travelling and unpack them when you get back. Their delivery service is free and will collect even a necktie. There is also a worldwide postal service and an overnight hatch through which you can drop clothes. Service takes a week and is very costly.

Lewis and Wayne, 13 Elystan Street, sw 3 (589-5730), are top-notch cleaners and launderers specializing in evening-wear. For collection ring 767-8777 or post to 9 Streatham High Street, sw 16. Expensive.

Watford Model Laundry, Whippendell Road, Watford (Watford 25277). This is a superior laundering and cleaning service, yet not staggeringly expensive. Laundry is hand-folded and hand-finished and there is a regular collection and delivery service.

Association of British Launderers and Cleaners, 319 Pinner Road, Harrow, Middlesex (863-7755), will provide a list of member firms and cleaners in your area, and specialist cleaners. They will also mediate controversies between customers and members of the Association and follow up customer complaints. (For self-service laundries see the Yellow Pages of the Telephone Directory.)

Leather Restorers, 22 Brompton Arcade, sw 3 (589-1580), clean leather, suede and fur. In operation for sixteen years they use a special patented process from

Sweden and cleaning takes around two weeks. They will also adjust hems, mend tears, sew on buttons and do other minor repair work.

James Smith, 53 New Oxford Street, WC1 (836-4731), repair umbrellas. They will re-cover umbrellas in nylon or silk, mend broken ribs and tips and replace handles.

Handbag Services, 183A Brompton Road, SW3 (589-4975), are specialists in handbag repairs. They will re-place frames, handles or clasps, re-line bags and bind edges, put new backing on *petit-point* and re-polish crocodile. Small repairs take a week, big ones a month. Handbag Services will also make handbags to your specifications.

Clements, 63 Burlington Arcade, W1 (493-0997), re-place natural bristles in old brushes.

Dylon Colour Advice Centre, Worsley Bridge Road, SE26 (650-4801), give free advice on dyeing any object at home. If you have trouble with any of their dyes, send them the item and they will sort it out for you, if possible.

Charing Cross Station and **Leicester Square** are about the only places left in London where you can get a shoe shine.

Royal School of Needlework, 25 Prince's Gate, SW7 (589-0077), will monogram clothes and accessories.

British Invisible Mending Service, 1 Hinde Street, W1 (935-2487), can repair any woven fabric except velvet; this includes woollens, knitwear, jersey, linen, printed fabrics, bridal veils, even chiffon. The normal service takes three days but unless the hole is quite small it is often not worth the cost.

Grange Training Centre, Great Bookham, Leather-head, Surrey (31-52608), monogram linens and other items by hand.

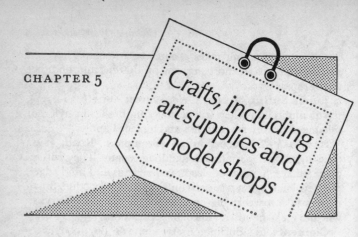

CHAPTER 5

Crafts, including art supplies and model shops

All craft shops will advise beginners on materials and most sell special beginners' kits. Craft shops also usually know where you can get instruction and where you can sell your handiwork.

The I.L.E.A. (Inner London Educational Authority) holds evening classes in most crafts and the fee is negligible. Details of I.L.E.A. courses are listed in their publication, *Floodlight*, available at news-stands, the I.L.E.A. office or your library.

Artists' materials

Rowney, 12 Percy Street, w 1 (636-8241), and
Winsor and Newton, 51 Rathbone Place, w 1 (636-4231), are top sources of art supplies for both professionals and amateurs. Each firm produces its own pigment in two grades, an 'artist' quality and a standard or 'student' grade called 'Winton' at Winsor and Newton and 'Georgian' at Rowney. Both shops carry portfolios, smocks, letraset, sketchbooks and poster boards as well as oils, watercolours, pastels, inks, brushes, easels and canvas either stretched or on the roll. Winsor and Newton have a little studio where customers can try out a new colour or material.

They also have oil colour boxes which cost anything from £10 to £170, depending on the number of oils and tools included. For real amateurs there are 'oilographs', pictures that have been sketched by professional artists for beginners to colour. Both firms have excellent mail-order catalogues.

Collet's Chinese Gallery, 40 Great Russell Street, wc1 (580-7538), sell Oriental paint brushes and Chinese ink sticks. They publish a brush catalogue which they will post on request.

Kantex, 20 Store Street, wc1 (636-0541), sell flax and linen canvas, also cotton duck and hessian, at reasonable prices.

Basket-making and raffia work

Eaton Bag Co., 16 Manette Street, w1 (437-9391), are the best suppliers of cane for basketwork and believe they are the only firm in London which has flat cane for caning chair seats. There are half a dozen different widths of basket cane in stock plus sea-grass and raffia. Eaton also undertake repairs of exotic baskets.

Hobby Horse, 15 Langton Street, sw10 (351-1913), sell natural cane, sea-grass and plywood bases for baskets in half a dozen shapes.

Bookbinding (see Book services, page 76)

Brass rubbing

Phillips and Page, 50 Kensington Church Street, w8 (937-5839). Everything a brass rubbing enthusiast needs: heelball (wax for rubbing with), suitable papers in several colours and grades, masking tape and a number of books on brass rubbing, including several county guides with locations of brasses and details on getting rubbing permission. (Phillips and Page stress that permission must be obtained in all locations recommended by them.) The firm frames rubbings and a stock list for mail orders is available through their office at 40 Elm Hill, Norwich.

Candle-making

Candle Makers Supplies, 28 Blythe Road, w14 (602-1812), can provide paraffin wax (granulated or in slabs,) beeswax, stearin, wax glue, wax dyes, wicks, thermometers, perfume and a number of books on candle-making. There are glass, metal and engraved or embossed plastic moulds. Candle Makers also market a kit which is available in most craft shops, contains everything except a thermometer, makes up to seventeen candles and costs about £3. Free illustrated brochure. The store is closed half day on Thursdays and every day during lunch.

Candles Shop, 89 Parkway, nw1 (485-3232). Candle-making supplies and ready-made candles, thirty-two perfumes for scenting candles and a kit which has everything, including a thermometer, and makes about twelve candles. The Candles Shop will buy back candles made from their kit, provided, of course, they are properly made.

Carpentry and metalwork (see also Household decoration, Chapter 11)

S. Tyzack, 341 Old Street, ec1 (739-8301). All woodworking tools including lathes. (For *woodcarving* tools, see Sculpture and woodcarving, page 129.)

Buck and Ryan, 101 Tottenham Court Road, w1 (636-7475), and 55 Harrow Road, w2, are Britain's most comprehensive tool merchants. A family-run business for the past 150 years, Buck and Ryan stock all woodworking hand-tools, plus tools for engraving, sculpting and metalwork (art metal hammers, repoussé hammers, etc.). They also carry engineers' precision tools, electric tools, light machine tools, wood lathes, centre lathes (for metal), light milling machines and cutlery. Scissors and saw sharpening service available. Free illustrated catalogue.

F. H. Brundle, 75 Culford Road, N 1 (254-2384). Nail specialists, selling wire nails, cut nails and tacks for every conceivable purpose. Oval wire nails, square twisted nails and annular ring nails designed to really stay put, lath nails, lost head and old-fashioned cut nails for floors and horseshoe nails. They even have square copper nails for boat-building. Mr Brundle is helpful and amiable.

Hire Technicians, 610 High Road, Wembley, Middlesex (902-3669) (and other suburban addresses), hire drills, saws, sanders, grinders, welders and other electrical tools for wood and metalwork. Rental is by the hour, day or week. There is a delivery service and items may be reserved in advance. A deposit is required. Hire Technicians also repair tools.

Crochet (see Needlework, page 125)

Enamelling (see Jewellery and beadwork, page 120)

Fabric painting and dyeing (see also Printing, page 128)

Hobby Horse, 15 Langton Street, SW 10 (351-1913), and **Candle Makers Supplies**, 28 Blythe Road, W 14 (602-1812), have all materials necessary for batik work: wax, dye, brushes, Tjantings (the pen with which the hot wax is applied), frames for holding the cloth and materials for cleansing it. They also have an introductory batik kit and sell hot- and cold-water dyes and books on fabric painting and dyeing. Hobby Horse sells suitable cloth for batik painting, Vat dyes.

Reeves, 178 Kensington High Street, W 8 (937-5370), sell Reeves and Deka colours that go on just about anything and stay there, they say. Wax for batiking, too.

Matheson, Marcon Place, E 8 (254-9684), sell materials

for making natural dyes, including indigo in both powder and extract form. Mordants too. They also stock synthetic dyes of all kinds and biological dyes for use in medicine and pathology. Large mail-order business. Price list on request.

Jewellery and beadwork

Ells and Farrier, 5 Princes Street, w1 (629-9964), is a scruffy little shop with an enormous stock of beads for stringing, weaving and embroidering: Indian-style beads and bead-looms, glass beads, *diamanté*, pearls, sequins and sequin motifs (the shop will make up any design in sequins). They also sell a kit for making beaded flowers. Ideal for jewellery and other decorative or theatrical uses.

Hobby Horse, 15 Langton Street, sw10 (351-1913), have a sizeable stock of wood, glass and ceramic beads; bead-looms and bead-loom kits too. Also jewellery 'findings', basic jewellery-making tools and horseshoe nails for bending into ornamental shapes.

Baku Trading Company, 80 Portobello Road, w8 (229-2787). Antique and reproduction African trading beads of multi-coloured glass. Baku beads cost from a few pence to a pound or more and were used as currency in Africa until the beginning of the century.

Reeves, 178 Kensington High Street, w8 (937-5370), sell materials for enamelling including copper by the square foot and a variety of 'blanks' suitable for enamel jewellery. Also enamelling kilns and paints, and jewellery findings in silver and gilt. Catalogue 50p.

Leisurecraft Centre, 2–10 Jerdan Place, sw6. Opaque and transparent enamel in powdered form or crushed lumps; tools, copper blanks and small kilns. An enamelling catalogue is available.

Hirsh Jacobson, 91 Marylebone High Street, w1 (935-4709) Stone-polishing machines or 'tumblers', wholesale or retail. Also diamond saws and grinders. Send a self-addressed envelope for stocklist.

Hydebourne, 46 Rainham Road, nw10 (960-1404),

manufacture simplified machines for craft work, especially kilns and control units for enamelling, metal-casting and glass fusing. Their metal-casting kiln has a vacuum casting unit and vibrator. They also make electro-plating and polishing machines. Free catalogue.

Mineral Stones, 111 Hatton Garden, EC1 (405-0197). Hatton Garden is the centre of the jewellery trade and several fascinating shops and workshops involved in the craft exist. Mineral Stones deal in semi-precious and precious stones, cut and uncut, and also sell metal detectors (for hunting old coins, etc.). They will cut stones.

Charles Cooper, 23 Hatton Wall, Hatton Garden, EC1 (278-8167). Gold and silver fittings, findings, and chain, plus piercing saws and other jewellery-making tools; also tripoli and rouge for polishing. Catalogue 50p.

J. Blundell, 199 Wardour Street, W1 (437-4746). Gold and silver for making jewellery can be bought in sheets of varying thickness or in chains, wires and findings for mounting, connecting and fastening.

Gemrocks, 7 Brunswick Shopping Centre, WC1 (837-7350), are specialists in precious and semi-precious stones; some rough, some cut and polished. (Other minerals too.) 75 per cent of Gemrocks' business is stones, the rest is related machinery: flat laps (for polishing flat surfaces), rock rascals (combination saw, grinder and polisher), diamond drills and cutters and assorted tumblers. Books on jewellery-making and on stones in general; findings in gilt, nickel plate and silver.

Knitting (see Needlework, page 125)

Leather

Connolly Bros., 39 Chalton Street, NW1 (387-1661). Whether you want to upholster a chair, or make a dress, suitcase, handbag or belt in leather you can find the right type at Connolly's. The firm sells cow-hide for every purpose except shoes and they will dye a skin to order. One skin measures about 45 square feet and half a hide is normally the smallest quantity they deal in, but they do have left-over bits and, being a helpful firm, will usually sell these to a customer who only needs enough for a watchband or a spectacle case.

Taylor and Co., 54 Old Street, EC1 (253-3319), have every kind of tool for working with leather: hole-punchers, needles, modellers, creasers; also leather fittings like buckles, rivets and press studs.

Barrow Hepburn Leathercraft, 29 King Street, Crieff, Perthshire (0764-2421). Barrow Hepburn own tanneries and operate a mail-order outlet selling tools and all sorts of leather (except reptile) for clothing, upholstery and other craft purposes. Catalogue costs about 50p.

H. Band and Co., Brent Way, High Street, Brentford, Middlesex (560-2025). Finest vellum and parchment for books, documents, lampshades and drumheads. Also chamois for export only, Band specialize in medieval and Kelmscott vellum – Kelmscott was first produced by them for William Morris.

J. T. Batchelor, 146 Fleet Road, NW3 (267-0593), sell special aniline dyes for leather (by the ounce) and other leather supplies.

John T. Marshall, Canonbury Works, Dove Road, N1 (226-7957), sell bookbinding tools for leather engraving. Also gold blocking presses and gold leaf.

Macramé

Hobby Horse, 15 Langton Street, SW10 (351-1913). Cord and string in various thicknesses, fasteners for belts, bamboo handles for macramé bags and sticks for macramé wall hangings. For beginners they have a basic kit with board, clip, pins, beads, twine and a leaflet on knots. A macramé belt kit is also on sale. Catalogue.

Models and model-making

Beatties, 112 High Holborn, w1 (405-6285), are England's biggest model shop, selling kits for model cars, aeroplanes, boats, motorcycles and weapons; their prices range from 40p for a plastic plane or small tank to £125 for a Rolls Royce. They have a full range of model railway equipment, and a secondhand and discount department. Beatties also stock Meccano parts.

Hamblings, 29 Cecil Court, wc2 (836-4704), specialize in N and OO gauge railways: kits or ready-made. They stock their own driving wheels and cardboard buildings, and have lots of odds and ends for locomotives and coaches plus paints, tools for tinkering and transformers and controls.

W. and H. Models, 14 New Cavendish Street, w1 (486-3561), are chock-a-block with kits for boats, cars and planes; also narrow gauge railways in N, OO and O sizes. Mail-order catalogue costs 25p. Models start under £1, although a Cumulus 2800 glider kit is £60 and a finished galleon model is £135. W. and H. also stock a random supply of balsa wood.

Tradition, 5A Shepherd Street, w1 (493-7452). Metal model soldiers in seven sizes (120 mm to 25 mm), painted and ready-to-paint. (Humbrol paint stocked.) There are Greek, Spartan, Roman and 'Roman enemies', medieval and modern soldiers. War game enthusiasts will find British involvements like the Seven Years War, and the Napoleonic, Zulu, Indian and Crimean campaigns fully represented. Unpainted soldiers in the standard 54 mm size cost about £1 each. Painted, they are about £10. Books and antique lead soldiers too. Tradition publish a mail-order list. They also have a small supply of antique military uniforms and antique swords.

Under Two Flags, 4 St Christopher's Place, w1 (935-6934). Six different sizes of lead soldiers (54 mm to 100 mm). British, continental and American makes. Several kinds of paint. Books and prints on military subjects, antique lead soldiers and plastic soldier kits.

Motor Books, 33 St Martin's Court, WC2 (836-5376). Exclusively books about cars, motorcycles and aircraft – life-size and model. In an annexe around the corner they also sell military books and model automobile and motorcycle kits. These are mostly in plastic or a combination of metal and plastic. Ready-made dyecast models sold too.

Steam Age, 59 Cadogan Street, SW3 (584-4357), have a wonderful array of old model railways for collectors, steamboat models and stationary engines. Steam Age make 5 inch gauge railways and locomotives that are actually big enough to carry passengers. [££+]

Henry J. Nicholls, 308 Holloway Road, N7 (607-4272). Model aircraft and radio control specialist with over 400 kits in plastic and balsa. The cheapest radio-controlled model is £100. Proportional radio controls and models can cost up to £600.

Aeronautical Modellers, 39 Parkway, NW1 (485-1818). Model boat and aeroplane kits plus engines and radio controls. They have some forty boat kits mostly in wood and costing from 80p. (H.M.S. *Victory* is £80.) Engines cost from £6 to £100 and controls are £41 to £350. Closed Mondays and Thursdays.

Mosaic

Edgar Udny, 83–5 Bondway, SW8 (735-2821), sell vitreous glass mosaic by the square foot, also *smalti* and ceramic and agglomerated marble tiles. They stock the necessary tools for cutting and laying mosaic and will mount it on paper facing if required. Postal orders are welcome but there is no catalogue.

Needlework (see also Fabrics and sewing
  accessories, Chapter 6)

The Needlewoman, 146 Regent Street, w1 (734-1727),
is the undisputed centre for general needlework supplies,
and both beginners and old hands can get what they need
here. Embroidery materials of every kind including kits for
embroidering pillows and panels, damask cloths with designs marked out for embroidering, or plain cloths, place
mats, napkins and handkerchiefs for your own embroidery
designs. Workbaskets, needles, scissors, frames, etc. All sorts
of books on handwork from soft toys to patchwork and
church embroidery. The Needlewoman have various kits
covering macramé, patchwork, doll-making and other
crafts. They stock knitting and crochet materials and a
variety of canvases for tapestry work. These tend towards
'middlebrow' flower patterns and reproductions of famous
paintings. Catalogues cost 20p and no mail order under £3
is accepted.
  W. H. I. Tapestry Shop, 85 Pimlico Road, sw1
(730-5366), sells hand-painted canvases and thread for
cushions, bell pulls, handbags, chair seats etc. These are exclusive to the shop and designs are more interesting than the
conventional flower canvases. The shop will also copy your
own design on to canvas and make up customers' work into
cushions, bags, framed pictures, screens and table tops.
Thread is available in both crewel and tapestry weight, and
Bargello designs can be rented.
  Luxury Needlepoint, 36 Beauchamp Place, sw3
(584-0499), is a family-run business selling *petit point* and
gros point tapestry canvases and thread and specializing in
tramé. Most are the shop's own designs. They will also make
work into cushions, frames and bags.
  Laura Ashley, 40 Sloane Street, sw1 (235-9728), sells
bundles of left-over cotton scraps for patchwork. Laura
Ashley prints are just right for old-fashioned quilt designs.
  Royal School of Needlework, 25 Prince's Gate, sw7

(589-0077), gives instruction in all forms of embroidery; I.L.E.A. evening classes, half-day classes and private tuition are available. They have a shop on the first floor with embroidery requisites: backs, frames, thimbles, Appleton wools, filofloss and hand-painted canvases. They will loan counted patterns and will copy designs on to canvas, or create designs to order.

Wools and Embroideries Ltd, 3 Queen's Parade, NW4 (202-9488). Mail-order knitting, tapestry and rug yarns. Unfortunately there is no catalogue but they stock the entire range of Paton and Jaeger knitting yarns and Coates' tapestry yarns, among others. Orders sent all over the world.

Anything Left Handed, 65 Beak Street, W1 (437-3910). Left-handed scissors and much-needed instruction books on how to do needlework or crochet if you're left-handed.

Papercraft

Paperchase, 216 Tottenham Court Road, W1 (637-1121), and 167 Fulham Road, SW3 (589-7839). Paper for origami, masks, pattern-making, decorating and drawing: coated papers, coloured papers, Japanese papers, tissue papers and foil – to name a few. Poster boards and books on papercraft.

Pottery

Fulham Pottery, 210 New King's Road, SW6 (736-1188), is believed to be the oldest pottery in England. Founded in 1671, it is now a sales warehouse for pottery supplies and has the widest variety of clays available in London, plus a complete selection of pottery tools, brushes, glazes, wheels and kilns. A preliminary trip isn't necessary as they publish an excellent catalogue, well-illustrated and highly informative. They also have kits for beginners.

Alec Tiranti, 21 Goodge Place, w1 (636-8565), is a centrally-located source of grey and terracotta clay; also some turning tools and an 8-inch diameter banding wheel, but most materials are really for sculptors.

Podmores, 105 Minet Road, sw9 (737-3636). This shop, located in Brixton, is highly recommended as a source of supplies for craftsmen potters. Podmores stock all raw materials and equipment necessary to the craft – clays, glazes, tools, kilns, wheels, moulds – and are happy to give free technical advice. They also repair equipment. Catalogue available.

Chelsea Pottery, 13 Radnor Walk, sw3 (352-1366), gives lessons in pottery and is a sort of club for pottery enthusiasts. For less than £10 per year anyone can join and use the facilities any time between 9 a.m. and 9 p.m. six days a week for only sixpence an hour. Children's subscription fees are half price. Lessons are on an individual basis for adults and a group basis for children and are not expensive. The director, Mr Hubbard, says that since pottery is largely a matter of practice it makes sense for beginners to join the pottery club and then take a lesson every now and then rather than sign up for regular lessons. Materials are available on the premises and there is a pottery saleroom of wares by professional potters who work there. Seconds are sold for practically nothing. The pottery will undertake commissions for all kinds of ceramic work.

Craftsmen Potters Association, William Blake House, Marshall Street, w1 (437-7605), exhibit and sell the work of Association members. The C.P.A. also sell books on pottery technique and history and a selection of specially-designed turning tools.

Note: value for money, pottery is about the least expensive hand-made artifact you can buy. Some other places to buy pottery are:

Craft Centre of Great Britain, 43 Earlham Street, wc2 (836-6993), which exhibits the work of contemporary potters.

Leach Pottery, St Ives, Cornwall (073 670 6398). One

of the world's greatest potters, Bernard Leach has developed several standard designs of bowls, cups, jugs and ovenproof stoneware. All are available in four choices of glaze. A tall jug costs around £3 and a lidded casserole dish about £2. Illustrated catalogue and brief history of Bernard Leach's pottery, 60p.

Printing (see also Fabric painting and dyeing, page 119)

Selectasine Silk Screens, 22 Bulstrode Street, WI (935-0768). Basic equipment for amateur and professional silk screen printers: printing frames, mesh for covering frames, inks for paper and fabric printing (ink for other mediums can be ordered). Also photographic, hand-cut and basic block stencils. Selectasine carry special ultra-violet lights, acetate film, opaque ink, gelatin and screen emulsion for making and developing photographic stencils. Free catalogue.

E. T. Marler, Deer Park Road, SW19 (540-8531), sell transfer papers for screen printing on ceramics and all screen-printing materials. Mail orders accepted.

C. J. Graphic Supplies, 4 Ganton Street, WI (439-3489). Complete selection of Mecanorma letterpress for printing. Various types of print – alphabet, numerals, symbols. Excellent catalogue.

Hunter, Penrose and Littlejohn, Spa Road, SE16 (237-6636). Engraving and lithography supplies: metals, etchants, resin for coating plates, film for exposure, metal engraving tools and a variety of inks and processing chemicals. Catalogue on request.

Falkiner Fine Papers, 4 Mart Street, WC2 (240-2339), behind the Royal Opera House, are paper specialists for art and craft work: Japanese, watercolour, fine printing, marbled papers and vellum off-cuts.

Hobby Horse, 15 Langton Street, SW10 (351-1913), sell silk-screen printing frames and squeegees. Catalogue.

Sculpture and woodcarving

Alec Tiranti, 21 Goodge Place, w1 (636-8565). Number one suppliers of woodcarving and sculpting materials. Alec Tiranti have every sort of tool needed for working in wood or stone, plus sculpting supplies like lead pipe, wire, clay, turntables, modelling stands, goggles, and polyester resin and glass fibre for cold casting. Comprehensive catalogue.

Marble and Onyx, 465 Finchley Road, nw3 (435-1827), have Carrara marble and onyx in sizes suitable for carving.

J. Bysouth, Dorset Road, Tottenham, n15 (800-3403), supply Portland, Bath, Ancaster and Clipsham stone in blocks and slabs for sculpture and engraving.

Morris Singer Foundry, 18 South Parade, sw3 (352-6452), will cast any work in bronze, brass, aluminium – even gold or silver – provided the cast belongs to the person who brings it in. A life-size head in bronze takes eight to ten weeks.

Stobart and Son, 67 Worship Street, ec2 (247-8671), specializes in books on wood and metalworking. Over seventy titles on woodcarving alone. Catalogue by request.

Shellcraft

Eaton Bag Co., 16 Manette Street, w1 (437-9391), sell all sizes of shells, common and rare, for decoration and design.

Weaving

Handweavers Studio and Gallery, 29 Haroldstone Road, e17 (521-2281), located in Walthamstow, is a complete service for hand-weavers; spinning wheels (for flax, wool and cotton) and table and floor looms for sale or for hire by the hour, day or week. Depending on what stage you wish to begin there is yarn or fleece, raw flax, cotton and silk for spinning and dyeing. Handweavers give instruction in spinning, dyeing and weaving and sell customers' hand-woven fabrics in a little gallery that is part of the shop. Closed Mondays.

Hobby Horse, 15 Langton Street, sw10 (351-1913), sell Lervad looms from Denmark, wool and cotton thread.

Reeves, 178 Kensington High Street, w8 (937-5370). Braid looms, table looms and foot-powered floor looms; rug frames and looms. Cotton and wool yarn and fleece for spinning. Catalogue 50p.

Fabrics and sewing accessories

Dress and suit fabrics

John Lewis, Oxford Street, w 1 (629-7711), have the biggest fabric department in Europe: cottons, silks, woollens, synthetics, tartans, fabrics suitable for saris. Although there is less variety in each *type* of fabric than in some specialty shops, anything you buy at John Lewis cannot be got retail for less elsewhere. In fact, it often is less at John Lewis. The fabric department caters for home sewing and a dressmaking adviser is on duty to answer questions. [££]

Jason's, 53 New Bond Street, w 1 (629-2606), claim to be the most exclusive silk shop in London. The staff is helpful and the stock is by no means limited to silks; there are a variety of imported fabrics for ladies' suits. Bolts of solid-coloured silk and some of the more delicate fabrics are kept in covered boxes and must be brought out for inspection. Prices are high to sky-high. Jason's clientele are rarely amateur seamstresses sewing for amusement or economy, they are ladies who have dressmakers, who want originality and can pay for it. [£££]

Simmonds at Stanley Lowe, 42 New Bond Street, w 1 (629-3866), are like Jason's above – elegant fabrics and

131

elegant clientele – but Lowe's have no desire to encourage new customers. [£££]

Laura Ashley, 71 Lower Sloane Street, sw1 (730-1771), sell inexpensive cottons in solid colours and prints. Fabrics are dyed and printed in the shop's factory in Wales and designs are delicate, traditional and very popular with the young. [£]

Jacob Gordon Ltd, 19 South Molton Street, w1 (629-5947), is a good source of fabrics at bargain prices. The shop specializes in selling clearing lots from model fashion houses and 90 per cent of the tweeds, cottons, silks, synthetics and men's suiting fabrics are well below retail price. Sizeable remnants are available at even greater reductions and the firm will let you talk them down further on these. Display space has been sacrificed to provide more room for stock but the staff will point you in the right direction and it is well worth the effort to look around. [££+]

All Woollens Ltd, 32 Great Marlborough Street, w1 (437-5751), and the

Tax Free Shop, 99 Regent Street, w1 (408-2068), are exactly what they sound like. Both specialize in woollen and cashmere cloth for men and women and both give discounts (V.A.T. exemption) to anyone who can produce a foreign passport and a foreign destination. The average man's suit, incidentally, takes about three and a half yards of material. [££]

Allan's, 56 Duke Street, w1 (629-3781). According to the Guinness Book of Records, the most expensive fabric in the world is sold by Allan's and costs £135 a yard. But this should not put off those who want to pay a lot less. Allan's is a well-rounded shop and devotes its basement to selling broken ranges at 30 per cent and more below retail prices. Allan's specialize in evening fabrics but they also stock many beautiful silks, cottons, novelty tweeds and fine woollens. Light-weight suiting for men is another speciality. The staff are well equipped to help and advise you and if you don't want to make a garment yourself, they will give you the name of a dressmaker. [££+]

G. Wood, 162 New Cavendish Street, w 1 (636-7488), sell very inexpensive cottons, woollens and synthetics. Located in the basement of a run-down building, G. Wood's is recommended to those whose main consideration is to save money. It is a bargain basement in every sense of the word. [£]

Jane Halkin, 45 Sloane Avenue, sw3 (589-2919), has been selling English tweeds and silk and cotton prints for over twenty years. There is a dressmaker in residence who will make things up to your design or the shop's. Prices are medium to fairly high but there are clearance sales in January and June when remnants in generous dress and skirt lengths are greatly reduced. [££+]

Liberty and Co. Ltd, Regent Street, w 1 (734-1234). No list of English fabric houses is complete without Liberty's. In the 100 years since they began by selling Japanese silks, Liberty's have become world-famous for fabrics. True to their beginnings they still maintain a special department of Oriental silks and cottons but most of their fabrics are designed, dyed and printed in this country. They still produce the traditional flower prints and Tana lawn which became a Liberty trademark between the wars, but they also design new and contemporary prints and produce the old ones in new colour combinations. [££+]

Hunt and Winterbotham, 4 Old Bond Street, w 1 (493-0940), were weavers in the sixteenth century and are now affiliated with the nation's largest textile manufacturers. They have literally thousands of quality suiting fabrics – tweeds, cashmere, vicuna and worsteds – and will send samples by post. [££+]

Kopelovitch, 84 Berwick Street, w 1 (437-6194), sell machine-made lace ranging from inexpensive borders to elegant re-embroidered lace fabrics. [££+]

Note on metric conversions: 36 in. = 90 cm, 45 in. = 115 cm, 48 in. = 120 cm, 54 in. = 140 cm.

Furnishing fabrics

(See also Curtains, blinds, and upholstery services, page 190.)

Afia, 85 Baker Street, w1 (935-5013), has appeal for everyone – savers and spenders alike. Afia's stock is huge: there are four basements plus the showroom and if that isn't enough there are sample books to order from. Afia *specialize* in selling clearing lots, particularly Dralon velvet, and prices are often reduced by as much as 50 per cent on quality goods. Furthermore, if your curtains or covers are worn out and you like the design but can't get it any more, Afia will copy it for you. They do this for the National Trust and Victoria and Albert Museum as well as private customers and, needless to say, it is costly. [££, ££+]

Laura Ashley, 40 Sloane Street, sw1 (235-9728), sell inexpensive furnishing fabrics at this address and dress fabrics at another. All fabrics are cotton and are printed in Wales. Prints usually have two colours and designs have a simple and traditional flavour. Prices start at 60p and run to about £2. [£]

The Fabric Shop, 6 Cale Street, sw7 (584-8495), was started by two interior designers to provide a selection of fabrics from international sources. Customers can help themselves to free cigarettes and make their choice while puffing away on a comfortable Chesterfield sofa. The fabrics – many of which take about three weeks to get – are from America, France, Switzerland and Italy. Original designs produced by London art students are also available and the shop will make up a customer's own design and even arrange for walls and blinds to be painted in it. These services are, of course, expensive. The Fabric Shop also has a special range of nursery prints and some vivid complementary coloured prints drawn from natural subjects. [£££]

John Lewis, Oxford Street, w1 (629-7711), has a big range of furnishing fabrics at unbeatable prices. Before you buy any fabric you may have chosen elsewhere, check with John Lewis. If they stock it, you will probably get it for less (for example, Sanderson's William Morris prints are, on average, 20 per cent cheaper here). John Lewis have a curtain-making and upholstery service but there is a long wait and it is advisable to get such work done elsewhere. There are clearance sales in January and July. [£+]

Peter Jones, Sloane Square, sw3 (730-3434), is part of the John Lewis Partnership and its policy is therefore about the same. But while John Lewis tends to range from the inexpensive to the medium lines, Peter Jones goes from the medium to the somewhat more expensive. [££]

Curtains and Crafts, 7 Westbourne Grove, w2 (229-7877). If economy is a big consideration then the cottons and synthetics here are well worth looking at. A good percentage of the stock is sometimes reduced and the shop will make unlined curtains free of charge to readers of the *London Shopping Guide*. They also make loose covers. [£]

The Designers Guild, 277 King's Road, sw3 (351-1271), stocks its own designs and specializes in things that match. Fabrics have matching and complementary wallpaper, paint, carpets, lamp-bases and patchwork. Mostly cotton and linen, some Indian crewel-work. [££+]

Watts, 7 Tufton Street, sw1 (222-7169), are church furnishers who also stock Victorian damask and a selection of trimmings and tassels. Free catalogue. [££+]

Tamasa Fabrics Ltd, 343 King's Road, sw3 (351-1126), have a handsome range of bold, modern designs which are created in their workshop. They also stock several sheer fabrics of their own design. [££+]

Colefax and Fowler, 39 Brook Street, w1 (493-2231) and 25 Walton Street, sw3 (589-3795), is the place to go for exclusive chintzes. There are some eighty patterns all reproduced from old documents, 36 inch and 50 inch widths, from £4. [££+]

Frederick Clarke, 68 Pembroke Road, w8 (603-0022), is another good source of quality chintz – English, French and American designs. [££+]

Heal's, 196 Tottenham Court Road, W1 (636-1666), sell contemporary fabrics of their own design and from other manufacturers. Wide selection. [££+]

Kantex, 20 Store Street, WC1 (636-0541). Cotton duck and hessian at very reasonable prices. [£+]

Felt and Hessian Shop, 34 Greville Street, EC1 (405-6215), stock 107 shades of 72 inch felt and forty of hessian. [££]

Note on metric conversions: 48 in. = 120 cm, 54 in. = 140 cm, 72 in. = 182 cm.

Sewing accessories, trimmings and related services

John Lewis, Oxford Street, W1 (629-7711), have what is probably the best selection of dress trimmings including lace, sequins, woollen braid, velvet and embroidered ribbons and ostrich feathers. They also sell curtain tapes, hooks, lining, tracks and 'how-to' brochures on the ground floor.

Carlton Embroideries, 63 Berwick Street, W1 (437-7946), are the people to go to for elaborately embroidered bead collars and cuffs, sequin motifs, and bead embroidery of all kinds. They have their own workrooms and make up their own trimming designs.

Distinctive Trimmings, 17D Kensington Church Street, W8 (937-6174), and 11 Marylebone Lane, W1 (486-6456). Furnishing trimmings exclusively. There is a wide variety of braid, tassels and fringes and the shop will custom dye any design to match your fabric. This takes three weeks (or ten days if you want express service) and is not especially costly.

Nu-Life Upholstery Repairs Ltd, 39 Praed Street, W2 (723-4491). Do-it-yourself upholsterers can get webbing, springs, hessian, twine and other necessary sundries here.

Siegal and Stockman, Drayton House, Gordon Street, wcı (387-4879), sell tailor's and dressmaking dummies with toile, jersey and felt finishes.

A. Taylor, 1 Silver Place, wı (437-5343), have the largest selection of buttons at retail prices in London: pearl, leather, horn, plastic and self-cover buttons – and these can cost up to 50p each. Taylor's also sell belt buckle sand do permanent pleating. They will cover and dye buttons and make button-holes, and are inexpensive and anxious to please.

The Button Queen, 19 Marylebone Lane, wı (935-1505), specialize in antique buttons but stock some contemporary ones. They will make buttons into cuff-links.

Paris House, 41 South Molton Street, wı (629-5065), belt-makers to the Queen and button-makers *par excellence*. Paris House buttons start at 15p but are more likely to cost £1. All are hand-made in either the customer's design or the store's. Special orders take about ten days. Belts are stocked in a variety of leather and evening-wear styles, and can be made in the customer's fabrics.

R. D. Franks, Kent House, Market Place, wı (636-1244), near Oxford Circus, carry sewing accessories and books and magazines on fashion, fashion design, dress-making, pattern cutting and related subjects; also lots of American and continental fashion magazines. Mannikins, pressing hems, velvet pressing mats, yardsticks, and dress-makers' scissors of all sizes.

Inner London Education Authority (I.L.E.A.) (633-3441), hold evening classes in dressmaking, dress de-sign and pattern cutting. For details telephone or write to the Education Officer (GP2), County Hall, se1.

Anything Left Handed, 65 Beak Street, wı (437-3910), have dressmaking and tailoring shears, also irons, for left-handed people.

Felix Sollen, 8 Spring Street, w2 (262-0436), is recom-mended for alterations.

CHAPTER 7

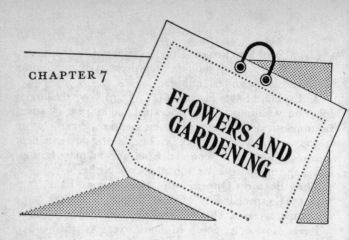

FLOWERS AND GARDENING

Although a lot more Englishmen are at home in gardens than castles these days, comparatively few, complain nurserymen, know what plants cost. They are staggered by estimates for a window box, let alone an entire garden. Plants and flowers are getting more and more expensive – especially things like palms where the demand grows quicker than the plant – and many Londoners feel they can get them more cheaply and find a bigger selection in the country. They are unaware that stashed away behind the city's façade of stone is an array of plants, flowers and garden services unequalled in Britain – and there are discounts, too, if you know where to go.

Garden and house plants

New Covent Garden Market, Vauxhall, sw8 (720-2211), is the most inexpensive place in London to buy plants and, contrary to popular opinion, the public can get in and you don't have to go there at 4 o'clock in the morning. The Flower Market is open until 11 a.m. Monday to Friday.

Plants and flowers cost about 50 per cent less at New Covent Garden than elsewhere but since this is a wholesale market small plants and cut flowers must be bought by the box. Some people team up with their neighbours and each household buys part of the box-load and goes to fetch them in turn. Big plants like palms are sold singly in the market and it doesn't make economic sense to buy a palm anywhere else if you can recognize a healthy specimen. Two leading merchants in the Flower Market are **Stuart Low** and **Rochford**.

After New Covent Garden there are two main sources of house and garden plants:

Clifton's, Clifton Villas, w9 (286-9888), central London's biggest nursery, occupies three quarters of an acre and has another two acres in North Kensington as a feeding ground. Clifton's real speciality is house plants and there are four greenhouses full of them. There is a huge selection of garden plants, basic tools and outdoor urns and tubs. Clifton's has a landscape gardening service that handles decorative planting on any scale. There is usually a charge for drawing up an estimate but this is refunded if the work goes ahead. Other advantages: Clifton's is open on Sundays till 1 p.m. and will take C.O.D. orders on the telephone. Delivery is free on any order over £2. Smaller orders cost a few pence.

Rassell's, 80 Earl's Court Road, w8 (937-0481), are a complete gardening service, selling trees, shrubs, bulbs, moss, herbs, etc. Many people think they have the best geraniums in London; they also have excellent rhododendrons and camellias. Pots, urns, tubs and other ornaments in terracotta and cement are always in stock. Window boxes come in wood, fibreglass, cement and other mixtures and can be made to order. Rassell's make up indoor and outdoor hanging baskets and have an experienced shop staff and landscape gardening staff, many of whom have been with the firm for years. They deliver free to most, but not all, parts of London – Putney but not Mayfair, for example. They also publish a catalogue of roses, trees, shrubs and climbing plants in October and one of bulbs in August. If they don't have it, they claim they will get it.

Some other recommended nurseries around London are:

Southwood Village Nurseries, Townsend Yard, Highgate High Street, N6 (340-1041).

Chelsea Nurseries, 408 King's Road, SW10 (352-5519).

Granville Nursery, 170 Granville Road, NW2 (455-3654).

Syon Park, Brentford, Middlesex (568-0134).

Woolworth's have a reputation for the least expensive house and garden plants to be had at retail prices. Many of these are grown exclusively for them. Woolworth's chief buyer recommends the Kingston-on-Thames branch for perhaps the widest variety, but all London branches have some plants on sale.

Flower House, 228 Fulham Road, SW10 (351-0195) and branches, is an expensive but highly reputable source of house-plants, especially unusual ones like medinella and orange trees.

Tropical Plants Display, 64 Emlyn Road, W12 (743-8777), sell palms and exotic tropical plants of all kinds. C.O.D. orders, free delivery.

S. R. Millward, 36 Tavistock Street, WC2 (836-6489), rent subtropical plants like *ficus layrata* and *ficus benjamina* and palms up to twelve feet high. A six-foot palm costs £3 a week. Millwards will maintain their hired-out plants for an additional fee.

Thompson and Morgan, London Road, Ipswich, Suffolk (0473-214-226), are the country's leading seedmen for both flowers and vegetables. Though not a London firm, most of their business is mail-order from their excellent free 175-page seed catalogue.

Richelle, 5 Chiltern Court Apartments, Baker Street, NW1 (935-1863), is the place for cacti and succulents. Cactus plants are imported from Mexico and prices start at 50p. A big 300-year-old cactus can cost £200 and according to the shop, the bigger they are, the faster they sell. Richelle also make up little cactus gardens with bonsai and tiny Oriental figures.

Selwyn Davidson, 31 Berwick Street, w1 (437-0881), makes and sells bottle gardens.

Royal Horticultural Society, Vincent Square, sw1 (834-4333), have a library which anyone can use to look up information about gardening.

170 Ring this number between 8 a.m. and 6 p.m. for recorded gardening information.

499-4191 Ring this number to find out the best flower and plant buy of the week. The recording also tells how to look after the flowers it recommends and even has some tips on arranging them. The service is sponsored by the Flowers and Plants Council.

Cut flowers

Moyses Stevens, Berkeley Square, w1 (493-8171) have been in the flower business for a hundred years. They are famous for floral arrangements for parties, receptions and weddings (they did Princess Anne's wedding bouquet). They also sell cut flowers, wreaths and flowering plants and they will send almost anything anywhere. This includes Christmas trees and (of possible interest to Welsh nationalists) bunches of leeks. Moyses Stevens sell dried flowers and silk flowers, but according to Mrs Simmons, who runs the firm, the best-selling flower of all is the Baccara rose. 80 per cent of those who buy flowers at Moyses Stevens, she says, are men, and 20 per cent of those who get them are dead.

Felton's, 220 Brompton Road, sw3 (589-4433) and 5 Cheapside, ec2 (236-7261), also in Leadenhall Market and at London Bridge. A lot of people in the flower business believe the best cut flowers at the most reasonable prices come from Felton's. Mr Rutledge, who runs the main shop in the Brompton Road and has been with the firm nearly thirty years, says Felton's aim at freshness. They never cut their flowers with scissors, always with a knife, since scissors close the stem, nor do they put arrangements in shallow bowls because this will shorten a flower's life. Over seventy years old, Felton's are a founder member of Interflora, and they have contracts to provide flowers regularly at many churches, hospitals and hotels. Felton's are also noted for their cut-rate hydrangeas which they sell *for planting* when they are returned from hotel displays.

Constance Spry, 64 South Audley Street, w1 (499-7201) and 88 Pimlico Road, sw1 (730-7632), are highly recommended for fresh flowers. Constance Spry also have a flower school at the first address, where short courses in flower-arranging are held. Six sessions cost about £13. Hand-made crêpe paper flowers are also available at the Flower School and can be made to order.

Pugh and Carr, 26 Gloucester Road, sw7 (584-7181). Weekly or fortnightly deliveries of flowers or plants at special prices are available from Pugh and Carr's flower club. The membership is free and flowers cost from £1 delivered, depending on how many bunches you want. Members have a say about colour, type, length of stem, etc. Some members have been subscribing for twenty years.

Pulbrook & Gould, 181 Sloane Street, sw1 (235-3920), is the best shop for cut flowers in London and is noted for flowers grown in private gardens as well as exotica.

René, 32 Carnaby Street, w1 (734-1855). Dried flowers and grasses and some composite 'fantasy' flowers made from several types of dried material.

Selfridges, Oxford Street, w1 (629-1234), sell dried flowers and grasses and floral foam on the ground floor.

Lyndeau Fleur Rentals, 8 Rickett Street, sw6 (385-6800), rent plastic flowers by the day, week or month. If you go in for the Italian and Irish custom of putting plastic flowers on graves, why not rent rather than buy them?

Chivers, 43 Charlotte Street, w1 (580-1761), 68 March-mont Street, wc1, and 129 Tottenham Court Road, w1. If you need a bunch of flowers after the shops have closed you can get them from vending machines outside any Chivers' shop. They cost 50p or £1.

The Handicraft Shop, 83 Northgate, Canterbury, Kent (0227-69888). Floral stem wires, binding wire and gutta percha (sticky tape) are very difficult to buy retail. They can be ordered here, as can artificial leaves and stamens. Free catalogue.

Garden ornaments and tools

Garden Crafts, 158 New King's Road, sw6 (736-1615), sell garden ornaments and wrought ironwork: cast cement urns, statues, birdbaths, fountains, medallions and bas re-liefs; they are mostly classical reproductions, but there are also a few gnomes for those who like that sort of thing. Garden Crafts also supply painted wrought iron tables, chairs, railings and benches.

Crowther of Syon Lodge, Busch Corner, Isleworth, Middlesex (560-7987), have a fine selection of antique garden ornaments and furnishings, but they are expensive.

Christopher Wray's Pot Shop, 606 King's Road, sw6 (736-8008) is a welcome extension of Wray's lighting em-porium and sells Spanish terracotta pots, unglazed and hand-thrown. A few are antiques. Sizes range from flower-pot size to giant Ali Baba storage jars.

Army and Navy, 105 Victoria Street, sw1 (834-1234), have the best selection of gardening tools: wheelbarrows, sprayers, and special plastic gardening shoes as well as the usual digging and trimming equipment. *Spear and Jackson* and *Wilkinson Sword* brands predominate.

Hire Service Shops, 192 Campden Hill Road, w11 (727-0897), and other addresses in and out of London, rent powered mowers, hedge-cutters, sprayers, tree winches, turf-rollers, cultivators, fertilizers and chain saws plus useful hand-tools like spades, shears, axes. Rental is for twenty-four hours or by the week. Free catalogue. Delivery service.

Adrian Hall, Hanworth Garden Centre, Feltham Hill Road, Feltham, Middlesex (890-1778), is a stone, soil and turf specialist. All kinds of stone for paving, walling and rockeries, sold by the ton or by the yard, depending on what it's for. Soil is sold by the *cubic* yard. Free delivery. Mr Hall also sells water plants and fibre-glass garden pools. He will build or put down any of these materials in a customer's garden, but he is usually over-booked. Open on Sundays.

Ross Ltd, 23 Wardle Avenue, Tilehurst, Reading (0734-27243), is one of the few sources of bottles for bottle gardens. Mail order. Free brochure.

W. Richardson (688-0629). Timber-framed, modular and custom-built conservatories.

Landscape gardening and window boxes

Helen Hockey, 3 Pixham Court, Lake Road, Wimbledon, sw 19 (946-4752), is a landscape gardener famous for her traditional English gardens, 'woolly and full of roses'. Prospective clients must be prepared to accept her ideas and to give her her head after basic discussions. Miss Hockey does not just stick to grand gardens, but enjoys doing tiny plots too. She has designed and planted gardens for as little as £50 or as much as £7,000.

D.I.G., Hugon Road, sw6 (736-2299), are landscape gardeners specializing in the unusual and sometimes way-out. D.I.G. believe gardens should be more like 'outdoor rooms'. They supply everything from imaginative fibre-glass constructions to simple innovations like putting castors on patio tubs. A basic design fee is about £125. The fee for

an average size London garden from scratch is around
£1,000.

Rassell's, 80 Earl's Court Road, w8 (937-0481), sell
window boxes. For details see under Garden and house
plants, page 139.

Clifton's, Clifton Villas, w9 (286-9888), sell hanging
baskets, terracotta and plastic window boxes, and wooden
window boxes to order. They are also landscape gardeners.
New branch in Bishop's Bridge Road.

Flowerdell, 595 Harrow Road, w10 (969-0317), specialize in window-box planting. Installation of one window
box plus compost is £10, and quarterly plantings cost about
£25 a year.

Inchbald School of Design, 7 Eaton Gate, sw1
(730-5508), run a ten-week introductory course in garden
design. Students learn about different soils and the funda-
mental principles of garden design: how to integrate plants,
ornaments and basic garden structures like walls and paving.
The course is from 10 a.m. to 4 p.m. five days a week.

Solve Your Problem, 25A Kensington Church Street,
w8 (937-0906),

London Domestics, 313 Brompton Road, sw3
(584-0161) and

Gentle Ghosts, 33 Norland Road, w11 (603-2871), provide gardening help generally of a willing rather than a
skilled nature. (For more details of these firms see under
Domestic services, page 261.)

Trees and tree surgeons

Longman's, 154 Fenchurch Street, EC3 (623-8414), are
London agents for Interarbor, an Essex firm that will send a
tree to any destination. There is a list of twenty-two varieties
readily available but others can be got: deciduous trees up
to ten feet high, evergreens much smaller. All orders are

delivered during the planting season only but notification is sent at once along with planting instructions. Prices are standard: trees sent anywhere in Britain cost around £8 each including postage. Anywhere overseas costs £12 or thereabouts.

J. W. Beattie, 36 Parkside, Dollis Hill, NW2 (452-8348). A tree surgeon, Mr Beattie is employed by the G.L.C. among others. He fills holes, feeds trees by boring little holes around the base and is an expert at thinning trees yet keeping their natural shape. The cost of his services depends on size and location since some trees are more accessible than others. Mr Beattie uses a ladder to get into trees, explaining he is of the old school when it comes to hydraulic lifts, etc. He likes being up in the tree and he likes getting there by himself.

T. N. Harrison, 14 Barlby Gardens, W10 (969-6223), is another expert surgeon who has been curing trees for many years by feeding, pruning, fertilizing and spraying them. Clients include the Grosvenor estates. Mr Harrison still recommends the London plane tree as the hardiest tree for the city.

C. E. Henderson, 48 Leadenhall Market, EC3 (626-4740), are specialists in bonsai, the Oriental art of tree miniaturization. Everything is grown in Japan and this includes evergreens and deciduous trees like apples, pomegranates, wisteria and Japanese maples. A two- or three-year-old tree costs about £2 while a ninety-year-old 20-inch-high juniper is £100.

Southwood Village Nurseries, Townsend Yard, Highgate High Street, N6 (340-1041). Huge two-and-a-half-acre garden centre stocking over 1,000 trees, including fruit trees and conifers.

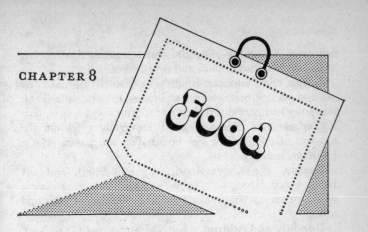

CHAPTER 8

Food is a commodity which is normally acquired locally, if only for the sake of convenience. This chapter concentrates on the extraordinary foods, that is, foods which are unusual because of their exotic nature or comparative rarity, or because they are of exceptional quality and worth going out of the way for – at least, occasionally.

London visitors in search of those delicacies which favour both transport and exchange rates should also find this chapter useful, while many of the addresses should be of help to those who cannot visit London but wish to order by mail.

Bread and cake

Cranks, 8 Marshall Street, W 1 (437-2915). Many people think this health food shop is the best place in London to get heavy-textured 100 per cent wholewheat bread. Cranks have their own bakery round the corner and several types of breads in different sizes and shapes are available in the shop. Especially useful are mini-loaves suitable for single people's needs. Cranks also make and sell barley bread, rye, bran and a number of special concoctions such as cheese, malt, nut and fruit breads, and sweet cakes.

Ceres, 269 Portobello Road, w11 (229-0817), make and sell 100 per cent wholewheat and mixed grain breads. Their harmony loaf contains five different grains – rye, oats, barley, wheat and maize. Ceres is especially proud of the amount of rye in their rye bread. Pies are baked on the premises, breads near by.

Beaton, 134 King's Road, sw3 (589-6263), and 151 Earl's Court Road, sw5 (370-1020), are famous for their white loaves but also make good scofa, croissants, rolls and cakes.

Dugdale and Adams, 3 Gerrard Street, w1 (437-3864), have been baking breads in their underground Vienna ovens since the 1890s and make London's nearest equivalent of French bread. They use English flour, however, since French flour does not combine well with hard London water.

Clark's, 27 Peter Street, w1 (437-6622), general bakers who are noted for their dark rye which is baked on the premises using sour dough. This is more of a German black bread than a traditional Jewish rye and does not contain carraway seeds. (They do have a white rye with carraway seeds.)

Grodzinski, 13 Brewer Street, w1 (437-3302), and many branches, are kosher bakers selling a variety of breads including bulka, cholla, rye and streusel cake.

Hygienic, 46 Walton Street, sw3 (589-4734), a bakery for over a hundred years, is now owned by food doyen Justin de Blank. It is noted for traditional English crusted bread but also makes rye and 100 per cent wholewheat bread from compost grown wheat. The ovens are located beneath the shop and brioches and flaky croissants made with butter, not fat, are also produced here. Hygienic breads can be bought in Justin de Blank shops in Elizabeth Street, Duke Street and Brompton Road as well as over the tiny counter in Walton Street.

Bouquillon, 45 Moscow Road, w2 (229-8684), and

Le Relais Basque, 28 Westbourne Grove, W2 (229-2107), are both under the same management and produce some of the best pastry available in London. Tarts, éclairs, Napoleons, marzipan, profiteroles – to name a few. The croissants and brioches are made with Normandy butter. Special orders undertaken. Le Relais Basque provides full catering facilities.

Floris, 39 Brewer Street, W1 (437-5155), hold the Royal Warrant for pastry and although there is a worn look about the shop, they can turn out some amazing concoctions. They have a book of cake designs for inspiration, but try to adapt these to individual requirements and will also undertake original design ideas. Floris are noted for their petits fours and chocolates. Complete catering facilities for small or large parties.

Maison Verlon, 12 Bute Street, SW7 (584-0485). Even Marie Antoinette would think twice about letting the peasants in on this. Verlon cakes and pastries are exquisitely made and the patisserie is kept on its toes by the surrounding French community who frequent it.

Cheese

Harrods, Knightsbridge, SW1 (730-1234), has reputedly the largest cheese department in Europe and stocks some 500 varieties. These include the traditional English cheeses – Wensleydale, Leicester, Cheshire, Caerphilly, double Gloucester, blue Wensleydale, Derby, Stilton and Cheddar. There are several modern variations on these cheeses such as red, white and also blue Cheshire, Cotswold (a new cheese made of double Gloucester with chives) and Walton (a combination of Stilton, Cheddar and walnuts). Harrods stock multifarious French cheeses and are sometimes able to get local French cheeses not generally available outside the particular region. French goat cheeses are a speciality.

Other national cheeses such as feta and haloumi are also available, and the *pièce de résistance* is Roquefort pâté cheese, specially made up for Harrods, and very expensive too.

Paxton and Whitfield, 93 Jermyn Street, sw1 (930-3380), is one of the most evocative and delightful small shops in London. Old-fashioned and plain, its only decoration is its products – smoked hams and rounds of golden cheese which fill the window and shelves behind the counter. Paxton's is justifiably famous for all its cheeses, but particularly for English cheeses, and above all (and everyone) for Stilton. They sell about 500 lbs. of it a week. Whole Stiltons can be bought in three sizes ranging from 5 to 18 lbs. Half a large round can also be ordered and there are jars of Stilton in four sizes.

Cheddar is the next most popular Paxton cheese and all Cheddar sold has been matured for at least eleven months – some for eighteen months. There is a Christmas price list. All cheeses can be exported.

G. Parmigiano Figlio, 43 Frith Street, w1 (437-4728), specialize in Italian cheeses: dolcelatte, bel paese, fontina, gorgonzola cadempatori, parmesan, provolone, ricotta, straccino, taleggio and mozzarella (the mozzarella is made in England and not with traditional buffalo milk). There is also a selection of French and English cheeses.

Scandinavian Shop, 170 Brompton Road, sw3 (589-7804). Norwegian goat cheese and Danish cheeses.

Hellenic Provision Stores, 25 Charlotte Street, w1 (666-2933). Authentic Greek feta is sold here.

Selfridges, Oxford Street, w1 (629-1234), have a superior cheese department with a good variety of English and imported cheeses always in stock.

Justin de Blank, 42B Elizabeth Street, w1 (730-0605), sell unpasteurized brie and mature their own Cheddar for at least a year – sometimes eighteen months – before sale.

Note: Never put cheese in the refrigerator unless it is a very hot day and then put it in the vegetable bin or lowest shelf. Take it out an hour or two before you need it so that the flavour can be revived somewhat. Cheese can be wrapped in tinfoil but ideally it should be able to breathe and either muslin or a paper with tiny perforations is desirable. Stilton should be covered with a damp cloth which has been dipped in vinegar and water, then wrung out.

Chocolates

Bendicks, 3 Grosvenor Street, w1 (629-1812), also 20 Royal Exchange, ec3, 55 Wigmore Street, w1, and 195 Sloane Street, sw1. Bendicks hold the Royal Warrant as chocolate makers and claim to be the largest producers of handmade chocolates in the world. Chocolates are made near Winchester: the centres are cut out first with devices similar to pastry cutters. Then these are hand-dipped into melted chocolate and fished out with a special fork. Squiggles are made on the tops to indicate the contents. Bendicks are especially famous for their Bittermints and Mint Crisps, but assorted chocolates of many kinds can be bought in boxes weighing between 200 g and 5 lbs. A 5 lb. box of chocolates costs about £16. Although Bendicks' chocolates can be bought in over thirty countries, there is something special about buying them fresh in London. Handmade chocolates do not have the amount of preservatives that other types contain, so freshness is important. Bendicks do not make liqueur chocolates.

Prestat, 24 South Molton Street, w1 (629-4838), makers of handmade chocolates, are noted for their truffles in three flavours and for their brandy cherries. The cherries are soaked for eighteen months before being dipped in chocolate. Prestat chocolates are made on the premises and, as well as liqueur chocolates, there are fancy chocolate Easter eggs, assorted chocolates and special gift boxes. Price list on request.

Clare's, 3 Park Road, w1 (262-1906), and 163 George

Street, w1 has been owned and operated by Max Dobrin for twenty-five years. Clare's make handmade after-dinner mints, mint crèmes, marzipan and assorted chocolates on the premises; their chocolates tend to be marginally less expensive than other West End competitors'. They also sell weighed-out chocolates and will prepare an assorted box according to customer's desires, but the order must be given in advance.

Charbonnel et Walker, 31 Old Bond Street, w1 (629-4396), have been making chocolates for English addicts for just over a hundred years. Most are handmade and hand-moulded (you get a more even covering by hand). Almost as famous as their chocolates are their boxes, which are often handmade too, and are certainly unique. Sizes range from ¼ lb. to a giant, round 10 lb. size which must be the ultimate gift for a sweet-toothed friend.

Coffee and tea

Whittard and Co., 111 Fulham Road, sw3 (589-4261), near South Kensington underground, are coffee and tea specialists selling about twenty blends of coffee and over fifty teas. They do their own roasting and blending of beans from coffee-producing areas throughout the world. As well as traditional blends of Chinese, Indian and Ceylon teas, Whittard sell several *tisanes* or herb teas – lemon verbena, camomile, lime tree, vervain, peppermint, rubbed mint. Traditional teas include darjeeling, ceylon, assam, lapsang, keemun, jasmine, white rose and gunpowder or green teas. Mail order accepted for orders of 5 lbs. Orders of 8 lbs. or more are shipped postage free. Price list on request.

H. R. Higgins, 42 South Molton Street, w1 (499-5912), are coffee specialists. Unlike many coffee merchants they believe in unblended coffees as well as blended varieties.

Higgins stock beans from around the world and even have a coffee grown specially for them by the Chagga tribe on the slopes of Mount Kilimanjaro. Another African coffee stocked is Ethiopian Mocha which, pulverized, is traditionally used for Turkish coffee. Higgins sell two types of coffee-making machine – a Melitta filter and La Cafetière, a jar with a plunger. Mail orders over 5 lbs. sent postage free.

Algerian Coffee Stores, 52 Old Compton Street, WC2 (437-2480), do *not* specialize in Algerian coffee. The name comes from the original owner in 1887, who was Algerian. The shop sells a number of medium and high roast coffees (medium tends to be a breakfast coffee while high roast is a stronger, after-dinner type.) Coffees in stock are Java, esotico, Boston, velluto nero, mocha parfait, connoisseur, Algerian special, gourmet mulatte, gourmet noir and brunette. Also eight types of tea. Several makes of coffee pots are on sale and the shop will repair those which were bought there. To keep beans fresh the management recommend screw-top jars.

L. Fern, 27 Rathbone Place, W1 (636-2237), blend their own coffees and teas and do their own roasting. Price list available. Mail orders over 3 lbs. accepted.

Markus, 13 Connaught Street, W2 (723-4020), sell thirty-five different coffees and six kinds of tea.

Fish and meat

Fish

Harrods, Knightsbridge, SW1 (730-1234). This fish department, located on the ground floor, must have the most spectacular terrestial display of marine life outside a museum: like the fish supply, the display is changed daily. Fresh dressed crab is perhaps the most unusual thing available here, but fish or shellfish in season is usually in stock. [£££]

Cecil and Co., 1 Duke of York Street, SW1 (930-2658). Fish is an unusual commodity to be purveying at this posh address, but Cecil's sell some of the best. Hotels and restaurants are the main clientele but other customers will find a broad selection of freshwater and sea fish, shellfish, and native oysters (also game in season). Closed half day Mondays and Saturdays. All fish is fresh daily. Deliveries throughout central London. [£££]

Richards, 11 Brewer Street, W1 (437-1358), is Soho's leading fishmonger and among the fish you are likely to see here are halibut, cod, sole, red mullet, sea bream, monk fish; also squid, cuttlefish, langoustine, crabs (live and cooked), mussels and Helford oysters. Richards tends to sell Dover sole at specially reasonable prices. [££+]

Hamburger, 1 Brewer Street, W1 (437-7119). Down the street from Richards (above) is London's best smoked fish shop. Hamburger smoke all their own fish and will smoke customers' fish too. Large stoneware crocks fill the window and counter, containing smoked mackerel, halibut, haddock, herring rollmops and roe, eels, trout, sturgeon, kippers, sprats and salmon. There is a snack bar open from 1 p.m. to 3 p.m. [££]

Sam Stoller and Son, 8 Stamford Hill, N16 (806-2102), 28 Temple Fortune, NW11 and 33 Market Place, NW11. Fresh fish is available on Sunday mornings at Stoller's. This is a kosher fishmonger's, therefore only scaled fish is sold. Israeli carp is flown in from Israel every week. [££]

Bentley's, 15 Swallow Street, W1 (734-0431), has a take-away service selling smoked salmon, West Mersea oysters and lobsters alive or cooked. [£££]

Meat, game and poultry

Slater and Cooke, Bisney and Jones, 67 Brewer Street, W1 (437-2026), is a mini department store in that there is a separate counter for each kind of meat. S and C, B and J sell English lamb, Scotch beef, Dutch veal, poultry and game in season. It is a pleasure to see the elegant and decorative ways they dress their produce – racks of lamb with ruffled rosettes of fat and a kidney at either end, oven-ready pheasants with tail feathers replaced. There are a number of prepared meats including steak tartare, shish kebab, haggis, stuffed peppers and tomatoes. This is one of the most appetizing butchers in London. [£££]

Bifulco, 24 Frith Street, w 1 (437-5279), and 82 St John's Wood High Street, NW8 (722-8101), are as well known for their friendliness as for their quality meats at prices which are not exorbitant. Bifulco sell Dutch veal, Scotch beef and English lamb, and rely somewhat on bulk for their profits. At the St John's Wood branch are some fancy, prepared things such as chicken Kiev, and they have a delivery service covering most of London. [££+]

Harrods, Knightsbridge, sw 1 (730-1234). The meat department at Harrods should be visited by everyone. Produce is displayed on a grand scale – increasingly appropriate in times when a roast threatens to become as much a luxury as a château-bottled wine. Harrods have a representative in Scotland who selects Aberdeen Angus which are then sent to Smithfield markets where the Harrods buyer has an option on them. All Harrods beef is hung for at least ten days before selling. Lamb and pork come from Harrods' own flocks and herds near Cambridge. Harrods will cut meat in American or French styles as well as traditional English joints, saddles and crown roasts. Free delivery daily within a three-mile radius. Harrods also sell frozen meat in bulk and export meat to countries where the law permits it. Their Christmas turkeys and hams are justifiably famous and they stock a wide selection of game in season. [£££]

Randall and Aubin, 16 Brewer Street, w 1 (437-3507). Top quality French cuts of meat. Randall and Aubin make their own sausages which include 'Toulouse' pork sausages. Phone orders accepted. Daily delivery within one mile. [£££]

Smithfield Market, EC 1, is the wholesale centre for meat in London but this is also a public market and there-

Food

fore not limited to professional wholesale trade. The market is open from 5 a.m. until noon but most buying takes place between 6.30 and about 8 a.m. Smithfield is a fairly formidable place and is not recommended as a source for a few chops or a single joint. If, however, you want a side of beef for your freezer it is worthwhile, provided you can communicate your needs and the kinds of cuts you want. One dealer who is highly recommended for providing quality cuts is **J. T. Hart**, 301 Central Markets, EC1 (236-0055). [££]

Fulton Frozen Foods, 18 Randlesdown Road, SE6 (698-9197), specialize in foods for the freezer. Quality English and Scotch meat and poultry. Meat can be specially cut to customers' orders if two days' notice is given. Send for price list of ready-frozen cuts. Delivery free for orders over 10 lbs. (reduction if you collect). Mr Fulton guarantees satisfaction, or your money back. Frozen fish, vegetables and ice cream available too. [££]

John Baily, 116 Mount Street, W1 (499-1833), are the country's oldest poulterers and its finest: their spacious old-fashioned premises, knowledgeable service and high standards are without equal in this trade. Baily's sell free-range chickens, ducks and Christmas turkeys. They also sell geese, both farm reared and wild (in season) but point out that this is the most uneconomical bird you can buy, pound for pound, because the yield is so low. Other game in season includes pheasant, grouse, woodcock, snipe, partridge and, on occasion, *rarae aves* like young capercailzie (a Scottish bird similiar to grouse) and blackgame. Game can be hung to suit the preference of the buyer since Baily's hang their own. You can get it fresh or well hung. [£££]

W. Fenn, 27 Frith Street, W1 (437-4181). Specialists in fresh poultry and game. Venison in season and from time to time, other rarities such as gulls' eggs. No delivery service. [££]

Wholefood Butchers, 24 Paddington Street, W1 (486-1390), are 'health food' butchers and all meat comes from animals reared naturally 'at their own pace', without hormones, confined quarters or other artificial means. Free-range chickens and eggs, hams from pigs raised by a member of the board. No delivery. [££+]

I. Robatkin, 24A Hessel Street, E1 (481-2347). Kosher butcher selling only the fore-quarters of lamb, beef, oxen. Pre-packed food for freezers. Open half-day Sunday, Monday and Friday. Full day Tuesday, Wednesday and Thursday. Delivery service. [££, ££+]

Richard Parker, Portobello Farm, Christmas Common, near Watlington, Oxfordshire (049-161-2372), is a farmer who sells game from his home and his prices considerably undercut London market rates. Most of the pheasant, part-ridges, rabbits and hares come from local shoots, but Mr Parker also has grouse in season and a steady supply of venison. About an hour's drive from London. Telephone first. [££]

Foreign foods

Fratelli Camisa, 1A Berwick Street, W1 (437-7120),

I. Camisa, 61 Old Compton Street, W1 (437-7610),

G. Parmigiano Figlio, 43 Frith Street, W1 (437-4728), and

Lina, 18 Brewer Street, W1 (437-6482), are located in the heart of Soho and are family-run Italian food shops. All have charming 'country' atmospheres: parma hams and salamis hang from the ceilings, marble-topped counters are loaded with cheeses, freshly made ravioli and bread, while bins, barrels, bags and shelves store coffee beans, golden pasta, dried peas and beans and innumerable tinned and preserved Italian specialities.

A. Gomez Ortega, 74 Old Compton Street, W1 (437-2521). Spanish food and wine: polenta, paella rice and pans, *chorizas* (sausages), Serrano hams, white beans, *olivas alinadas*, couscous, manchego cheese and Spanish olive oil (which can be bought in bulk very reasonably). Also various tinned and packaged foods including chick peas, *bacalao* (cod) and traditional Mexican foods.

Randall and Aubin, 16 Brewer Street, w1 (437-3507), French butchers and grocers since 1906, supply top-quality French cuts of meat and French-style sausages, pâtés and quiches which they make themselves. All the ingredients for a true cassoulet can be bought here, including the pot. Delicatessen counter. Phone orders taken, free delivery within one mile radius. Expensive.

Scandinavian Shop, 170 Brompton Road, sw3 (589-7804), sells foods peculiar to Denmark, Norway and Sweden. Herring (sild) is available whole for marinating. already marinated in different-sized pieces, or packed in spices. There is Norwegian goat cheese, a dozen Danish cheeses, salamis without garlic, crispbreads, fish cakes and puddings and fenelar (smoked lamb leg).

Osaka, 17 Goldhurst Terrace, nw6 (624-4983). Indian, Chinese, Japanese, West Indian and Middle Eastern foods. Huge variety of spices and a diverse selection of native foods – chillis, okra, lychees, dates, houmous, fresh noodles, dried mushrooms, paw paw, bitter gourd, white pumpkin, basmati and patna rice, and so on. Mail order and price list available.

J. D. Shah, 161 Drummond Street, nw1 (387-9856). Indian vegetarian foods only: spices, pickles, cereals, savouries and poppadoms. Prepared food to take away, or ingredients.

Dein, 191 Shepherd's Bush Market, w12 (743-5389). West Indian and West African specialities, many flown in from abroad – waterleaf, bitterleaf, West Indian peppers, Nigerian gari (pudding), smoked fish and condo flour from Ghana, and live snails; cassava flour, bean flour, cola nuts and bitternuts, also home remedies such as Nigerian ori for rheumatism and alligator pepper for tummy aches, etc. Open six days a week.

Cheong Leen, 4 Tower Street, wc2 (240-3857). Large Chinese emporium selling Chinese food and fresh vegetables as well as other wares imported from China.

Nippon Food Centre, 483 Finchley Road, NW3 (794-2933), also 61 Wimbledon High Street, SW19 and 193 Upper Richmond Road, SW15. Over 500 items of Japanese food, mainly tinned or prepared, and including *shirataki* and *konnyaku* (yam noodles), frozen fish cakes, saki and Japanese whisky. Also Japanese crockery. London deliveries, mail order. Price list usually available.

Hellenic Provision Stores, 25 Charlotte Street, W1 (636-4406). Feta, Greek olives, taramasalata and pitta bread are only a few of the comestibles available in this shop catering for Greek food enthusiasts.

General provisions

Harrods, Knightsbridge, SW1 (730-1234). The food departments at Harrods are on a palatial scale and for the widest variety of quality foods as well as for the appetising, even aesthetic effect they can produce, Harrods should be experienced: meat, fish, dairy produce, fruit and vegetables, bread, tinned and packaged goods. Despite the high prices there are always queues at nearly every counter. Free delivery service, phone orders taken, export service. [£££]

Fortnum and Mason, 181 Piccadilly, SW1 (734-8040). Fortnum's has been a purveyor to upper-class palates for so long that although many other fine delicatessen and speciality food shops have arisen there is still a special *cachet* about Fortnum's. A Fortnum label on a jar of pâté or Stilton is somehow quintessentially English and any tourist in search of Imperial flavour should go there. The ground floor is packed with fancy tinned food, baskets of fruit, jams, gentleman's relish, cheeses and meat pies. You will be served by a man in a tailcoat, but don't try and give him the money. This task is reserved for the cashier. [£££]

Marks and Spencer, 458 Oxford Street, W1 (486-6141), All Marks and Spencer food is sold under their own St

Michael's label and, true to form, the quality is very good and the prices very reasonable. There is not a great range within each category, but what there is, you can rely on. Of special interest are the unusual cuts from familiar birds and beasts: turkey and pork escalopes, for example – a clever way of producing an impressive dinner without the exorbitant costs that go with it these days. [££]

Selfridges, Oxford Street, w1 (629-1234). The food department has its own entrance on the left-hand side of the building. Inside is a complete range of comestibles, both staples and delicacies. Kosher department, too. [££+]

Justin de Blank, 42b Elizabeth Street, sw1 (730-0605), and 136 Brompton Road, sw3 (584-8144). Justin de Blank has done as much to improve the availability of first-class foods in England as anyone. His shops are not large but what they have is excellent. He is specially proud of his fruits and vegetables and claims they are the best in London – also about the most expensive, but that is the price of creaming the crop. The shops stock their own sausages, pâtés and bread as well as superior take-away dishes such as puddings, tarts, quiches, salads, hams, etc. De Blank's also do catering. [£££]

Jacksons, 172 Piccadilly, sw1 (228-2332), and 6a Sloane Street, sw3 (235-9355), grocers to the Queen, have an expensive but fine selection of first-class foods which are bound to satisfy consuming passions of superior taste. Fresh and tinned foods and a complete delicatessen. No fresh meat. Jacksons are noted, among other things, for fresh and dried herbs, wines and teas. Catering facilities. [£££]

Sainsbury, 98 Marylebone High Street, w1 (935-1827), and numerous other addresses, is a supermarket chain whose prices are kept reasonable by the sheer bulk of their business. Sainsbury's often have 'specials' on commodities such as instant coffee or sugar at prices that make hoarding a tempting proposition. [££]

Berwick Street Market, w1, is an excellent fruit and vegetable street market in the heart of food-conscious Soho. The area south of Brewer Street is inclined to have more unusual produce such as *mange tout* peas, fennel or expensive melons. Meat, which hygiene laws generally prohibit from outside sale, is available in several shops along the upper end of the street, as are game, fish, cheeses and other foods. Open on Saturday, but this is really a Monday-to-Friday market and prices are often a bit cheaper in the afternoon, especially on Fridays. [££]

New Covent Garden Market, Vauxhall, sw8 (720-2211), London's central wholesale fruit and vegetable market, is open from 4 a.m. till midday and if you wish to buy in bulk it is well worth the effort to get up and go there. You cannot of course buy a lettuce or a cabbage, you must buy a box-full, but if several neighbours band together and take turns going, it is possible to save quite a lot of money. The market authority does not encourage individual trade, but it doesn't discourage it either – though retail tradesmen buying in the market understandably don't like it. Because of their 'lobby' you cannot take your car into the market area without a special sticker, but must park outside. This makes it more difficult to take away a lot of produce. [£+]

Spitalfields Market, E1 (247-7331), is another whole-sale fruit and vegetable market which will sell in bulk to private customers. This is a covered market and is open six days a week, roughly between 5 a.m. and 11 a.m. Located between Commercial Road and Bishopsgate. [£+]

Portobello Road, w11. At the lower end of this famous antiques market road, between Colville Terrace and Tavistock Road, is a bustling food market open Monday to Saturday (half-day Thursday). Fruits and vegetables are sold from barrows at very reasonable prices, while meat can be bought from butchers' shops along the way. Friday and Saturday are the big days. [££]

A shortlist of markets:

Electric Avenue, Brixton. Monday to Saturday, half-day Wednesday. West Indian specialities.

North End Road, w12, from Lilly Road to Fulham

Broadway. Monday to Saturday, half-day Thursday. 92 pitches.

Leadenhall Market, EC3. Covered market. Monday to Friday. Bank underground.

Inverness Street Market, NW1. Monday to Saturday. 30 food pitches.

Health foods

Cranks, 8 Marshall Street, W1 (437-2915). Complete range of general health foods, including bread, dairy products, some fresh vegetables, health drinks, remedies and books.

Cranks Whole Grain, 37 Marshall Street, W1 (439-1809). Almost opposite the shop above, this branch is essentially for bulk buying of flour, grain, beans, fruit, dried herbs and rice. These can be bought by the pound but larger orders are encouraged here and smaller ones should be bought across the street.

Ceres, 269 Portobello Road, W11 (229-5571), is many people's favourite health shop. Organically grown vegetables and whole-grain products – rice, millet, beans, pressed oil, fruit and nuts. Clean, country atmosphere. Whole-grain bakery next door.

Wholefood, 112 Baker Street, W1 (935-3924). Full stock of health foods, cosmetics, books, remedies. Salad and juice bar.

Wholefood Butchers, 24 Paddington Street, W1 (486-1390). Free-range meat and poultry. For details, see Fish and Meat.

A shortlist of health food shops:

Sesame, 128 Regent's Park Road, NW1 (586-3779).

Hampstead Village Health Foods, 2 Flask Walk, NW3 (435-0959).

Holland and Barrett, 260 Kensington High Street, w8 (602-3627), and 86 Camden High Street, nw1 (388-0808).

Special Services

Fresh Orange Juice Supplies, 5b Thames Road, e16 (476-8202). Freshly squeezed orange juice delivered to your door. Half a gallon costs about £2 and keeps for four days in the refrigerator. Grapefruit and lemon juice, too.

    Dish of the Day. Dial 246-8071 for a daily recipe.

    Lunch Box, 17 Swallow Street, w1 (730-5326). Boxed lunches for one or more. Free delivery for orders of ten. Luxury lunches for occasions such as Glyndebourne can be arranged in advance.

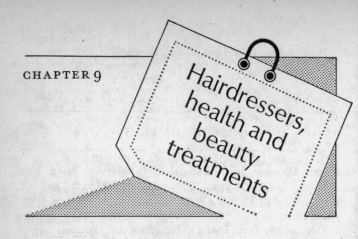

CHAPTER 9

Hairdressers,
health and
beauty
treatments

Hairdressers

Most people either go regularly to a hairdresser who is located near by or do their hair at home. The following directory is intended for the remainder: those who live out of town and want to know where to go and what to expect when they get there, those who want the occasional tint, cut or special service and those who either want to splurge or to do just the opposite – find a really cut-rate service.

All hairdressers provide the same basic service but the degree of skill, decor, sanitation and the type of product used varies greatly. The cost varies even more. You can get a haircut and set in London for 20p or you can pay £12. Because comparative price is such an important factor in choosing a hairdresser the exact prices of many services are quoted below in the hope that although dated they will at least give a more precise index for comparison. A word of warning about posh salons: most have several grades of shampoo, conditioners and even stylists on hand and there is a tendency to load the unsuspecting client with the more expensive of these. So ask about all prices before you begin. If you are quoted only one price for a particular service, ask if it is the only one. As for tipping, 10 per cent of the cost is adequate for stylists, manicurists and other operators with the exception of the stylist's assistant (if there is one). He or she gets a standard 10p or so depending on how elegant the salon is and how much help you get.

Women, children and unisex

Leonard, 6 Upper Grosvenor Street, w1 (629-5757), is London's top hairdresser and its most expensive. Leonard only *cuts* hair himself and he has almost stopped that. Running a highly-successful salon for women and another for men (see below) keeps him occupied more with shares than shears, but if you can't get Leonard, there are three other categories of stylists on hand: a cut, shampoo and set by an 'artistic director' is £12, by a 'top stylist' is £9 and by a run-of-the-mill 'stylist' is £6. Colour costs from £9.75, and highlights from £27. Elegant decor with a chi-chi boutique on the ground floor. Leonard uses his own products and these can be purchased. [£££]

Harrods, Knightsbridge, sw1 (584-8881), located on the fourth floor of the department store, has a non-stop lift service. Few people know that this salon is in fact owned by another firm who simply rent space in Harrods. One of the largest ladies' salons in Europe, it employs forty-five stylists plus many others who give additional treatments (see Special treatments, page 168). A shampoo and set costs £2·75 with a 'senior' stylist and £4 upwards with a 'style director'. Harrods have all hair services including straightening hair and cleaning and dressing wigs. They boast a special children's salon with a fishpond and sound-proof walls. Open all day Saturday. [££+]

Vidal Sassoon, 60 South Molton Street, w1 (629-6403), 171 Bond Street, w1 (629-9665), 44 Sloane Street, sw1 (235-7791), and Grosvenor House, Park Lane, w1 (629-2463), are world-famous for cutting hair and don't like to work on hair they haven't cut themselves. A cut, shampoo and blow dry costs upward of £4·50, depending on the status of the stylist. However, if you go to Sassoon's hairdressing school as a model or guinea-pig, the same treatment by a student costs only £1.20. The school is located at 56 Davies Mews, w1 (493-2291). [££+]

Cut In, Carnaby Court, Carnaby Street, w1 (437-1227), are an informal, easy, first-floor unisex salon with music. They specialize in cutting and blowing dry, at a starting price of £4·50. There is a model night after 6 p.m. on Tuesdays when a cut and blow dry costs only £1. Open all day Saturday. [££]

Annie Russell, 398 King's Road, sw10 (352-5693). Popular, medium-priced salon. Unisex, but men are downstairs and women upstairs. A cut and blow dry costs from about £6 for a woman and £5 for a man. Good colour department. Open Saturdays. [££]

Judy Arnold, (505-0465), will do your hair in your own home. She brings all supplies including a hair-drier. Miss Arnold also gives facials and does make-up, and is increasingly hard to get. [££]

D. Harris Salon, 108 Clapham Road, sw9 (735-1395). Mrs Harris is a travelling hairdresser who has been in the trade for thirty-five years. She gives preference to those who are homebound by illness or small children. Appointments day or evening. [££]

College of Fashion and Clothing Technology, 20 John Prince's Street, w1 (493-0790). You can get a cut, shampoo and set or blow dry for only 20p performed by students under the supervision of a professional. If you go in the evening you can get a stylist who is already in the trade but doing an advanced course. Tints and perms cost under £1. Service is available during term time only. Ring first for an appointment. [£]

Cheevers, 46 Shepherd's Market, w1 (629-3752), is unisex and informal, with modern surroundings, and music. It was originally for men but changed to unisex. Trendy cuts and sets: men £6·50, women £7·50. Cheevers also straighten hair. There is a model day on Wednesdays and those who are willing to submit to treatment by a student can get their hair done for £1. [**££+**]

Hairquipment, 59 Frith Street, w1 (437-6344), sells professional hair-driers and other salon equipment for serious do-it-yourselfers. Both hood and hand driers. (These can be repaired by **Hairdressers Electrical Service**, 51 Islip Road, nw5 (267-1677).)

Men only (for unisex, see page 165)

Michael John, 6 Carlos Place, w1 (499-7529), highly-fashionable hairdresser whose clientele include a few royal heads as well as some famous commoners'. If you can get either Michael or John the cost of re-styling and a blow dry is £6. Otherwise, there is Frank at £5·25 and several others at £4·25. You can get a shave at Michael John, and the salon also does permanent waving and handles special trichological problems. [**£££**]

Trumper, 9 Curzon Street, w1 (499-1850). Tory ministers, peers and rich businessmen from Detroit go to Trumper's for their 'short back and sides'. Haircuts cost from £1·50. Trumper's are conservative by nature but they offer services a lot of their clients wouldn't dream of having, like face massage, manicure, razor cut, and moustache curling. They use their own preparations exclusively and these are on sale in the salon at retail prices. [**££+**]

Austin Reed, 103 Regent Street, w1 (734-6789), located in the basement of the men's store, is one of the biggest barber-shops in London and one of the most reasonable. There are twenty chairs and an appointment is not usually necessary. Haircuts cost £1·10. Shaves, manicures, mud packs and high frequency scalp massage are all about £1. Styling, shampoo and blow dry are £2·50. Austin Reed believe they have the best chiropodist in London. He does whatever needs doing for £3. [**££**]

Penhaligon's, 41 Wellington Street, wc2 (836-2150), have been making perfumes, toilet waters and pomades for men for a hundred years. The shop is thoroughly English: its gleaming mahogany cabinets and glass-fronted cases display Edwardian-style bottles labelled English Fern, Blenheim Bouquet, Extract of Limes. The atmosphere is one of elegant masculinity. Penhaligon's have a mail-order service and produce a superbly designed catalogue. They will also find unusual dressing-table bottles for clients [£££]

College of Fashion and Clothing Technology, 20 John Prince's Street, w1 (493-0790). During term time you can get a haircut, shampoo and blow dry for 20p as a student's guinea-pig. [£]

Special treatments

Note: most beauty treatments are for women but several centres have services for men too. These are marked with an asterisk for easy reference.

Elizabeth Arden, 20 New Bond Street, w1 (629-8211), offers a four-hour 'Top to Toe' treatment consisting of massage, shampoo and set, manicure, facial and make-up. The cost is £18·50. Or, if you have the time, there is a full day 'Maine Chance'. You get a massage, vibro-therapy or steam bath, haircut, shampoo and set, manicure, face treatment and special make-up for £28·50 with lunch thrown in. Arden's give an oil manicure for dry hands (£2·50) and a paraffin wax manicure for ageing or rheumatic hands (£2·50). Arden's dye eyelashes and attach individual false lashes that you can sleep or swim in. A one-hour facial using their own cremes is £5·50 including a light make-up: with special Venteuse electrical apparatus it is £6. Paraffin baths, wax removal of hair and spot reducing massage by the electrical stimulation of involuntary muscles (ideal for lazy people) are also available. [£££]

Countess Csaky, (629-3732) (address withheld),

apparently has the magic touch. Her famous facials which she gives in her home cost £13·20, yet unless you are lucky enough to get a cancellation, booking is about four months in advance. The countess's treatments consist of a back and neck massage to stimulate circulation, steaming, face mask and rest. She uses her own cremes, and treatments are one and a half hours long. A hand and arm massage is £2·20. [£££]

*Hand and Nail Culture Institute, 35 Old Bond Street, W1 (493-7561), provides treatment for infections of hands or nails and for special problems like nail splitting or biting, large knuckles, rheumatic problems, hangnails and inflamed cuticles. The service is for men, women and children. The institute has been going for over forty years and many clients are sent by doctors while others come for cosmetic reasons. A course of seven treatments costs between £7 and £9. Treatment by post is also available. Write for details. [££]

Angele Curtin, 70 Duke Street, W1 (493-5619), specializes in nail treatments for problem hands. She performs all the treatments personally. [££+]

Tao Clinic, 153 Brompton Road, SW1 (589-4847), and branches throughout Britain. For the past thirty years the Tao Clinic has specialized in hair removal by electrolysis. The process is not painful and hair does not reappear. Sessions last from ten to sixty minutes and cost from £1·50 to £3·90 (more on Saturdays). If you are prepared to be a guinea-pig, you can get free treatments from technologists in training and under the careful supervision of two professionals. Moles and warts can also be removed at the clinic but require a doctor's certificate first. Electrology apart, the Tao has some of the most reasonably priced facials in town: forty minutes, £3·25, one hour with make-up, £3·90. Cremes used are specially made up for the clinic. [££]

*The Institute of Trichologists, 228 Stockwell Road, SW9 (733-2056), operate a daily clinic to treat hair and scalp problems. The Institute also functions as a standards-setting body for electrologists. To get the Institute's approval electrologists must train for three years and practise for three more. They will give you the address of an approved clinic near you. [££]

*Hair Extension Centre, 37 Warwick Street, w1 (734-3347), replaces hair by linking new hairs on to existing ones. This is an American method which involves literally weaving hairs together. For bald heads, a fine mesh is attached to hair on the side of the head and the mesh is stretched across the scalp. Then hairs are woven into the mesh much as they are in a wig. Readjustment is required at regular intervals but wearers can lead a more active life than a toupee allows. [££+]

Micheline Arcier, 4 Albert Gate Court, 124 Knightsbridge, sw1 (589-3225), is an aromatherapist. Practised by the ancient Egyptians and Greeks, aromatherapy involves the massage of face and body using pure aromatics and natural oils from plants, trees and flowers. Mme Arcier is an intelligent, articulate Frenchwoman who has been practising aromatherapy for over ten years. She examines a client from head to foot in an initial consultation lasting one and a half hours (costing about £25). Each treatment is designed for the client's particular needs, and a course of six costs £56 and is said to be extremely relaxing. Mme Arcier's special oils a d floral incenses can be bought retail from her salon. Detailed information sent on request. [£££]

Harrods, Knightsbridge, sw1 (584-8881), provides beauty treatments using Rose Laird or Orlane products. Sessions vary from a half-hour cleanse and make-up to a one-and-a-half-hour revitalizing treatment. There is a reduction in price if you take a course of treatments. Harrods offer a B.21 treatment especially for ageing skin, and a budget (comparatively speaking) face treatment lasting thirty minutes and including bio-peeling and a supervised make-up which you do yourself with Orlane products. Harrods also remove hair by wax or by electrolysis and give body massage either by hand or with a G Five machine. [££+]

Mavala Manicure School, 139A New Bond Street, w1

(629-6174). Manicures using Swiss-made Mavala products are performed by students for only 40p. Ring for an appointment. [£]

*Elizabeth Flair, 13A Alma Square, NW8 (286-0111), is a specialist in the treatment of acne. Miss Flair promises to clear the skin and claims she has never yet had a failure. Treatments at the clinic are £4·25 each, a course of six for the price of five. A home treatment pack is also available. This has seven preparations, includes a mild diet and costs £6. [££]

*Beauty Clinic Training Centre, 118 Baker Street, W1 (486-6291). Free treatments for acne and other skin problems are administered by trainees. [£]

Linda Turner, (505-0465), gives a one-hour massage or facial in your own home using natural oils extracted from almonds, wheatgerm, witch-hazel and the like. [££+]

College of Fashion and Clothing Technology, 20 John Prince's Street, W1 (493-8341), gives a one-and-a-half hour facials and body massage during term time for 20p. Telephone to find out class schedules. [£]

Porchester Baths, Queensway, W2 (229-3226). Sauna and full Turkish bath facilities, including cubicles for napping. Turkish bath clients can stay for up to three hours and the price, £3, includes a body shampoo. The hours are 9 a.m. to 7 p.m. (closing at 9 p.m.). Women on Tuesday, Thurdsay, Friday. Men on Monday, Wednesday, Saturday.

Exercise

---

*West Side Health Club, 201 Kensington High Street, W8 (937-7979), runs a health-food restaurant and a fully equipped gymnasium, and provides saunas and massage for women and men. Men use the club on Tuesdays, Thursdays and Saturdays, women on Mondays, Wednesdays and Fridays. Hours are 9 a.m. to 9 p.m. and a year's membership is £120. Membership entitles you to the use of gymnasium and sauna, plus a course of special exercises designed for individual needs. The gymnasium has instructors on duty at all times and regular classes are held in body movement. Non-members may also use the club. They pay £4 for a gym work-out and sauna. Massage is extra. There is a solarium and on the days the opposite sex are using the club, you can still come in for a sauna upstairs.

Beauty Farm Ltd, The Grange, Henlow, Bedfordshire (0462-811111), is a health farm located amid parkland in a Georgian house about an hour out of London. It provides weekly programmes, Sunday to Saturday, for men and women who want to slim, gain weight, get or keep fit. Exercises to music and custom diets are standard fare, but patrons also have access to an indoor swimming pool, badminton and tennis courts and various treatments such as wax and thermal baths, hydro-massage, solaria, mud heat and Finnish sauna. There are 32 rooms, six with private baths, and a week's residence costs between £165 and £250, depending on the room, which must vary quite a bit.

Shenley Lodge, Ridge Hill, Radlett, Herts. (Potters Bar 4242), is only 16 miles from London and offers exercise, relaxation and beauty treatments weekly or over a long weekend – Friday to Sunday.

Lotte Berk, 29 Manchester Street, w1 (935-8905), runs exercise classes for women only. Miss Berk's method combines modern ballet and a bit of yoga with exercise techniques. These are practised to music which makes working-out less boring. Classes last forty-five minutes. Ten lessons per course.

Town and Country Health Club, 2 Yeoman's Row, sw3 (584-7702), is for women only. In operation for seventeen years, the club is owned and operated by Marina Anderson, author of *What Have I Got to Lose? The ABZ of Slimming* (Dent). Town and Country specializes in slimming but is popular with models and women who just want to keep the shapes they've got. A year's membership to the club is £99.50.

Each member receives a written-out programme of exercises designed for her plus a special diet when required. Body massage, facials, manicures and pedicures, wax baths and hair removal. Miss Anderson welcomes visitors who want to have a look round.

*Dance Centre, 12 Floral Street, WC2 (836-6544), is about the cheapest place to get exercise in town. Classes are 80p and you can show up and join a class whenever you feel like it. Classical and modern ballet, jazz, soul, rock, mime, movement, go-go as well as exercise and limbering up classes. Also yoga.

*Body Control Studio, The Place, 17 Duke's Road, WC1 (387-3578), runs classes based on the Pilates method and designed for men and women, young and old, dancers and housewives. Body control exercises are done with light equipment and on an individual basis but in a room with other people. Good for keeping in shape, aligning the body and developing proper posture. Not muscle building. £2 for an hour.

*Ravelle's Health Centre, Portsea Hall, Portsea Place, W2 (402-5704), operates on a membership basis but is one of the most reasonably-priced gymnasium and sauna establishments in London. It has a well-designed studio with good equipment. Membership is £40 a year for women, £55 for men. Men use the facilities Mondays, Wednesdays, Fridays and Saturday morning, women on alternate days and Saturday afternoon. Open weekdays till 9 p.m., Saturday until 6 p.m. Most of the clientele are under thirty. The owner, Mr Lou Ravelle, has written several books on exercise and will write out the programme you need. There is a branch for men only at 52 Brunswick Centre, WC1.

The Sanctuary, 12 Floral Street, WC2 (240-2744). Located inside the Dance Centre, this new club is a veritable Xanadu. Balmy water-gardens and flamingoes provide an atmosphere which must be one of the most beautiful and relaxing anywhere in London. Tucked tastefully away are a solarium, gymnasium, sauna, and several treatment rooms. There is a swimming pool, restaurant and bar, and the club is open from 10 a.m. to 10 p.m. Membership is £200 a year.

Lillywhites, Piccadilly Circus, SW1 (930-3181), sell equipment to exercise with at home. They have things to lift and pull and get jiggled on.

Special cosmetic and make-up services

Cosmetics À La Carte, 16 Motcomb Street, SW1 (235-0596). If your lipstick or foundation has been discontinued, take what's left of it to Cosmetics à la Carte and they will copy it. The firm is run by two young women who do make-up diagnosis, create custom cosmetics, and give lessons in make-up. They cater to sensitive skins and the cosmetics are their own brand.

Floris, 89 Jermyn Street, SW1 (930-2885). A family business for five generations, Floris is England's answer to French perfume. The firm makes a dozen scents derived from English flowers – roses, violets, honeysuckle, geraniums and lilies of the valley, to name a few. Nearly all can be bought as toilet water, perfume, bath oil, sachet or talc. Six scents are available in soap. Floris also sells sponges and some men's preparations.

Joan Price's Face Place, 33 Cadogan Street, SW3 (589-9062), and 31 Connaught Street, W2 (723-6671). If you're tired of your cosmetics and want to try something different you can get the best idea about what you look like in a new shade at the Face Place. There are some twenty different brands and an assistant will try several on you free of charge and give you some advice about making-up too. Naturally it's hoped you'll buy a couple of items in the end. The Face Place gives private make-up lessons (£2·75), no appointment needed except on Saturdays. A cleanse and make-up costs £2·25, facials £3·50. Acne facials and herbal peeling are a bit more.

Culpeper, 21 Bruton Street, w1 (629-4559), 59 Ebury Street, sw1 (730-0361), and 9 Flask Walk, nw3 (794-7263), are herbalists. Elder flower cream moisturizer, red elm night cream, rose water astringent, and rosemary soapless shampoo are just a few of Culpeper's cosmetics. If you prefer to make them yourself there are how-to books plus herbs and oils in their original state.

Many health food shops stock cosmetics made from natural oils: two recommended sources are:

Westminster Health Food Centre, 81 Rochester Row, sw1 (834-2711), have a variety of brands of cremes, lotions, foundations and astringents.

Wholefood Bookshop, 114 Baker Street, w1 (935-9903). Nettle shampoo, seaweed bath preparations, and simple soap from makers like Weleda, Hofels and Countrified Products.

CHAPTER 10

see also Auctions,
Chapter 2 and
Kitchen units
page 214; for
radios and television
see Stereo, radio and
TV, Chapter 19

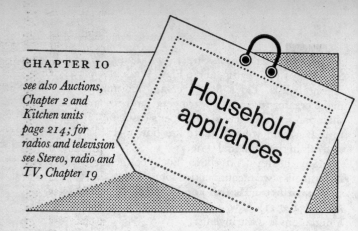

Household
appliances

Household appliances have *recommended retail prices* put on them by manufacturers and most retailers stick roughly to them. Yet there is virtually no reason to pay the recommended retail price for any appliance unless you are extremely lazy or it is so exotic that only one store sells it. Everything else can be got on average at 20 per cent off through discount warehouses and, sometimes, by 'special offers' and mail order.

Curiously enough, no matter where you live in Britain it makes sense to buy your appliances in London. According to a survey made by the Consumers' Association of ten cities in which a variety of household appliances and electrical goods were purchased, London averaged 20 per cent below list prices; the others were between only 8 and 14 per cent.

Effective discount buying involves some shopping around since no warehouse or store consistently undersells any other. Discount stores operate by bulk buying and their prices depend on what and how much of an item they can get. Prices fluctuate from store to store accordingly. Therefore you should telephone all or several of the discount houses listed below. When you find the right model at the best price make sure the appliance is actually *in stock* or you may get there and discover it is on order and there is a long waiting period. Another important thing to ask about is after-sales servicing. Under the Supply of Goods Act, 1973, the retailer is responsible for providing repairs, but many are reluctant to admit this. Also the speed of repair service varies enormously, so unless you have a local repair man or know the brand you are buying has a servicing division in London (as most do), it is worth taking this into consideration as well as price. And remember, the manufacturer's guarantee covers the appliance no matter where you buy it.

To find out what model or brand suits you, visit the displays in manufacturers' showrooms or have a look in some of the department stores. The *London Electricity Board* gives free advice. An excellent source of information is *Which* magazine, published by the Consumers' Association and available by subscription or in your local library. *Which* tests and reports in detail on all kinds of appliances, always recommending the best model to get value for your money. Surveys are constantly being brought up to date as new models appear on the market. **The Design Centre** in the Haymarket keeps an illustrated index of appliances whose design meets their standards of performance, safety, beauty, and value for money.

Finally, remember that most department and many appliance stores have sales in January and July and if you can wait until then to buy, your chances of both getting what you want and saving money are further increased.

Discount houses

(See also Miscellaneous bargain shops, reconditioned appliances and rental services, page 180)

Note: owing to the competition between discount houses and the difficulties in getting bulk orders from manufacturers, the percentages of discount mentioned below are subject to fluctuation and should be treated as guidelines only. In fact, one appliance may be 50 per cent below list price and another only 15 per cent. Telephoning around is strongly recommended.

Comet, 190 London Road, Hackbridge, Surrey (669-4321), the biggest discount warehouse in the London area, has 125 outlets across the country and prices average between 25 and 30 per cent below list prices. Comet stock both large and small appliances. There are no showrooms but goods are often advertised in the *Evening Standard*. They will accept advance orders and rather a lot of the items they advertise are not in stock, so telephone first. Not only are popular lines like Indesit, Hoover, Tricity and Philips stocked, there are occasionally discounted luxury appliances too. All goods are guaranteed for twelve months. Delivery charge.

Argos, 80–110 New Oxford Street, w1 (637-1869) and various branches round London and throughout the country, stock over 4,000 different items at discount prices but only a proportion are 'white goods', as all household appliances except radio and television are called in the trade. (Radio and television are known as 'brown goods'.) Many Argos showrooms have all items on display, others have about half. There is a fully-illustrated catalogue in colour which is free to customers who call in. Electric curlers, coffee percolators and steam irons as well as dishwashers, electric cookers, etc., average about 30 per cent below recommended prices and most can be collected on the spot. Flat rate for deliveries. Argos have servicing arrangements with all their manufacturers. They also have a credit plan, take several credit cards and can arrange Hire Purchase. See the telephone directory for the showroom nearest to you.

Discount Buying Agency, 111 South Farm Road, Worthing, Sussex (from London, 0903-31415), are a mail-order discount house giving 10 and 20 per cent off retail prices. On becoming a member, which costs nothing, you get regular lists of discounted goods. All their appliances are nationally-known brands and the Agency takes special orders for items which are not on the list. Free delivery in the London area. Own after-sales servicing, H.P. and account facilities. Members can cancel an order any time before it is actually dispatched.

Country Gentleman's Association, Icknield Way West, Letchworth, Herts. (046-26-2377), is an organization with shopping opportunities which may appeal to Londoners of all sorts as well as country gentlemen. Membership includes a subscription to a monthly magazine – admittedly on country matters, but with numerous advertisements for discounted goods. Members also get a catalogue of goods discounted at 10 per cent. There are household and garden things – also wine – and there is a list of shops which automatically give CGA members discounts on all purchases.

Avon, 124 Uxbridge Road, w7 (579-2741), sell electric blankets, heaters, freezers, washing machines, driers, etc. at between 10 per cent and 30 per cent off retail prices. C.O.D. orders taken. Minimal delivery charge. Own servicing facilities.

Discount and Delivery, 15 Approach Road, sw20 (540-3855), have mostly large appliances – fridges, dishwashers, washing machines and cookers (when they can get them). Delivery costs extra. Goods on order can be cancelled at any time and your deposit will be refunded.

London Electrical, 557 Battersea Park Road, sw11 (223-3344), are smaller than many discount houses but what they do have is usually about 30 per cent off. Free delivery.

Sewcraft, 150 King Street, w6 (748-0808). Sewing and knitting machines at 30 per cent to 50 per cent off list prices: Frister and Rossmann, Elna, Pfaff, New Home, Bernina, Necchi, Viking, Novum and Knitmaster. Sewcraft guarantee all their machines and parts for ten years and will deliver free anywhere in Britain. Detailed brochures and price list on request. All machines listed are in stock. Delivery in about one week.

Miscellaneous bargain shops, reconditioned appliances and rental services

John Lewis, Oxford Street, w 1 (629-7711). Stores in the John Lewis partnership keep their prices low by buying through a central buying department. Occasionally they put their trade-name, Jonelle, on another brand of appliance in order to sell it even more cheaply. Their policy is never to be undersold and should you find an appliance you bought from them on sale for less elsewhere, they will refund the difference. A few of the appliances on display must be ordered but most are ready for delivery which is free within thirty miles radius of London. Credit facilities available.

Buyers and Sellers, 120 Ladbroke Grove, w 10 (229-1947), specialize in fridges, freezers, washing machines, dishwashers and driers that have been rejected by the manufacturer because of minor *exterior* blemishes. They carry the same warranty as any new machine yet discounts often exceed what you get at warehouses. Only models in stock are for sale: they take no advance orders; as a result most deliveries are within twenty-four hours. Buyers and Sellers also sell reconditioned Hoover and Electrolux cleaners. All brands have servicing depots in London.

Refrigerator Rentals, 139 Sloane Street, sw 1 (730-0448), rent all sizes of electric fridges short and long term. They are ideal for people whose fridge has broken down or those sharing furnished flats, as there is no capital outlay and rent is monthly (about £2 per month for a four-cubic-foot size). Same day deliveries. The firm also rent freezers.

Calor Gas, 29 Stacey Avenue, n 18 (807-5801), hire gas cookers by the week. Three-, four- and six-burner models are supplied, together with their own cylinder of gas. Delivery is free within a five-mile radius.

Cooker Centre, 420 Edgware Road, w 2 (723-2975),

usually have several secondhand gas cookers repaired to working order and priced at a fraction of their original cost. All have a sixty-day warranty. The Centre also stock new gas and electric cookers at about 10 per cent below list prices, and you can trade your old model in. Most brands are in less expensive ranges. Deliveries are free and the firm will install and service its models. Installation is by a licensed CORGI installer. (See Installation, repairs and servicing, page 183.)

Reconditioned Gas Appliances, 4A Camden Road, NW1 (485-4016), and 38 Stamford Hill, N16 (806-5274), have fully-reconditioned cookers, gas fires and water heaters. All have a three-month warranty and are installed by a registered CORGI serviceman. Prices are well below normal. Delivery free locally.

Hire Service Shops, 192 Campden Hill Road, W8 (385-1841) and other branches, rent vacuum cleaners, carpet shampooers, steam irons, sewing machines, fans and typewriters by the day or week. Pick up and delivery service.

D. S. Levey, 33 Camden Passage, N1 (226-3711), one of the oldest residents in Camden Passage, was born in the room over his shop. Mr Levey sells reconditioned sewing machines. Most are electric but there are some treadle-operated ones too. All have a twelve-month guarantee and each purchaser gets a demonstration of how to operate and care for his machine.

Note: to find out about the best sewing machines in straight stitch or zig-zag see *Which* consumer reports, June 1973.

Posh appliances

Harrods, Knightsbridge, sw1 (730-1234), is the place to see the latest thing in domestic appliances. It's worth a visit for sheer technological wonder or just to see how the other half (per cent) lives. Harrods have microwave ovens that will cook a potato in five minutes, and a 5-lb joint in half an hour. There are high temperature self-cleaning ovens which literally incinerate old food and grime. You merely brush out the ashes afterwards. Most exotic of all is the Cool-Top hob which looks like part of the kitchen counter and can be used like it. The 'cool-top' only heats up when it comes into contact with a saucepan. If it comes into contact with a person who wears a heart pacemaker, however, it can kill them. The price is £1,600. Harrods also have double-door American fridges by Westinghouse and Amana (£800). One model gives you either ice-water or ice for only £200 extra. Just press a lever and it plops into your glass. De-luxe dishwashers and automatically defrosting freezers are also on display. Small appliances include electric waffle irons, frying pans, rotisseries, trolleys and humidifiers – items not normally stocked by discount houses.

David MacIlwaine and Rose Gray, 113 Warwick Avenue, w9 (289-1667), have a house full of old French stoves made of cast iron, enamel and porcelain. Their heating stoves and cookers come in all shapes and sizes, and can burn wood or coal. Ring first for an appointment.

Aga, 26 Brook Street, w1 (499-8941). In spite of all the new-fangled cookers on the market, the Aga is still the favourite of a lot of cooks. Its old-fashioned shape has been slightly streamlined and it is now available in gas- and oil-burning models as well as the traditional solid fuel version. It comes in eight colours, and costs from £500 to £600. Agas can operate as hot water boilers but an attachment costing £250 to £300 is required.

Installation, repairs and servicing

A note about electricity: most branded appliances have servicing depots in London and throughout the country. Either ring the manufacturer or check with the dealer from whom you bought the appliance. Remember, under the Sale of Goods Act, 1973 it is the *retailer* who is legally responsible for the working order of all goods he has sold. Many appliances have a list of repair and servicing depots attached.

A note about gas: all gas installations should be done by registered CORGI installers. They meet the standards set by the Gas Board and are fully qualified to work with North Sea gas.

Electrical Contractors Association, 34 Palace Court, N2 (229-1266). If an old appliance needs re-wiring or you want special wiring done, the Association will give you the name of an electrician in your area. By using an Association member you are automatically insured for up to £5,000 against faulty workmanship.

London Electricity Board (look under 'Electricity' in the telephone directory for the number nearest you). The L.E.B. have a twenty-four-hour emergency service and don't charge for genuine emergencies. The L.E.B. will also give advice about what electrical goods would be best for your needs.

National Association of Plumbers and Domestic Heating Engineers, 6 Gate Street, WC2 (405-2678). This is an industrial relations group, not a trade association, but if you write to them about the job you want done they will send names and addresses of plumbers to get in touch with, and any complaints can be filed through them.

North Thames Gas Co. See 'Gas' in the telephone directory for the number of the emergency service nearest you or for installation and repairs.

Electric Razor Hospital, 491 Commercial Road, E1

(790-2906), will repair any electric or battery-operated razor. Also Ronson electric toothbrushes. Either send the razor in by post or ring and find out where the collection depot for your area is located.

L. Apple, 60 Brewer Street, w1 (437-8184), repair small appliances like curlers, hair-driers, vacuum cleaners and mixers, usually within three weeks. They keep a supply of spare parts for out-of-date models.

D. S. Levey, 33 Camden Passage, n1 (226-3711), repairs and services sewing machines.

Problem Ltd, 179 Vauxhall Bridge Road, sw1 (828-8181), is a good service for those who are willing to pay extra for prompt, competent assistance. For £10 a year, plus £5 deposit, you become a member of Problem and when you need a plumber or electrician, among other things, they will send a reliable one at once.

Electrical Association for Women, 25 Foubert's Place, w1 (437-5212), was established in 1924 to give instruction to women about electrical equipment. The Association distributes information on re-wiring and has a 'Ready Reference Kitchen Chart' explaining electrical terms, and giving information on how to change fuses and plugs and read meters. The Association also offers a three-lesson course of basic electrical training, costing 50p.

CHAPTER 11

see also
Household
furnishings,
Chapter 12

Household
decoration

When getting a price from a painter or builder remember there is a difference between an 'estimate' and a 'quotation'. An estimate, as the name suggests, is merely a rough idea of what the cost will be, while a quotation is a guaranteed price and therefore more desirable if you can get it.

Architectural and structural items

(See also Chapter 1, Antiques, and Antique repairs and restoration, page 51)

Doors and windows

W. H. Newson, 61 Pimlico Road, sw1 (730-6262). Interior and exterior doors of all kinds: panel doors, louvre doors, Georgian styles complete with surrounds, sliding glass doors, garage doors, wood folding doors. Also windows in many sizes and styles including Georgian sash and bow windows. Excellent illustrated catalogue.

Louvre Centre and Door Store, 61 Judd Street, wc1 (387-0091). Cupboard or full-size pine louvre doors, and interior and exterior panel doors in Philippine mahogany. Brochure on request.

Open Sesame, 1 The Broadway, Barnes, sw13 (876-8322). Nothing but doors for inside and out; a few secondhand ones.

Chelsea Glassworks, 105 Fulham Road, sw3 (581-2501), supply window glass cut to size. They stock several thicknesses and types. The Glassworks will mend broken windows, install new ones or provide double glazing.

Alcan, 352 Neasden Lane, nw10 (450-8246), are double glazing experts. They will make aluminium frames to measure, and give a ten-year guarantee on labour and fittings. Double glazing is a good way to keep noise out as well as heat in and in some of the noisier parts of greater London you can get a government grant to have it installed. Complete double glazing for an average semi-detached house costs between £600 and £700.

Fireplaces

Fireplace Designers, 157c Great Portland Street, w1 (580-9893), build and install fireplaces from scratch or alter existing ones. You can make up your own design or choose from their modern and period selection. They will get the materials and craftsmen required for whatever needs doing, and can install electric and gas fireplaces as well as open ones.

Hart of Knightsbridge, 3 Beauchamp Place, sw3 (584-5770), make hand-carved reproduction mantelpieces to special order or from a comprehensive catalogue of period designs; also painted wooden mantels with composite decoration, and reproduction grates.

Goslett, 55 Great Marlborough Street, w1 (437-7890), display a series of contemporary fireplaces designed by top European designers and commissioned by the Coal Board. The Coal Board will arrange for installation. Write to either Goslett or the Coal Board for illustrated brochures.

Bufalini, 31A Bedford Street, WC2 (836-1633), cut marble to any size for hearths or surrounds. They also clean, restore and match marble.

Flooring

A. Vigers, 59 Poland Street, W1 (437-5724). Hardwood flooring in blocks, mosaics, tongue-and-groove strips and parquet. Mostly African and Malayan woods, but their parquet is all oak. Flooring is sold by the square yard and can, with the exception of parquet, say Vigers, be laid by amateurs.

Gloster Parquet, 36 Maxwell Road, SW6 (731-0533). All types of hardwood flooring including $\frac{1}{4}$ inch oak parquet in strip or batten. (Hardwood mosaic is the least expensive.) Gloster lay floors too.

Robinson Ltd., 8 Bowater Road, Woolwich, SE18 (317-8192). Specialists in cork floor and wall tiles. Over forty different designs and textures.

Wincilate, Town Hall, Bow Road, E3 (980-2203). Slate for floors, patios, fireplaces in rectangular or random shapes or cut to size. Wincilate also lay slate floors.

Alpha Mosaic and Terrazzo, 42 Caversham Road, NW5 (485-7227), supply and lay-in terrazzo and mosaic designs. They use cement sand exclusively and believe other adhesives are inferior.

Bufalini, 31A Bedford Street, WC2 (836-1633), cut marble flooring to size and lay it.

John Lewis, Oxford Street, W1 (629-7711), sell Amtico and Armstrong vinyl tiles, cushion vinyl sheet flooring and self-adhesive do-it-yourself vinyl tiles. If you want to see the complete Armstrong or Amtico range both manufacturers have London showrooms but they do not sell tiles. Amtico's range includes patterned vinyl floor tiles with matching ceramic wall tiles.

Tile Mart, 151 Great Portland Street, W1 (580-3814), and branches, have some 200 hand-painted designs which are reproductions of old Dutch Makkum tiles. Free illustrated brochure. Tile Mart also carry reproductions of antique French and Italian tiles. Sizes vary from $3\frac{1}{2}$ cm square to 30 cm square. Most of the stock is exclusive to the firm.

Domus, 260 Brompton Road, sw3 (589-9457). Exclusively Italian ceramic tiles. There are 120 designs in stock; most of them hand-finished. Domus have an illustrated brochure of some eighty designs, and the colours of some match kitchen and bath units by Wrighton, Adamsez and others.

World's End Tiles and Flooring, 9 Langton Street, sw10 (351-0279). Quarry tiles in different sizes and colours, cork tiles for floors and walls and ceramic tiles that include some fifty patterns exclusive to World's End: silk-screened reproductions of old Delft, art deco and art nouveau tiles.

U.B.M. and Pratt, 123 Caledonian Road, n1 (837-2781). Inexpensive quarry tiles 6 inches by 6 inches by $\frac{5}{8}$ inch; ten for only 60p. They lay tiles too.

Chelsea Pottery, 13 Radnor Walk, sw3 (352-1366), will produce hand-painted tiles to any design or specification or create original tiles.

Continental Tiling, 141 Sherwood Park Avenue, Sidcup, Kent (304-3332), lay floor and wall tiles of all kinds.

Heating

National Heating Centre, 26 Store Street, wc1 (580-3238), will advise you on the best heating system for your needs. Consultations are £5 an hour. Bring house plans or dimensions of rooms and windows. You can write in for advice too. This costs £6. The Centre is part of the Building Centre and displays examples of gas, oil and electrically-fired central heating systems. If you would like a heating consultant to visit your home ask for Mr Beer at the same number.

Iron and metalwork

Bayswater Architectural and Sheet Metal Works, 2 Pond Place, sw3 (589-4191). Mr O'Meagher and his craftsmen can make almost anything in brass, steel, aluminium or iron from staircases to cooker hoods, gazebos, and finials. Finest workmanship.

J. J. Contracts, 787 Wandsworth Road, sw8 (622-9604), are architectural metal workers who will make, copy, or repair balustrade railings, grilles, staircases, grates, firedogs, or 'any metal work that shows a profit'.

T. F. Buckle, 427 King's Road, sw10 (352-0952), sells a reproduction spiral iron staircase winding clockwise or anti-clockwise and rising to any height. It is 4 foot in diameter clockwise and 4 foot 6 inches anti-clockwise, and costs around £270.

Lifts

Barron and Shepherd, 134 King Street, w6 (748-0311), supply and install home lifts in three standard sizes, or to measure. A two-floor lift costs around £1,600 installed.

Mouldings and trim

Skirting, banister railing, sills and decorative mouldings in many widths can be found at most timber merchants. Many also supply panel board, and all deliver. Check the yellow pages for the nearest supplier to you. A few centrally-located firms are:

R. G. Watkins, 323 Euston Road, NW1 (387-6909).

Joseph Yates, 146 Kensington Church Street, w8 (229-4276).

Latchford, 61 Endell Street, wc2 (836-6556).

W. H. Newson, 61 Pimlico Road, sw1 (730-6262).

G. Jackson and Son, Rathbone Works, Rainville Road, w6 (385-6616), are expert plasterers who can produce or replace an elaborate baroque ceiling or a delicate Adam frieze.

J. G. McDonough, 347 New King's Road, sw6 (736-5146), plasterwork specialists who will tackle jobs on any scale. They have plaster columns, friezes, etc. already cast (free catalogue) but custom work is the larger part of their business. They can match cornices, make columns of almost any size and they also do pargeting, i.e. exterior plaster-work.

Trollope and Sons, 26 Voltaire Road, Clapham, sw4 (622-9481), make and install hard and softwood panelling; dados or entire rooms. They will copy a period design or create a modern one.

Curtains, blinds and upholstery services

(See also Furnishing fabrics, page 134)

De Winter, 223 Kensington Church Street, w8 (229-4949), run a complete soft furnishings service. They make lined and unlined curtains, bed hangings and loose covers and do all types of upholstery work. They stock curtain rods and tracks, have several pelmet designs and will give decorating advice to customers. They also lay carpets and apply fabric to walls. The store is chock-a-block with fabrics and sample books of traditional and, to a lesser extent, ultra-modern designs on cotton.

They will make curtains or covers in your own fabric if you prefer. Standards of workmanship are high. [££+]

C. H. Frost, 67A Abingdon Road, w8 (937-0451), make curtains and pelmets, upholstery and loose covers in your own or their material. (Sample books in stock are mostly velvets, damasks, etc.) Frost also collect and clean curtains. [££]

Decor Furnishings, 44 Stanhope Grove, Beckenham, Kent (658-6975), provide a complete in-your-home service for lined curtains. They bring the samples to you and hold them up so you can see how they will really look. Delivery takes three to four weeks. [££+]

Enriqueta, 4 Barley Mow Passage, w4 (995-6659), runs an in-the-home service for all soft furnishings. She brings a van full of fabrics, carpet and paper samples to you. Enriqueta makes loose covers and curtains and has a carpet laying and paper hanging service. She also has a reputation for good workmanship and for meeting deadlines. [££+]

John Lewis, Oxford Street, w1 (629-7711), and

Peter Jones, Sloane Square, sw3 (730-3434) and other branches of the Partnership sell ready-made and custom-made curtains. The custom service includes both machine and hand-made curtains. (Custom-machined curtains must be between 9 and 12 feet long.) All fancy headings are done by hand and all custom curtains are cotton-lined. There are ready-made ranges available in Jonelle and Sanderson fabrics, among others. John Lewis stores will send a man to measure and give a free estimate within a radius of forty miles of London. [££, ££+]

Net Centre, 46 Goodge Street, w1 (580-1915), sell nothing but net – by the yard or already made up into curtains. The Centre make to measure, hire and maintain net curtains. [£+]

Antique Leathers, 4 Park End, South Hill Park, nw3 (435-8582). Upholsterers in leather on horsehair. Expensive, but workmanship is excellent. [£££]

Canonbury Antiques, 13 Canonbury Place, n1 (359-2246). Mr Holyome is one of the few upholsterers who still stock a selection of horsehair fabric for covering chairs. The widest is 27 inches and there are colours as well as traditional black. Horsehair is one of the toughest coverings you can get. Mr Holyome also re-upholsters old furniture. This is a one-man operation and can take a lot of time. [££]

Charles Hammond, 165 Sloane Street, SW1 (235-2151). Complete decorating service of the highest quality. Expensive. Hammond's make curtains and have a fine selection of English and continental fabrics; chintzes, brocades, velvets. Elegant and traditional. [£££]

Association of Master Upholsterers, 4 Sutherland Avenue, W9 (965-3565), have a membership of craftsmen providing soft furnishing services. Send them details of the work you want done – curtains, loose covers, carpet laying – and they will give you a short list of Association members in your area. Specify what price range, since registered members range from finest quality handcraftsmen to those who do a thorough but workaday job. Should a dispute arise over work done, the Association will act as a mediator.

Putney Blinds, 317 Putney Bridge Road, SW15 (789-0015), make and install interior and exterior blinds in any style to any specification; awnings, continental blinds, venetian blinds, roller blinds and shutters. Roller blinds can be made up in your own material. [££+]

Radiant Venetian Blinds, 1 Hartfield Crescent, SW19 (540-0211), make venetian blinds to order or collect them for laundering. They also make roller blinds. [££+]

Whiteleys, Queensway, W2 (229-1234), stock interior spring rollers, canvas, and spray fabric stiffener for do-it-yourself blind makers. Roller sizes are 36 inches to 108 inches wide and cost less than similar kits elsewhere. Whiteleys also have a wide range of colours and patterns in made-to-measure roller blinds. [££]

Blind Alley, 119 Regent's Park Road, NW1 (586-3911), will hand-paint or print roller blinds and chair canvas in any design or colour. They also paint murals. [££+]

Starcraft, 88 New King's Road, SW6 (736-7411), reglaze chintz and provide a complete curtain service.

Decorative hardware

(See also Bathroom fixtures, page 199)

Beardmore, 4 Percy Street, w1 (636-1214). Over 35,000 brass reproductions of furniture mounts (finials, hinges, drawer pulls, beading, casters and feet), decorative keys, stair carpet rods and brass grilles in Jacobean to modern styles. They also have gold plated bath fixtures and porcelain and glass door knobs. Beardmore's sell to trade and retail customers and will fill custom-made orders when they have the time. They also stock reproduction fire furniture and locks. Usually crowded and queueing is to be expected.

Knobs and Knockers, 65 Judd Street, wc1 (387-0091), specialize in brass door furniture but stock wrought iron and chrome designs and some bath fittings in chrome, gold plate and Porcelaine de Paris. Mahogany toilet seats.

Comyn Ching, 15 Shelton Street, wc2 (836-9123). Ironmongers for over 200 years, their premises don't seem to have changed, just aged. There is nothing on display; you choose what you want from a catalogue and they dig it out for you. Myriad brasses and odds and ends.

Habitat, 206 King's Road, sw10 (351-1211), seem to have the least expensive brass knobs around for drawers and doors.

Paint and wall-coverings

(For wall tiles see Flooring, page 187)

Note: most British wallpaper rolls are 11 yards long and 21 inches wide.

Sanderson, 49–57 Berners Street, w1 (636-7800), Britain's largest decorating suppliers, stock wallpaper in over 1,000 colours. Patterns include the famous William Morris prints made from Morris's own blocks, plus flocks, stripes, solids and a vast number of miscellaneous designs, including Triad and Rasch Maison papers with matching fabric. Prices start about £1·50 a roll. Sanderson's have their own line of paint which is mixed on the spot, and comes in 1,350 shades. They also sell Hadrian and Crown paints. [££]

Cole and Son, 18 Mortimer Street, W1 (580-1066). Traditional hand-printed wallpapers and exclusive French papers, several with matching fabrics. Expensive. Cole's stock their own brand of paint in a limited number of shades. [££+]

Osborne and Little, 304 King's Road, SW3 (352-1456). Wallpaper designers and suppliers. Handsome, hand-printed papers, metallic papers, paper-backed felt and hessian. About sixty-five patterns, each in four colours, and prices average £4 to £6 a roll. Osborne and Little also have Designers Guild wallpapers. These tend to be small regular patterns with cotton fabric to match. [££+]

Watts, 7 Tufton Street, SW1 (222-7169), have a small but elegant selection of Victorian wallpapers handblocked from the original wood blocks. Catalogue. [££+]

John Lewis, Oxford Street, W1 (629-7711). A big section of Lewis's third floor is devoted to paints and related hardware and cleaning fluids. Generally speaking, this is the best place to buy Dulux, Crown Plus II, Brolac, Magicote and Vymura Colour-sheen. The selection is large (any of Dulux's 220 shades can be mixed while you wait) and you nearly always pay less than you would for the same paint in your local hardware store. [££]

Leyland, 125 Church Street, NW8 (262-6905), sell their own paint and wallpaper, often at discounted prices. Inexpensive wallpapers from 55p. [£+]

Mr Stone's Paint and Wallpaper Shop, 175 Muswell Hill Broadway, N10 (444-9562), isn't easy to get to (Highgate tube, then a 43 or 134 bus), but when you do get there it's worth it. Mr Stone's has one of the biggest selections of wallpapers and paints in London: Sanderson, Osborne and Little, and Cole wallpapers can all be seen here; also Sanserson, Carson and Dulux paints. [££]

Samuel French, 26 Southampton Street, wc2 (836-7513). Paper over your cultural gaps with wallpaper designed to look like well stocked bookshelves. Three shelves of books per sheet. Each sheet costs 45p and is 38 inches wide and 28 inches high. [£+]

John Oliver, 33 Pembridge Road, w11 (727-3735), will mix paint to match any colour sample you bring in. Custom matching takes a couple of days, but there are 1,341 shades of John Oliver paint that can be mixed in the shop. Mr Oliver also sells his own attractively-designed wallpaper and matching fabric, plus a few American and continental papers. [££+]

John T. Keep, 15 Theobald's Road, wc1 (242-7578), sell their own range of Victor paints in emulsion, eggshell and gloss. They will match any colour you bring in and are happy to do this even for small orders. They also stock translucent enamels for glass in six shades. [££]

J. W. Bollom, 107 Long Acre, wc2 (836-3727). This huge shop is both trade and retail outlet for Bromel paints and there are literally hundreds of shades already mixed in emulsion and eggshell finishes. Bollom also sell PVC in several colours (50 inches wide) and felt and fibreglass.

Hire Service Shops, 192 Campden Hill Road, w8 (727-0897), rent wallpaper steam strippers, paperhangers' tools and tables, ladders, paint sprayers and, for the more intrepid, scaffolding. [££]

Kantex, 20 Store Street, wc1 (636-0541). Paper-backed hessian at unbeatable prices. Each roll is 36 inches wide and 6 yards long and costs about £5. Ten shades. Mail-order sample card costs 15p. [£+]

Felt and Hessian Shop, 34 Greville Street, ec1 (405-6215). Twenty shades of paper-backed felt and hessian for walls. Hessian comes in 36 inch and 52 inch widths, and their felt is 31 inches wide. They have an even wider range of felt and hessian for other purposes (e.g. without backing): over 100 shades of felt and forty of hessian. [££]

Colefax and Fowler, 39 Brook Street, W1 (493-2231), sell their own wallpaper which is reproduced from old documents. Elegant Mauny designs from France – by special order only. [£££]

Dominique Regnier, 2 Priory Avenue, Bedford Park, W4 (995-1572), applies fabrics to walls without battens or paste. [££+]

Laura Ashley, 40 Sloane Street, SW3 (235-9728), stock about 16 different wallpapers which have in common that well-known Laura Ashley signature – small two-colour printed motifs reminiscent of the eighteenth and nineteenth centuries. Matching fabrics. [££]

Home Decorating Shop, 83 Walton Street, SW3 (584-6111). Good selection of British and continental papers. [££+]

Professional instruction

Inner London Education Authority, County Hall, SE1 (633-3441), hold evening classes in curtain and pelmet making, home decorating, home repairs, graining and marbling loose-cover cutting and upholstering. Each course runs from September to June and costs about £6. For details, contact the Authority or send for their publication *Floodlight*, which costs 5p.

Inchbald School of Design, 7 Eaton Gate, SW1 (730-5508), has a one-year intensive course in interior design which teaches drawing techniques for presentations and theoretical aspects of design and includes lectures on building, heating and lighting as well as furniture. This is a three-semester course. Classes are five days a week, from 10 a.m. to 4 p.m., and the cost is about £1,000. There is a short ten-week course for £235.

Reader's Digest Do-it-Yourself Manual comes in its own carrying-case and is divided into two sections: one on technique and another on projects – how to finish wood, lay tiles, use tools or how to build cabinets, tables and do plumbing. Available in bookshops, but if you order from the *Reader's Digest*, 22 Berkeley Square, w1 direct it costs £5·10 instead of £6·95.

Rhodec, Yelverton, Devon (Yelverton 2764), runs a correspondence diploma course in interior design. Rhodec is an accredited correspondence college. The diploma course takes an estimated two years (working part-time) and costs under £70. This includes manuals, art materials and tuition. There is a 'certificate' course for about half the price. Both can be paid for in instalments.

Professional advice

Design Centre, 28 Haymarket, sw1 (839-8000), is part of the Design Council, a government-sponsored organization whose aim is to encourage good British design. The Centre has a pictorial file, open to the public, of over 10,500 modern British designs which have been selected by the Council committee for their high standards of safety, performance, aesthetic appeal and value for money. The designs include fabrics, appliances, furniture, door furniture, carpets, tiles, and many other artifacts. If you see an item that you want, you fill out a postcard, which the Centre sends to the manufacturer and he in turn notifies you of local stockists. For a stiff fee of £10·50 the Centre will also advise on interior decorators. You give them details of what you want and they provide a shortlist of three names most likely to suit your taste and needs. There is always an exhibition in the Centre's gallery and their bookshop sells paperbacks called 'Kitchens', 'Heating', etc.

Building Centre, 26 Store Street, wc1 (637-4522), gives

information to architects, builders and the general public. Huge displays with relevant brochures. This is a good place to see some of the latest things on the market whether they are flooring, kitchen units, doorknobs or saunas. There is also a reference library containing building codes and standards and trade literature. **Note:** this is not an impartial body, since manufacturers buy space at the centre for display.

Art Workers Guild, 6 Queen's Square, wc1 (837-3474), is an educational charity organized in 1884 under the inspiration of William Morris and John Ruskin to bring together architects, artists and craftsmen. The Guild will recommend an architect, furniture designer, cabinet-maker, interior decorator or lighting designer.

Crafts Advisory Committee, 12 Waterloo Place, sw1 (839-8000), have an index of selected craftsmen in Britain which includes biographical information and colour slides of each craftsman's work. This is a free service, but an appointment is necessary. The Crafts Advisory Committee can advise on textile weaving, embroidery, printing, pottery, metalwork and furniture-making.

Skilled craftsmen

(See also under Antique repairs and restoration, page 51)

Three Bridges, Leighton Place, Kentish Town, nw5 (624-4748). Expert joinery and wood turning. Balusters or bedsteads made to order; also some four-poster and half-tester beds already constructed.

Alan Dadd, 295 Caledonian Road, n1 (607-8737), is a marbling specialist and will decorate anything from a small box to a pillared hall in the *faux marbre* of your choice.

Household furnishings

Bathroom fixtures (see Decorative hardware,
   page 193, for additional bath accessories; Flooring,
   page 187, for information about tile supplies and
   installation; and Linen, page 219, for towels, etc.)

Bath shops supply but do not normally install fixtures.
They seem to feel plumbers are too unreliable to get mixed
up with. But you must, and the best way to find one is to
rely on the advice of a friend who has used one. **The
National Association of Plumbers and Domestic
Heating Engineers**, 6 Gate Street, WC2 (405-2678), an
industrial relations group, will send a list of member
plumbers in your area. Be sure to give a description of the
job when you write. For emergency service, see the Yellow
Pages for the twenty-four hour service nearest to you. Another solution to the plumbing problem, if you can afford
it, is provided by **Problem Ltd**, 179 Vauxhall Bridge Road,
SW1 (828-8181). Their membership fee is £10 a year, but
they produce reliable plumbers, electricians, etc., at a
moment's notice.

   Boldings, 58 Davies Street, W1 (629-6617), were bath
merchants before there were bathrooms; the firm started in
1828. Today their first-floor showrooms display medium to
high-priced fixtures for every taste. There are baths in

several shapes, whole suites in a range of colours, bidets, showers, basins built into cabinets or with marble surrounds, taps in chrome or gold plate – even a gold-plated hot towel airer. Twyfords, Armitage Shanks and Johnson Bros. makes predominate. Showers cost from £90, loos from about £20. Boldings also stock mahogany lavatory seats. [££, ££+]

Aston and Matthews, 143 Essex Road, Islington, N1 (226-7220), give the public the same terms they give the building trade and the most inexpensive loo, for example, is about 25 per cent less than at most plumbing merchants. Like all mass-selling operations prices fluctuate according to what the firm can get. No advance orders. Fixtures are stacked warehouse style against the walls for customers' inspection: bathroom suites in colours, taps and mixers, even a few exotic items like corner baths incredibly below the usual prices. Free delivery within seventy-mile radius and, unlike most bathroom merchants, Aston and Matthews will recommend a plumber. [£+]

C. P. Hart, Newnham Terrace, Hercules Road, SE1 (928-5866), stock medium and low-priced fixtures and there are many items at sizeable discounts. A good place to find a bargain. Free delivery within a twenty-mile radius. [£+]

Evered, 18 North Audley Street, W1 (499-1845), has the widest range of posh bath fixtures in London. Their showroom covers two floors, and displays Armitage Shanks, Adamsez, Eric Pol, and Porcelaine de Paris baths, bidets and loos in off-beat colours and shapes, even flower patterns. There are both new and old styles (Adamsez make a 'Victorian' suite), and lots of small hand-basins and gold-plated accessories. There are also showers with thermostatic mixers which keep the temperature constant. Perhaps the most unusual item is a high-backed wooden 'lavatory chair' with decorated pull chain, built-in ashtray, candlestand reading light and musical seat (£700). [££+]

Bonsack, 14 Mount Street, W1 (629-9981), is London's most exclusive bath shop. Designs are all by Mr Bonsack and each one is made up specially for the client in absolutely any colour. The eight available bath styles include a round bath with towel-upholstered cushions around the edge, a double bath with head and foot rests, and a chair-backed fibre-glass model with its exterior covered in the laminated fabric of your choice. These designs cost from £300. Another sybaritic fitting is a giant clam-shaped basin with a crusty exterior and a mother-of-pearl inside; there are also taps cast in gold or shaped like animals, large turtles with water gushing from their mouths and flower vase backs, frogs, and improbable spouting rhinos. Bonsack will design a bathroom for £35 and should you buy the fixtures from them, your fee is refunded. [£££]

J. A. Distributors, 20 Leigh Hill, Leigh-on-Sea, Essex (0702-77733). Guaranteed lowest prices anywhere on bathroom fixtures and fittings of all qualities. 1,000 bathroom suites in stock. Kitchen fixtures and gas heating also. London deliveries. [£+, ££]

Nordic Saunas, 31 Lesbourne Road, Reigate, Surrey (Reigate 49451), sell and install domestic saunas in two styles and several sizes. The more expensive style is made of solid interlocking pine logs; the alternative is a 'sandwich' of panelled pine with 3 inches of insulation between. Heating is usually electric but gas and solid fuel are possible. Saunas start around £500 but a big outdoor model can cost thousands. Nordic also sell solariums – multi-light devices giving both ultra-violet and infra-red rays. Another device is Nordic's 'electronic impulse' shower: water shoots from several directions and can alternate hot and cold in rapid succession. Nordic supply a price list and free illustrated brochures. [£££]

Renubath, 596 Chiswick High Road, W4 (995-5252), re-surface pressed steel and cast iron baths and remove cracks and stains. They will also repaint baths in any of fifteen colours. [££]

Bufalini, 31A Bedford Street, WC2 (836-1633), cut and install marble on walls and bathroom floors or on the surrounds of baths and basins. They give free estimates, and their have own drawing offices for custom plans. [££+]

Beds

London Bedding Centre, 26 Sloane Street, SW1 (235-7542). Two floors of beds in the medium and upper price ranges and a budget department in the basement full of seconds and shop-soiled samples. All have individually-sprung or 'packeted' inner-spring mattresses available in three firmnesses. The Centre stocks Sleepeeze, Hypnos, Relyon, Dunlopillo, Staples, Slumberland and French Treca makes, and has sofa beds, round beds, trundle beds, bunk beds, divan beds and beds with manually- or electrically-operated frames to provide back and leg rests. Single beds cost from around £150 but you can pay £1,000 for a 9 foot by 9 foot size. The Centre sells headboards separately and will cover sofa-beds or headboards in your own fabric and make any style of bed to order. Delivery is free anywhere in Britain. Special export department. Excellent colour leaflets. [££+]

Bedlam, 114 Kensington Church Street, W8 (229-5360) and 811 Fulham Road, SW6 (731-2595), sell hanging beds and space-saving beds in fourteen designs. Their hanging models are suspended like swings from the ceiling, their space-saving models have drawers beneath. One model folds up, and they have bunk styles. Each is made to order and can be produced in special sizes at no extra cost. Bedlam make a small delivery and assembly charge, and delivery can take four to five weeks. Free illustrated leaflet and price list. Bedlam also sell nightshirts and caps. [££]

Wentelbed, 13 Golden Square, W1 (734-4246), are specialists in inexpensive space-saving beds that fold against the wall beneath an ordinary bookshelf or into a custom-built cabinet. Ideal for small flats or guest beds, Wentelbeds fold up horizontally or vertically and frames can be purchased without a mattress or shelf. Mattresses come in two types of inner-spring or in foam rubber and carry the 'kitemark' of the British Standards Institute. All beds and mattresses are fully guaranteed for five years. Mail-order catalogue on request. [££]

Secondhand City, Methodist Church, North End Road, W14 (385-7711), near West Kensington tube station, sell secondhand and shop-soiled beds in good condition for a fraction of the original cost. [£] (For secondhand beds see also Auctions, Chapter 2, especially 'Junk' Bonhams, Phillips West 2, Marylebone and Harrods auction rooms.) [£+]

Aquarius, 571 King's Road, SW6 (731-5121). Single, queen and kingsize waterbeds. They have a dozen standard models, and can make beds to order. Waterbeds have a heating apparatus to keep them warm and, contrary to popular opinion, do not need an especially sound floor to support their weight. Delivery is free in central London; installation is extra. [££]

And So To Bed, 7 New King's Road, SW6 (731-3593), and

Aristocat, 36 Westbourne Grove, W2 (229-5819), specialize in nineteenth-century brass beds. [££+] (For other antique beds, see Furniture, page 38.)

Heal's, 196 Tottenham Court Road, W1 (636-1666). Modern and reproduction beds for pop stars or county ladies. These are not only classic four-posters, but also suede-covered live-in beds complete with His and Hers cocktail cabinets, washbasins and reading lamps. Expensive but worth a visit. [££+]

Three Bridges, Leighton Place, Kentish Town, NW5 (624-4748), are joiners who will make beds to order. They also have some four-posters and half-testers in stock. [££+]

General Welfare for the Blind, 8 Curtain Road, EC2 (247-2405), re-cover mattresses and pillows and make new bedding. Price list on request. [££]

National Bedding Federation, 251 Brompton Road, SW3 (589-4888), a trade association, give advice on what to look for when buying a bed, mattress or bedding; for example, to be sure of a minimum standard of comfort look for the 'kitemark' of the British Standards Institute when buying an economy-priced mattress. For leaflets, send a stamp but no envelope.

Carpets and rugs (for antique and secondhand rugs see page 31. Also Auctions, Chapter 2)

Contrary to popular opinion, Axminster and Wilton are not brand names and do not necessarily mean quality. They are *types of looms* on which carpets of various qualities and fibres can be woven. Many inexpensive cord carpets, for example, are Wiltons. The main difference between Wilton and Axminster is that Wiltons are plain carpets and Axminsters are patterned. Both come in several thicknesses and in synthetic fibres as well as wool. Another popular type of carpet is the foam-backed or bonded into which the fibre has been implanted. Most shaggy carpets are foam-backed and these can be expensive, but no matter what type of carpet you choose, two things are important: firstly, make sure you get the correct quality for the amount of wear the carpet will receive. A drawing-room or hall carpet, for example, is likely to get more wear than a bedroom one. Secondly, a good underlay in felt or foam will add considerably to the life of any carpet.

Note: a *carpet* is 40 square feet or more in size. Anything smaller is a *rug*.

Resista Carpets, 148 Brompton Road, sw3 (589-3238), and three branches, claim to have the largest selection of plain carpets in London – Wiltons, cord and shaggy pile. Prices below many competitors and fitting within forty-eight hours. [££]

Afia, 81 Baker Street, w1 (935-0414), are a good place to buy quality carpets with assurance and also to get the occasional bargain. Special offers are always on sale and reductions can be as much as 50 per cent. They have Wilton samples in eighty colours and several grades, including cord. Axminsters, and shaggy, bonded carpets too. Afia have their own planners and fitters and all carpets installed by them are hand-stitched. Afia will dye carpets to any colour. Princess Margaret is a customer and while this may encourage the rich, it ought not to put off the poorer. [££, ££+]

Chatsworth, 227 Brompton Road, sw3 (584-1386) and 27 Brook Street, w1 (629-6300), are Wilton carpet specialists with over 100 colours in stock. Good service. They can lay a carpet within forty-eight hours of purchase. [££]

Liberty's, 210 Regent Street, w1 (734-1234). Still true to their original Oriental emphasis, Liberty's maintain one of the largest selections of new Oriental rugs and carpets in London. These are all good quality or better, and pure silk and silk and wool mixtures are available, as well as wool. A few are secondhand. Persian rugs and carpets predominate but there are also Turkish, Indian, Afghan, and even Greek Flokatis on sale. [££+, £££]

Tulleys, 289 Fulham Road, sw10 (352-1078), stock cord carpeting from Czechoslovakia at unbeatable prices. It comes in fifteen colours, and Tulleys also sell numdahs and rag rugs. [£+]

Whiteleys, Queensway, w2 (229-1234), always have carpets on sale at considerably reduced prices. Getting a good look can be difficult because of stacking but the effort is often worth it. [£+]

Sapphire, 14 Uxbridge Road, w5 (567-9969), have 13,000 square feet of warehouse filled with Wiltons, Axminsters, foam-backed, cord and sisal carpets which can be delivered and fitted almost at once. They have some exhibition stock at reduced prices, but Sapphire's reputation is primarily for quantity actually *in stock* and ready for delivery. [££]

Allied Carpets, 67 Kilburn High Road, nw6 (328-2266), and suburban branches. Some people feel Allied isn't the bargain centre it used to be before it went public. Admittedly, service is not always good but the emphasis is on quick turnover and the result is better than average prices and value for money. [££]

Many decorators have their own carpet range:

Zarach, 183 Sloane Street, sw1 (235-6146), carry the complete line of carpets designed by David Hicks. [£££]

Colefax and Fowler, 39 Brook Street, w1 (493-2231), have their own small line of recognizable patterns, mostly with matching borders. [£££]

Rooksmoor Mills, Stroud, Gloucester (Amberley 2577). Not a London firm but nevertheless a convenient and inexpensive source of rush and maize matting of any size. Rush mats cost about 20p a square foot. Maize is half as much again. Packing and shipping costs extra. Send for brochure. [£]

Caroline Bosly, 13 Princess Road, nw1 (722-7608), is an Oriental carpet broker with access to the largest stock of Oriental and Persian carpets in the world. These are located in twenty-two acres of bonded warehouse, once a part of Newgate prison. Here Persian, Turkish, Russian, Indian and Chinese rugs are sold to buyers from all over the world in bales of fifty each. Although this is a wholesale market, Mrs Bosly can, by special arrangement, take private customers round it and you can buy any rug through her at its *original* price plus a tiny commission. About 60 per cent of the rugs are new, the rest are mostly secondhand, but there are some antiques. Rugs start at £25 and go to thousands. Collectors looking for a special rug will find Mrs Bosly in a fine position to keep a look out for them. [££]

Persian Carpet Wharf, Regents Canal Dock, Commercial Road, e14 (589-4225), is a wholesale warehouse open to the public on Sundays only from 10 a.m. to 4 p.m. A good place to find a bargain. There are usually up to 1,000 pieces in stock and each is marked with its name and price. All are new and come from Persia and the Orient (India and China excepted), and cost from £25. The Persian Carpet Wharf is hard to get to: take the Underground to Aldgate East and a bus down Commercial Road. [££]

Patent Steam Carpet Cleaning, 49 Eagle Wharf Road, n1 (253-6121), and

London Carpet Cleaning, Furmage Street, sw18 (874-4333), are owned by the same management and both of them clean carpets in your home or in their factory. They also dye carpets.

Hire Service Shops, 192 Campden Hill Road, w8 (727-0897) and branches around London, rent carpet shampooers, vacuum cleaners and carpet-laying tools. Delivery service.

China and glass (for antique china and glass see pages 46 and 40, see also Kitchenware, page 215)

English china and earthenware are recommended buys for foreign visitors. Prices are about 50 per cent less than in America and Europe and there is a further reduction when exported, because of tax exemption. Shipping and duty charges must be added to this but savings are still as much as 25 per cent.

Most of the great names in china are English. Bone china was invented here in the late eighteenth century by Josiah Spode, who added bone ash to porcelain, giving it an increased translucence, whiteness and toughness. Bone china is incredibly hard-wearing despite its delicate appearance and, provided one has the nerve to try it, rings like a bell when struck with force.

A final note: there are acute shortages in china stocks and customers may have to wait months for orders. It is advisable, if possible, to pay in advance since prices may have gone up by the time delivery is made.

Gered, 134 Regent Street, w1 (734-2828), are specialists in Wedgwood, Spode and Coalport china and earthenware and this is the best place to see them. Examples are well displayed in glass cases on two floors and prices are clearly marked. Gered also sell Stuart crystal. [££]

Chinacraft, 499 Oxford Street, w1 (499-9881), 50 Brompton Road, sw3 (584-8512) and branches. Wide display of primarily English china: Minton, Royal Worcester, Royal Doulton, Crown Derby, Aynsley and Wedgwood. 80 per cent of Chinacraft's business is export. They also stock limited editions of Royal Worcester figures, some Coalport decorative pieces, and Tudor, Royal Brierly, Waterford and Edinburgh glass. [££+]

Thomas Goode, 19 South Audley Street, w1 (499-2823) sell the most elegant china being made today. In business for 150 years, Goode's were commissioned to make crested china for Queen Victoria and for a host of other monarchs and maharajahs. (Examples from these services can be seen.) Goode's can design china with your crest or monogram, or sell you a dozen service plates for £600 or a Minton pattern for £300 *a place setting*. But there are more reasonably-priced patterns too, by Spode, Royal Worcester, Staffordshire, Hammersley, Abbeydale, Coalport, Crown Derby, Haviland and Royal Copenhagen. Goode's carry limited series of Royal Worcester figures and Boehm figures. There are several rooms of china on display, containing tea, coffee and breakfast services as well as dinner services. An excellent up-market glass department stocks Baccarat, Val St Lambert, Tudor, Webb, Stuart and St Louis crystal. The staff are mostly middle-aged men who know their stuff, and service is in the old style. [£££]

Lawleys, 154 Regent Street, w1 (734-3184), is an established name in china shops. Many makes are on display but the general tone is suburban. [££]

Royal Worcester, 6 New Bond Street, w1 (629-0402),

Royal Copenhagen, 5 Old Bond Street, w1 (629-3622) and

Rosenthal, 137 Regent Street, w1 (734-3076), display and sell their own china. [££+]

Harrods, Knightsbridge, sw1 (730-1234), have a broad range of china and earthenware, including continental makes like Herend and modern Scandinavian pottery. They also export 'American place settings' consisting of plates in three sizes and a tea-cup. [££, ££+]

China Reject Shop, 33 Beauchamp Place, sw1 (584-9409), with annexes scattered along Beauchamp Place, specialize in seconds of china, pottery, glass and crystal; also discounted pieces in first-class condition. Several complete services usually on sale. Will ship anywhere. [£, ££]

Merchant Chandler, 72 New King's Road, sw6 (736-6141), have four floors of inexpensive household goods; one devoted entirely to glassware and one to really low-priced china in conventional but attractive patterns. Also crockery, utensils and baskets galore. [£+]

House and Bargain, 31 Brewer Street, w1 (734-9628), 142 Notting Hill Gate, w11 (229-9797), and 54 Chalk Farm Road, nw1 (485-8030). China, glass and housewares at bargain prices. Worth a visit. Stock constantly changing. (Wooden salad bowls, when available, are far below usual prices.) [£+]

Habitat, 206 King's Road, sw10 (351-1211), and 156 Tottenham Court Road, w1 (388-1721), carry well-designed glassware and a few designs in china at moderate to low prices. Mail-order catalogue costs 20p. [£+]

Central Bazaar, 70 Westbourne Grove, w2 (229-3388). Bargain china in generally attractive designs. Most is replaceable (continuous lines), but ends of lines and seconds are stocked too. [£]

The Reject Shop, 245 Brompton Road, sw3 (584-7611). China and glass as well as other household items at reduced prices. [££]

Glasshouse, 27 Neal Street, wc2 (836-9785). Hand-blown table and decorative glass. There is a gallery in front and workshop behind where you can see glassblowers at work. [££+]

Ironsware, 48 Parkway, n1 (485-7248). Seconds in china and glass, also some linen seconds.

Curtains and upholstery (see Chapter 11)

Furniture and general furnishings (see also Antiques, Chapter 1, and Curtains, blinds and upholstery services, page 190)

Habitat, 206 King's Road, sw10 (351-1211), and 156 Tottenham Court Road, w1 (388-1721), have brought good contemporary design within the reach of most people. Chairs, tables, sofas in inexpensive and in medium-priced lines. Fitted cupboards and kitchen units. There is a Habitat 'look' owing more to the general dearth of good design at moderate prices than to a narrowness of taste in Habitat wares. Large mail-order catalogue costs 20p. General furnishings: carpets to bookends. [££]

Heal's, 196 Tottenham Court Road, w1 (636-1666). Contemporary furniture and furnishings, all fairly expensive. A wide selection of sofas, chairs, tables, desks and beds and a special department for built-in furniture. Planning and installation service for bedroom and kitchen fitted units. Complete decorating service. [££+]

Harrods, Knightsbridge, sw1 (730-1234), have perhaps the widest *range* of furniture styles in the medium to high price brackets to be seen in London; contemporary, reproduction, antique and lots of upholstered furniture. Eclectic tastes might start looking here. The most recent addition is the *Way In* shop on the fourth floor which has a well-chosen range of comparatively inexpensive furniture in wicker, pine and plastics. Good simple design and worth a visit. [££, ££+]

Ciancimino, 307 King's Road, sw3 (352-2016), is a potter and sculptor turned furniture designer, who sells tables and chairs of wood and aluminium construction based on an interlocking system which makes their size adaptable. Ciancimino is a 'name' in modern English furniture. [£££]

Zarach, 183 Sloane Street, sw1 (235-6146). Sleek, modern furniture in chrome, perspex, leather and fabric. Most of it is imported and exclusive to Zarach. Also Eames and Corbusier chairs, fine contemporary lighting, specially designed bubble TV, and Sander mirrors and plate glass. Custom sizes are possible in several items. Complete home decorating service. [££+]

Albrizzi, 1 Sloane Square, sw1 (730-6119), carry elegant modern furniture, including upholstered chairs and sofas, and some small items like Chinese basketware. [££+]

Conran, 77 Fulham Road, sw3 (240-3474), are part of the Habitat group but are slightly more up-market. Their stock is either too pricey for Habitat stores or not available in large enough quantities. [££+]

Brown's Living, 26 South Molton Street, w1 (629-4049), next door to Brown's dress shop, caters most pleasantly to the tertiary needs of life – decorative ceramics, cushions and knick-knacks. Most are one-offs by fine craft designers whose work is chosen with the comforts of home in mind. [££+]

C. H. Frost, 67A Abingdon Road, w8 (937-0451). This is the address of Frost's upholstery shop, but an appointment will take you to their workshops in Ladbroke Grove where you can buy quality secondhand upholstered chairs ready-to-go or select old frames for re-upholstering. A money-saver. [££]

Tulleys, 289 Fulham Road, sw10 (352-1078), sell upholstered chairs and couches covered in muslin; also secondhand upholstered furniture in excellent condition at about half price. Simple, good design. Catalogue of new furniture on request. [£+, ££]

Secondhand City, Methodist Church, North End Road, w14 (385-7711), is near West Kensington tube station. It consists of the basement and interior of an old church crammed full of secondhand furniture and furnishings: tables, chairs, beds, mirrors and used cookers and water heaters. Stock constantly changing. [£]

Simmonds, 180 North Gower Street, nw1 (387-4746). Huge rabbit-warren of used furniture and furnishings. One floor is all chairs. Departments for used carpets, curtains, beds and appliances. [£+]

John Alan, 75 Parkway, nw1 (267-1313), sell bentwood chairs: hand-made Thonet rockers in a wood or painted finish, Osborne dining chairs and a few contemporary styles. They also have the Isokon long chair designed by Marcel Breuer and some upholstered pieces. [££]

Peter Dudgeon, 1A Brompton Place, sw3 (589-6291), supply custom-made upholstered furniture of fine workmanship, to order only. Traditional or modern styles. Four month delivery. [££+, £££]

Abode, 781 Fulham Road, SW6 (736-3161). Cane, pine and woven willow furniture to order. Bring in a photo of any cane chair, for example, and Abode will make it. (Cane refers to bamboo, not 'french cane' which is used to make chair bottoms.) Showrooms have examples for sale. [££]

Dodson Bull, Barbican Furnishing Centre, 100 Aldersgate Street, EC2 (628-3456), are a furniture discount house with 20,000 feet of display space, but many items still require waiting for. Stock includes furnishing fabrics (2,000 styles). Everything is $17\frac{1}{2}$ per cent below recommended retail prices. Delivery charge. [££]

Oscar Woollens, 421 Finchley Road, NW3 (435-7750). Top contemporary designs in furniture and a complete decorating service. Furniture is displayed on four floors in room settings so you can get decorating ideas. [££+, £££]

Zeev Aram, 3 Keen Street, WC2 (240-3933). The very best of modern furniture. Their chairs by Le Corbusier and Breuer are sculptures in themselves, and their Simon International collection includes Takahama's elegantly simple designs. They also have the variable height and width Altra table system, and floss lighting. Tomorrow's antiques. [£££]

Martin Barnett, 11 Bulstrode Street, Marylebone Lane, W1 (935-2353), specialize in quality leather furniture. [££, ££+]

CubeStore, 58 Pembroke Road, W8 (994-6016). Modular storage units and shelving in melamine finishes. Boxes, drawers, cupboards are sold flat for self-assembly. Free mail-order catalogue lists all dimensions. [££]

Old Times Furnishing Co., 135 Lower Richmond Road, SW15 (788-3551), rents period and reproduction furniture and furnishings. Hire one piece or a whole room including the carpet and curtains in whatever period you desire. If you take an unfurnished flat and don't have anything to put in it for a while, try Old Times; they are especially useful for expense-account businessmen from abroad. [££+]

Homeworks, Dover Walk, 107 Pimlico Road, sw1 (730-9116). This converted warehouse consists of about twenty 'rooms' completely decorated to give customers ideas about fabrics as well as furniture. All contents can be ordered. The style is modern and well suited to contemporary living. Homeworks is worth a visit before you begin to decorate. [££+]

Lexterten, 16 The Causeway. Teddington, Middlesex (977-9244). Leather Chesterfields and Regency leather armchairs for less money than you're likely to pay elsewhere. Delivery takes six months, however. Brochure. [££]

Salvation Army, 124 Spa Road, se16 (237-1107), sell used furniture and furnishings, all of which have been donated to the Army – so prices are generally rock-bottom, as are a lot of the items. Worth combing through. [£]

New Dimension, Manor Road, West Ealing, w13 (998-2900) and several branches. Budget furniture, including storage units and lighting. Some designs are good, simple and presentable. Colour catalogue about 25p. [£+]

Copenhagen Furniture, 318 Wandsworth Bridge Road, sw6 (736-4555), and

Wharfside Furniture Supplies, 66 Buttesland Street, n1 (253-3206), both specialize in Scandinavian teak and rosewood finished wall units, tables and chairs and some upholstered pieces. Motel modern styles supposedly at warehouse prices. Everything can be delivered at once. [££]

Pentonville Rubber Company, 50 and 52 Pentonville Road, n1 (837-0283), have two types of chairs sculpted from foam which you cover yourself, and they will make any shape to order [£+]

La Cucaracha, 6 Halkin Arcade West Halkin Street, sw1 (235-6741), claim to have Europe's largest selection of hand-made Mexican furniture. [££+]

Adeptus, 9 Sicilian Avenue, wc1 (405-5603). Foam furniture shapes and kits for covering them yourself. £[+]

Glass (see China and glass, page 207)

Kitchen furnishings (see Household appliances, Chapter 10)

Kitchen units

Norman Glenn, 477 Finchley Road, NW3 (794-7801).
Complete kitchen installation service. Hygena and Wrighton units mostly, both self-assembly and conventional.
Drawings, measuring and estimates cost £25 or you can do your own measuring and buy straight from stock. Most deliveries within 10 days. Appliances too. [££]

Comet, 190 London Road, Hackbridge, Surrey (669-4321), and branches around the country, are a discount warehouse selling fitted kitchen units by Electrolux at up to 50 per cent off recommended retail prices. [£+]

John Prizeman, 53 Upper Montagu Street, W1 (262-5287). Designer of kitchens *par excellence*. Expensive. [£££]

Multiflex, 222 Elephant and Castle Shopping Centre, SE1 (701-3237), have a good choice of kitchen units in custom sizes. All are exclusive to Multiflex and every order over £300 gets a 25 per cent discount. Solid timber and melamine units in several colours. Excellent catalogue.
Planning and installation service. Appliances. [££, ££+]

Harrods, Knightsbridge, SW1 (730-1234), and

Heal's, 196 Tottenham Court Road, WC1 (636-1666), run kitchen planning services and have model kitchen exhibits permanently on display. [££+]

Note: If you want ideas about styles and designs for your kitchen try the following: the **Building Centre**, 26 Store Street, WC1, which has several displays of model kitchens arranged and exhibited by manufacturers; **Hygena** and **Wrighton**, two manufacturers who have their own showrooms and who, although they don't sell units directly, will give you the names of stockists; and finally, the **Design Centre**, 28 Haymarket, SW1, which often has kitchen units on display, and has an Index, open to the public, which lists recommended units. (For details see Professional advice, page 197.)

Kitchenware

William Page, 87 Shaftesbury Avenue, WC2 (437-8888), are a long-established firm of restaurant suppliers with plenty of big sizes: colanders up to three feet in diameter, wine racks up to five feet square. They also stock tin ware, slicers, grinders and assorted gadgetry, plus scrubbing brushes, cheesecloth and 'Gustav Emil ern' knives.

Divertimenti, 68 Marylebone Lane, W1 (935-0689), sell French fireproof earthenware and china, cooking utensils, pots and pans. Detailed catalogue. Divertimenti also have a knife-sharpening service.

French Kitchen and Tableware Supply Co., 60 Westbourne Grove, W2 (229-5530), owned by Divertimenti (above) specialize in the needs of restaurants and have big sizes and everything else too. Their ground floor and basement are crammed with brown glaze porcelain, tin plate, slicing, peeling and shredding machines, stainless steel tableware, stoneware, Sabatier knives, inexpensive glassware, 'Pyroblan' extra tough china, ham and cheese stands, presses and hibachis. Good prices; usually a number of things on special sale.

Merchant Chandler, 12 New King's Road, SW6 (736-6141), have four floors of inexpensive kitchen and tableware including cutlery, china and glass. Other notables are: wine racks in three sizes, covered iron pots and wooden plate racks.

Elizabeth David, 46 Bourne Street, SW1 (730-5577), stock earthenware jugs and crocks galore. They also have tin plate, including lots of biscuit tins and pastry cutters, rolling pins (one pastry model has special attachments for setting desired thickness of dough) and other kitchen utensils and supplies.

David Mellor, 4 Sloane Square, SW1 (730-4259). Basement cook shop with lots of baskets, a good selection of pots and pans and stainless steel cutlery, several designs of table-ware, Sheffield and Victorinox kitchen knives, scissors and pocket knives. Their glassware includes hand-blown designs.

Glenhurst, 51 Long Lane, EC1 (606-2156), located opposite Smithfield Market, are butchers' suppliers and keep meat-market hours (6.30 a.m. to 3.30 p.m.). Glenhurst stock steel rails and butcher's hooks (useful for hanging pots and pans on), butcher blocks in all sizes, cutting and boning knives and slicing machines. A two-foot-square butcher block on legs costs around £90.

Staines, 15 Brewer Street, W1 (437-7965). General kitchen and restaurant supplies. Glass and china. Ice trays with American-sized cubes and pull out levers.

Anything Left Handed, 65 Beak Street, W1 (437-3910), one of London's most specializing specialists: bread knives, slicing knives, sharpeners, spatulas, whisks and kitchen shears for left handers. Small catalogue.

Richard Dare, 93 Regent's Park Road, NW1 (722-9428), are a small, well-stocked kitchen supply shop with just about everything anybody living in the area might want: they stock Breton earthenware.

Plating and Tinning Service, 125 Broadley Street, NW8 (723-8630), re-line copper pots and pans in tin, re-rivet handles and do other necessary tinkering. Collection and delivery service.

A. Stewart McCracken, 69 Dean Street, W1 (437-8374) are catering and restaurant supply auctioneers. (For details see Auctions, Chapter 2.)

Lamps and lighting fixtures (see also Antiques, Chapter 1, and Furniture and general furnishings, page 209)

British Home Stores, 252 Oxford Street, W1 (629-2011) and branches,

Woolworth's, 311 Oxford Street, W1 (629-8611) and branches, and

Whiteley's, Queensway, w2 (229-1234), are the best sources of really inexpensive lighting in London. Although a certain amount of the stock seems designed to illuminate Victorian bordellos, there is much that is neither fussy, junky nor gaudy but has good, simple traditional or contemporary lines. Lampshades too. If you can find something to suit your taste you will save a considerable amount of money. [£+]

Peter Jones, Sloane Square, sw1 (730-3434), have the best selection of medium-priced lamps around. The problem is that you see them in everybody else's home. [££]

Arnold Montrose, 45 Berners Street, w1 (580-5316), sell lamps and lighting fixtures, trade and retail. There are two floors of samples: reproductions of classic candelabra, traditional urns and vases and contemporary glass and metal constructions. [££+]

Peter Burian, Hillview, Vale of Health, Hampstead, nw3 (435-4493). Professional advice, design, installation of all lighting – half a room to an office block. [££+]

Clare House, 35 Elizabeth Street, sw1 (730-8480), are expert lamp makers who can convert almost anything into a lamp. Bring them a vase, statue, or other form and they will advise you on the right base and shade and do the conversion. Lampshades in silk, card or your own fabric. Several vases and forms in stock. [££+]

Nita Miller, 63A Grosvenor Street, w1 (629-0951). All the lamps displayed in this basement shop are made in Miss Miller's own workshop and many are conversions from vases, candlesticks and the like. The shades vary to suit individual needs. [££+]

Ryness, 37 Goodge Street, w1 (636-0321), and 326 Edgware Road, w2 (723-4034), are electrical fixtures specialists, having a full range of Edison power track lights, spots, recessed ceiling lights and baffle lighting. Also sockets and plugs, dimmer switches, wiring and miscellaneous electrical supplies. [££]

Quip, 226 Westbourne Grove, w11 (727-5377). Contemporary cone lamps, spots, battens and clip lights. Free brochure and price list. [££]

H. Ponton, 55 Sloane Square, sw1 (730-0303) have picture lights with arms and length of bulb in several sizes to suit different-sized canvases. They also carry a candle light which looks just like a candle, and puts out exactly the same amount of light. It was designed for chandeliers and sconces and is used in the House of Lords and St Paul's Cathedral. [££]

Habitat, 206 King's Road, sw10 (351-1211). Medium-priced modern lighting, well-designed. Catalogue costs 20p. [££]

Liberty, Regent Street, w1 (734-1234). Expensive lamps in traditional styles. [££+]

London Lighting Co., 173 Fulham Road, sw3 (589-4270). Contemporary lighting at medium prices. Concord and Thorne designs, and imports. [££]

Christopher Wray, 600 King's Road, sw6 (736-8008). Reproduction and original Edwardian lighting. Enormous stock, mostly brass or cast metal with glass shades. 'Annexe', across the street, sells reproductions of Tiffany glass domes. There is also a repair shop which stocks miscellaneous chimneys, shade holders, burners for conversion to and from gas or oil and several types of glass shades. Detailed mail-order catalogue. [££+]

Ann's, 34A Kensington Church Street, w8 (937-5033). Conventional lamps and ceiling and wall lights. [££]

C. H. Kempton, New Road, Bittacy Hill, nw7 (346-2688), make old-fashioned copper street lamps like those in The Mall and Birdcage Walk. There are four basic models which can be adapted to individual needs, and fitted for gas or electricity. Brochure on request. £65–£75 per fixture. [££+]

John Lewis, Oxford Street, w1 (629-7711), stock lampshade frames, raffia, stiffened fabric and trimmings for do-it-yourself shades. Frames are in several sizes and shapes. The lampshade department is on the ground floor. [£]

Lampshade Supplies, 21 Jerdan Place, Fulham Broadway, sw6 (385-2981), supply frames for lampshades. They have over 100 models in stock, and will also cover any lampshade for you in your own material or in theirs. [£+]

H. Band and Co., Brent Way, High Street, Brentford, Middlesex (560-2025). It seems a luxurious idea nowadays, but Bands supply parchment suitable for lampshades. [£££]

Linen

Table, bath and bed linen can be bought in any department store. This section is confined to linen specialty shops or unusual services and supplies.

Irish Linen Company, 35 Burlington Arcade, w1 (493-8949), sell sheets, tablecloths, luncheon mats, napkins and handkerchiefs (plain or hand-embroidered). A pair of linen sheets for a double bed costs between £40 and £60, depending on the quality. [£££]

Reject Linen Shop, 13 Beauchamp Place, sw3 (589-8814), have mostly discontinued lines, and some seconds. Bed, bath and table linen. Tea towels, printed sheets, blankets. Small stock but prices are less than for the same stock elsewhere. [££]

Granny Goods, 6 Gray's Inn Road, wc1 (242-6676), supply handmade patchwork quilts and hand-crocheted quilts and coverlets in their design or in yours. Delivery of custom-made items takes about three weeks. A custom-made patchwork quilt costs about £80. This is not, strictly speaking, a shop, so ring first for information or their colour brochure. [££+]

White House, 51 New Bond Street, w1 (629-3521). Elegant and expensive linen, including bed and bath linen by Porthault of Paris, hand-appliquéd table sets and bed cushions, and handerchiefs for men and women in linen or Swiss lawn. [£££]

National Linen Co., 20 Brook Street, w1 (629-5000), is an up-market linen shop specializing in extra large sizes of sheets, blankets and tablecloths plus other hard-to-get items. Monograms or crests embroidered to order. Fine embroidery and appliqué work. [£££]

N. Pattichis, c/o Lloyds Bank, 53 King Street, Manchester, is a traveller dealing in fine Cypriot embroidered linens. If you write to him at the above address he will pay a visit on rounds that include St James's Palace and various country houses. Embroidered sheets, tablecloths, mats, etc. at lower prices than in shops. [££+]

Linen Cupboard, 21 Great Castle Street, W1 (629-4062). Household and baby linen of good quality at reasonable prices. Some seconds. Sheets, towels, dishcloths, cot linen, nappies, baby pillows and pram sets. The Linen Cupboard also sell several grades of feathers and down and pure down by the pound for stuffing pillow-cases, quilts and cushions. [££]

Karo-Step, 138 Marylebone Road, NW1 (935-0196), are continental quilt specialists. Quilts are filled to individual requirements: duck, goose, eiderdown or a combination of the three. They can fill quilts on the spot. Fifteen year guarantee. Cleaning service. [££+]

Aeonics, 92 Church Road, Mitcham, Surrey (640-1113), supply kits from which you can make your own continental quilts: down-proof tubular stitched cases, plus filling (down or polyester) if required; alternatively you can use the filling from an old eiderdown. [£+]

London Bedding Centre, 26 Sloane Street, SW1 (584-1777), carry bedding for odd-size beds and will make bedding to any size. [£££]

Advance Cleaners and Launderers, 77 Upper Richmond Road, SW15 (789-8231), re-cover eiderdowns and clean and re-cover pillows. [££]

A. Maitland, 175 Piccadilly, W1 (493-1975). If you're tired of linen, you can throw in the towel and get sponges and loofahs here. [££+]

Locks and safety devices

Chubb, 68 St James's Street, sw1 (493-5414), are the leading name in locks and several types are on display. They also have safes the size of a brick or a small room. Chubb's install locks and safes and have a 'lost and found' key service that owners of non-Chubb locks can subscribe to. Your keys are given a serial number by the firm and then tagged with *Chubb's* address and a notice that the finder will receive a reward (about £2) if the keys are returned to Chubb. They then get in touch with you, thus saving you the cost of key duplication or lock replacement.

Barry Bros., 123 Praed Street, w2 (262-2450), cut keys while you wait and have several makes of locks in stock.

Chloride Granley, 44 Great Eastern Street, EC2 (739-3433). Devices for protection against fire and burglary: fibreglass fire-resistant blankets for smothering fires, smoke-detector alarms, fire extinguishers, fire escapes, rope ladders, thermalarms that go off when rooms reach a certain temperature and burglar alarms. The systems can set off bells or sirens or automatically dial Chloride Granley, who then ring the police or fire department, as the case may be.

Instant Aid, 15 Portland Road, w11 (727-0292). Full range of burglar and fire alarms. Guards are also available for hire.

Deste Photography, 163 Seymour Place, w1 (262-7645). Miss Deste specializes in photographing valuables – furniture, pictures, jewellery, *objets* – on 35 mm film. This film is deposited in the customer's bank vault or in hers and should anything be stolen, it can be enlarged so the police can see exactly what the missing goods look like. Miss Deste performs this service for the National Trust and clearly it is useful for anyone with valuable possessions to look after.

Note: if you need emergency lock service, look in the Yellow Pages for the twenty-four-hour service nearest to you. In some cases the police will lend a hand for free.

Mirrors and plate glass (see also Framing, page 253, Antiques, Chapter 1, and Furniture and general furnishings, page 209)

Zarach, 183 Sloane Street, SW1 (235-6146), is the home of the Sander Mirror Company. Modern mirrors for walls, tables, etc. [££+]

Chelsea Glassworks, 105 Fulham Road, SW3 (581-2501) Mirrors and glass in several thicknesses cut to size. [££]

The Glass Shop, 216 North End Road, W14 (385-1545). Mirrors cut to size, re-polished and drilled for hanging. They also stock simply-framed dressing-mirrors, and mirror-flex (backed mirror tiles). Moderate prices. [£+]

Peter Jones, Sloane Square, SW1 (730-3434), have lots of reproduction and traditional mirrors, and some modern ones. [££+]

J. Preedy, 4A Ashland Place, W1 (935-3988), repair and restore mirrors. The firm bevels, cuts, 'antiques' and re-silvers. [££]

Silver (see also Antique silver, page 48, and for stainless steel tableware and cutlery, see Kitchenware, page 215)

All British sterling silver must contain 92·5 per cent pure silver and every piece is hallmarked with four stamps. The first gives the initials of the firm who made the piece, the second, a lion passant, is your guarantee of sterling. The third mark is a *symbol* for the town where the piece was made. (For example, the sign of London has been a leopard's head since 1300.) The final symbol, a letter of the alphabet surrounded by a shield, indicates the date.

Silver plate is silver mounted on a copper or nickel base and the quality depends upon the thickness of the silver applied. Unlike sterling silver, there are no laws governing the amount of silver that plate must contain so it is wise to buy silver plate from reputable manufacturers only.

The Silver Club, 57 Farringdon Road, EC1 (242-5538), have expertly-crafted reproductions of seventeenth- and eighteenth-century patterns – rat tail, Kings, thread and shell, fiddle – for up to 40 per cent below retail prices. By joining the club, which costs £5, you get trade prices. Trays, salvers, tea and coffee services as well as cutlery. Illustrated catalogue and price list with description, photograph and weight of each piece costs 50p. [££]

Mappin and Webb, 170 Regent Street, W1 (734-0906) and 63 Brompton Road, SW1 (589-2559), are renowned for their silver plate. Flatware and holloware in their own designs, and reproductions of classic patterns. Their plate is guaranteed against re-plating for thirty years. Both machine-made and hand-crafted pieces are available. Mappin's also repair silver and silver plate. [££+]

Garrard, 112 Regent Street, W1 (734-7072), are the crown jewellers. They supply the finest quality silver: some machine-made, and some hand-finished. Other pieces (including cutlery) are made entirely by hand. This is a much more expensive process and, according to Garrards, only a real expert can tell the difference; hand-made does last longer if one is thinking in centuries. [££]

Stuart Devlin, 90 St John's Street, EC1 (253-5471), is a designer-craftsman working in silver. Examples of Mr Devlin's modern creations in hand-forged cutlery and holloware are displayed in his showroom. Silver Easter eggs are a speciality. [£££]

Georg Jensen, 15B New Bond Street, W1 (499-6541), sell Danish silver, and are known for simple, modern designs. [££+]

The Tableware Centre, 50 Burlington Arcade, W1 (493-2151), sells complete services of cutlery for twelve to thirty-six settings in reproduction and antique silver. Also odd services for 'fork' suppers, etc. All sterling silver. [£££]

The Silver Vaults, Chancery House, Chancery Lane, WC1 (242-3844). Vastly over-rated but tourists seem to feel it's a must. Most of the stock is new, plated ware and is no bargain. [££]

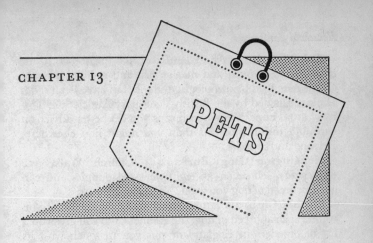

CHAPTER 13

Pets for sale

Regent Pet Stores, 35 Parkway, NW1 (485-5163). Rabies quarantine laws have discouraged Regent from keeping some of the exotic species they used to but they still have dogs and cats, cockatoos, pigeons, guinea-pigs, rabbits and fish, and, for more unusual tastes, iguanas, alligators, tarantulas, scorpions and snakes. A baby boa constrictor costs about £30 while a six- or seven-year-old eight-footer is around £100. Regent sell food and accessories for every kind of animal they keep and will tell you how to look after the pet you choose.

Battersea Dogs' Home, 4 Battersea Park Road, SW8 (622-4454), is an orphanage for stray dogs (and cats, as catch can). All animals are for sale but strays are retained for seven days in case owners turn up (for details about claiming lost pets see under Pet Services, page 228). The Dogs' Home also takes in dogs whose owners can no longer keep them. Puppies cost from £4 but there are dogs of all sizes and shapes in need of a good home: purebreeds, mongrels and appealing little hangdogs. Buses 170 and 44 go past the front door.

Animal Fair, 17 Abingdon Road, w8 (937-0011). Cats, dogs, birds, tropical and marine fish and rodents. Animal Fair is managed by a zoologist and the staff have Pet Trades Diplomas issued by the British Veterinary Association. This is *not* usual in pet shops and means you get better advice on care and training of pets than you might find elsewhere. Pet food and supplies.

Kensington Dog Bureau, 3 Church Walk, w8 (937-4522), sell seven- to eight-week-old puppies and can get any breed of dog you want. Not much in stock.

Kennel Club, 1 Clarges Street, w1 (493-6651). If you want a special breed of dog, the Kennel Club will give you a list of breeders in England or put you in touch with its Breed Club. The main function of the Kennel Club, however, is to register pedigree dogs for showing. Fashion-minded dog buyers might note that the most popular registered breed is the Alsatian, while the latest breed recognized by the Club is the Neapolitan Mastiff.

The Aviary, 74 Tachbrook Street, sw1 (834-3711). Canaries, budgies, parrots, mynahs, and love birds; young singles or breeding pairs. Bird-seed for both domestic and wild birds.

Tachbrook Tropical, 244 Vauxhall Bridge Road, sw1 (834-5179). Tropical fish specialists selling angels, discus, catfish, koi, carp and many others. Tachbrook make elaborately 'aquascaped' aquariums to order, and have an aquarium maintenance service and a packaging service for sending fish abroad.

Fish Tanks, 49 Blandford Street, w1 (935-3719), sell tropical and marine fish, aquariums varying in price from a few pounds to hundreds of pounds, marine plants, and fish food.

Queensborough Fisheries, 111 Goldhawk Road, w12 (743-2730). 200 tanks of tropical fish including discus, elephant fish and deadly piranha. Stock and custom-made aquariums.

Butterfly Farm, Bilsington, Ashford, Kent (023 373-2513). In business for eighty years, this is the world's oldest butterfly and moth farm. You can buy them in the egg, caterpillar or pupae stages. There are both domestic and foreign varieties like the beautiful blue morphidae or the rare birdwing from New Guinea (£4), and also some insects and silkworms. Lepidopterists will find everything they need for catching, mounting, displaying or breeding butterflies and moths. There are books for amateurs and specialists, and a detailed stocklist is sent on request. Most of the Farm's clientele are schools and naturalists but some people order butterflies for their gardens. Novice butterfly buyers will no doubt be relieved to hear that butterflies do not live for only one day, their average life-span is a fortnight.

Robert Lee, George Street, Uxbridge, Middlesex (893-3181). Beekeeping is both a sport and a pastime and Robert Lee can provide everything required for it. To start a hive you need a 'nucleus', consisting of four 'frames' of bee-infested honeycomb or a 'colony' consisting of six or eight frames. Frames measure 13 inches by 8 inches. Both types include a fertile Queen bee and you can pick your bees from several different varieties. Hives are available in both British and American styles, and the cost is between £30 and £40. Bees can be kept relatively easily in the average London garden, says Mr Lee, who also sells books on beekeeping and the necessary veils and gloves for tending bees. A hive gives honey once a year.

Some other conventional pet shops located centrally are:

Palace Gate Pets, 1 Gloucester Road, sw7 (584-7727),

Pets Parlour, 60 Chiltern Street, w1 (935-6195), grooming too, and

Duke Street Kennels, 14 Connaught Street, w2 (262-0299), dogs and grooming.

Harrods, Knightsbridge, sw1 (730-1234).

Pet services

There are several dog-grooming centres, or 'poodle parlours' as they are called, in and around London. See the Yellow Pages under Dog Grooming for the one nearest you.

Central Dog Registry, 9 Fenchurch Street, EC3 (602-4444), will tattoo your National Insurance number on your dog's leg and register it. This makes lost dogs easily identifiable and discourages kidnappers from stealing animals for sale to laboratories. Lifetime registration costs £6 but allows you to register as many animals as you wish.

Battersea Dogs' Home, 4 Battersea Park Road, SW8 (622-4454), takes in dogs you can no longer look after and also collects lost ones. If you have lost a dog you can call at the home between 2 p.m. and 4 p.m. including Saturday and Sunday, to see if it has been found. You *must* call within a week, however, or your dog may be sold to someone else.

Animal Action, 13 Tottenham Street, W1 (935-1118), rent trained animals and exotica to film companies. They will act as agents for your pet if it has special aptitudes or is unusual in any commercially viable way. They will also train your pet to do tricks for advertisements and other commercial purposes.

Animal Fair, 17 Abingdon Road, W8 (937-0011), will board any animal. A budgie, for example, costs 11p a day for bed and board; a parrot is twice as much. Large animals like dogs and cats are kept in the country. The staff is specially trained in pet care (see under Pets for Sale, page 226).

Gerrard Hire, 85B Royal College Street, NW1 (387-2765). If you like the idea of having a pet but can't be bothered to look after one, rent it stuffed from Gerrard. Dogs, cats, budgies, horses, cows – even an elephant. Long- or short-term rentals.

Dog Training Societies. These are local groups holding classes in general obedience and, on a higher level, retrieving and scent discrimination. They normally meet once a week and fees, if any, are negligible. All breeds welcome. For the group nearest you write to the Kennel Club, 1 Clarges Street, w1 (493-6651).

Animal Photography, 4 Marylebone Mews, w1 (935-0503). Pet portraits taken by a professional, at a cost of £10 for the first animal and £5 for any others on the spot. Show dogs are a speciality.

Pigeonhole Gallery, 13 Langton Street, sw10 (352-2677), are agents for pet portrait painter and miniaturist Rita Greer. Pets can be painted in a straightforward realistic manner or they can assume certain anthropomorphic, even eponymous aspects through fancy dress. Miss Greer has painted pugs named Napoleon in tricornes and is quite willing to put togas on terrier Caesars or tartan skirts on Lassies if owners want it.

J. H. Kenyon, 45 Edgware Road, w2 (723-3277), and branches, are funeral directors who will undertake pets. Kenyon will supply a coffin relative to the size of the pet, a hearse for transport to the pet cemetery, if required, and will make arrangements with the cemetery for a grave and headstone. (Petticists seeking a more tangible immortality are advised to see a taxidermist.)

Pet hospitals and vets

Canine Defence League, 10 Seymour Street, w1 (935-5511),

R.S.P.C.A., 105 Jermyn Street, w1 (930-0971),

Blue Cross, 1 Hugh Street, sw1 (834-4224) and

Peoples' Dispensary for Sick Animals, 201 Vauxhall Bridge Road, sw1 (834-0143 and nights, 550-6644), will treat animals whose owners cannot afford to pay for veterinary service or they will treat any animal in a genuine emergency. All have many branches and some have mobile units. See the telephone directory for the one nearest you or inquire at an office listed above.

British Veterinary Association, 7 Mansfield Street, w1 (636-6541), will give you the name of a local vet. All vets are qualified to deal with conventional pets whether bird or beast and, like GPs, will refer you to a specialist vet if the disease or injury requires it or if the animal is unusually exotic.

Zoological Society of London, Regent's Park, NW1 (722-3333), treat exotic animals but do *not* accept any animal direct. It must be vetted first.

CHAPTER 14

Photography, including motion picture services

Still cameras and camera services

Hundreds of shops sell new and secondhand cameras and buyers are strongly advised to shop around for the best price. The Edgware Road from Marble Arch north to the overpass is full of camera shops and good for browsing. Magazines like *Amateur Photographer* and *British Journal of Photography* carry equipment advertisements. A shortlist of camera shops where value-for-money is likely is given below. Good buys do not always go hand in hand with good service and advice, but no matter where you buy a new camera you do get a year's guarantee from the maker.

Secondhand cameras used to be a better buy than they are now. There were exempt from Purchase Tax but are now liable for V.A.T.

Cash N Carry, 8 Regency Parade, Finchley Road, NW3 (722-1031), is a discount house selling still and movie cameras, film, chemicals, etc., with reductions up to 35 per cent. They will take part exchange for your old camera and for a quick turnover establishment, appear surprisingly helpful. They also do repairs.

Direct Photographic Supplies, 224 Edgware Road,

231

w2 (262-4427), is another helpful shop selling photographic equipment of every description at good prices. You can buy a £4 Instamatic or a £2,000 reconnaissance camera, film, bromide paper, enlargers, and miscellaneous darkroom supplies. The large secondhand department includes out-of-date equipment. If they don't have it they say they can get it.

Teletape Photographic, 84 Shaftesbury Avenue, w1 (437-3287), and 33 Edgware Road, w2 (723-1942), sell still cameras for amateurs and professionals, especially the latter or the more serious amateur. Teletape do have Instamatics but the emphasis is on Nikon, Cannon, Pentax and Zenith, and many people think their prices can't be beaten on these makes. Secondhand goods too.

Dixon's, 88 Oxford Street, w1 (636-8511), and many other branches, are London's largest camera merchants. Dixon's is as good a place as any to get an Instamatic or other inexpensive amateur camera.

Express Camera Repair, 12 Greville Street, ec1 (405-0231), repair every kind of camera and will make a part if it can't be ordered. Express also polish lenses and repair editing equipment and exposure meters. Same day repairs when possible make it a good place for tourists. All work carries a six-month guarantee except for flash guns (only three months because the electrical parts are only guaranteed that long by the manufacturers). Visitors with broken cameras can put them in a taxi in the morning and Express will return them if possible by taxi in the evening.

Sendean, 6 D'Arblay Street, w1 (439-8418), is highly recommended as a repair shop and is patronized by many professional photographers.

R. G. Lewis, 217 Holborn, wc1 (242-2916), are unusual in that they carry a complete stock of Kodak colour materials for those who want to make their own colour prints. Lewis also sell cameras.

Slide City, 6 Kirby Street, ec1 (405-1323), can produce glass-mounted slides in twenty-four hours.

Studio 10, 56 Whitfield Street, w1 (323-1544). Top

quality special film lab services. Studio 10 retouch colour prints or transparencies, make 'C' Types (colour prints from slides) up to 12 feet by 4½ feet and make transparency dupes. Express service is available if required. This is work of professional quality and amateurs are warned that it is costly.

Ray Rathbone, Methodist Church, 6 Westbridge Road, SW11 (228-1163), rents studios and fully equipped dark-rooms in this old church in Battersea. Flexible terms, in-formal atmosphere, ample parking space.

Pelling and Cross Rentals, 104 Baker Street, W1 (487-5411), hire sophisticated cameras – Nikon, Pentax, Hasselblad – and their own large format equipment for 10 inch by 8 inch negatives, as well as exposure meters, special lenses, and still photography accessories. Minimum rental is one day. Pelling and Cross also repair fine cameras at 104 Baker Street, W1.

Piccadilly, 16 Piccadilly Arcade, SW1 (499-4617), specialize in one-off equipment and special rigs for special needs. This is also a recommended place to buy quality cameras.

Camera Club, 8 Great Newport Street, WC2 (240-1137), is a useful organization for anybody interested in photo-graphy. The club is open Monday to Saturday 11 a.m. to 11 p.m. and the membership fee gives you access to the club's studios and darkrooms, demonstrations and lectures on new equipment and techniques, and opportunities to chat with fellow enthusiasts. Members often trade equip-ment among themselves.

Royal Photographic Society, 14 South Audley Street, W1 (493-3967), gives lectures and demonstrations on all aspects of photography. Membership is open to anyone interested in photography whether amateur or professional. There are special interest groups in Colour Photography, Medical Photography, Photo-journalism and others. These cost a bit extra. There is a large reference library and fringe benefits like package travel deals. Reduced membership fee for students.

Photographers Gallery, 8 Great Newport Street, WC2 (836-7860), has the best selection of books on and about photography in London. Secondhand department. The front of the gallery is used for photographic exhibitions.

Rayco, Blackwater Way, Ash Road, Aldershot, Hants (Aldershot 22725). Not a London firm, but a very useful address for anyone interested in photographic processing on a small scale. Rayco sell chemicals in small amounts. They also supply photographic printing papers and processing equipment. Free catalogue.

Motion picture equipment and services

Unless you are making 'home movies' with an 8 mm camera, it usually makes sense to hire equipment. As film makers know, all 16 mm and some 8 mm cameras and accessories are very expensive, especially if they are of the standard needed to make experimental or documentary films which may eventually have a public life. Since the equipment needed to make a film varies at each stage, (e.g. camera and lighting, editing, lab work) it is pointless to buy equipment that will be left unused much of the time. Also, there are the problems of insurance and maintenance which in the case of rented equipment are usually the headache of the rental company. A good name for maintenance is of prime importance in hiring cameras since a breakdown during shooting can be extremely costly. So hire equipment either from recommended firms like those listed below or from a friend or cameraman you are sure of. So-called 'bargain rentals' can cost a lot of money in the end.

Samuelson Film Services, 303 Cricklewood Broadway, NW2 (452-8090), are the best film equipment company in London. Samuelson rent 16 mm and 35 mm professional cameras, lenses and accessories: Arriflexes, Mitchells', Bolex, Panavision cameras; and rigs for helicopter or under-water photography. They hire both Steenbeck and Moviola editing equipment, Nagra tape recorders for sync sound, dollys, tripods, filmstock – everything from clapboards to cranes. Their insurance broker will arrange an insurance policy, or you can. New customers should use the account of a friend, come up with some good references or be prepared to fork up a full cash value deposit. Delivery and collection service is by van or rail via the 'Red Star' system. The firm have a branch in the West End called **Renta Camera**, 8 Broadwick Street, w1 (437-2603), run by some nice young people. There is also a film bookshop at this address.

Sam Cine Sales, 267 Cricklewood Broadway, NW2 (452-8090) (a continuation of the Edgware Road), are the part of Samuelson that *sell* equipment. They are Steenbeck agents and many of the cameras and rigs for sale are special adaptations of factory models.

Direct Photographic Supplies, 224 Edgware Road, w2 (262-4427), sell new and secondhand 8 mm, Super 8 mm and 16 mm cameras and filmstock. They have less expensive ranges – mainly Bell and Howell, Bolex and Kodak – and old, out-of-date cameras.

Wallace Heaton Rentals, 127 New Bond Street, w1 (629-7511) (now owned by Dixon's), hire 8 mm and Super 8 mm Chinon cameras, editing equipment and projectors. They also rent 16 mm optical and optical-magnetic sound projectors with or without a projectionist, screens, slide projectors and video-tape recorders.

Lee Electrical, 1 Alderson Street, Kensal Road, w10 (969-3621), are specialists in motion picture lighting. Lees hire everything from modest sun guns to mighty Brutes (spots). They have their own insurance and there are no set rules about deposits and references. These can be worked out individually.

Rank Film Laboratories, North Orbital Road, Denham, Uxbridge, Middlesex (332-2323), and

Colour Film Services, 22 Portman Close, Baker Street, w1 (486-2881), process 16 mm and 35 mm film: black and white, Ektachrome, and Eastman Colour. All labs keep film makers on tenterhooks but these two are less hazardous than most. Coffee stains and technicians' fingerprints are not likely to impair the negatives, and both firms are helpful and friendly.

Colour Tone, 18 Oak End Way, Gerrards Cross, Bucks (49-85554), make copies of 8 mm and Super 8 mm prints. This does not involve a negative. There are discounts on orders of over ten copies. Colour Tone also do 8 mm and Super 8 mm reductions from 16 mm (reversal or inter-negative) or vice versa.

Mercury Theatres, 84 Wardour Street, w1 (437-2233), have seven preview theatres for hire, each fully equipped for either 16 mm or 35 mm film. Seating capacity varies from eight to 112. (Two theatres can handle extra tracks.) Minimum rental is fifteen minutes. Night rate is a bit more expensive.

British Film Institute, 81 Dean Street, w1 (437-4355), was set up by the Department of Education and Science to encourage the art of film and, subsequently, TV. It has an excellent reference library and information service which includes catalogues of films for hire and film teaching. The Production Board of the Institute accepts applications from film makers regarding films they would like to make. If an application is accepted, and this doesn't happen often, the Institute becomes the producer-distributor and the applicant directs the film.

Cinema Bookshop, 13 Great Russell Street, wc1 (637-0206). Specialist bookshop carrying books about every aspect of the cinema. For details see Books, Chapter 3.

Photographers

Choosing a photographer is finally a matter of personal taste but essentially one wants evidence of competence and some idea of cost. *The Institute of Incorporated Photographers* is one of the world's leading professional photographers' organizations and membership is based on thorough examination of each applicant, and if successful, admission to one of three grades of membership. In order of importance these grades are Fellow, Associate and Licentiate. Below is a shortlist of London members of the I.I.P. who specialize in portrait and wedding photography, giving the grade of membership in the Institute which they hold.

Arnold Behr, 22 Redington Road, NW3 (794-2535). Associate of I.I.P.

Clayton Evans, 51 Cadogan Place, SW1 (235-6578). Fellow of I.I.P.

Mark Gerson, 24 Cavendish Avenue, NW8 (286-5894). Fellow of I.I.P.

Kenneth Prater, 246A Green Lanes, N13 (886-3099). Associate of I.I.P.

The 'Big Three' in British photography are as follows, but it is unlikely that you will be able to persuade them to take your picture.

David Bailey (722-6615).

Patrick Lichfield, 20 Aubrey Walk, w8 (727-4468).

Lord Snowdon, *Sunday Times*, 200 Gray's Inn Road, WC1 (837-1234).

Desmond Groves, Harrods, Knightsbridge, SW1 (730-1234) is a well-known photographer specializing in portraits of individuals, family groups and weddings. All photographs are in colour. The fourth-floor studio has an office 'set' for executive portraits and you can order a special bonded canvas finish which looks like oils (sort of) as well as the more conventional finish. The Royal Family are among Mr Groves's clients and photos for the Royal Silver Wedding stamps were taken by him.

Norman Derrick, 2 York Road, Shenfield, Brentwood, Essex (0277-221628), is a photo-journalist who also does weddings and general photography. He is competent and more reasonably-priced than the above list.

Passport Photos, 449 Oxford Street, W1 (629-8540),

are opposite Selfridges, and can produce photos within ten minutes. British passport size (2 by 2½ inches) or to the requirements of a particular country. These are not polaroid photos and have proper negatives.

Animal Photography, 4 Marylebone Mews, w1 (935-0503). See page 229 for details.

Deste Photography, 163 Seymour Place, w1 (262-7645), photograph valuables on microfilm. In case of theft, the police and insurance can see what the missing items look like.

Alan Philip, 12B Suffolk House, George Street, Croydon, Surrey (688-0556), copy old photographs that are faded, torn or damaged. By making a new negative and often doing special filtering and art work, a sharp new image can be produced.

*Pictures, prints
and maps*

Picture galleries

This is a quick reference guide especially for those who do not know London but who do know something about pictures and want to find the type of art that suits their taste, be it old masters or the extremes of *avant-garde*.

Old masters

Agnew's, 43 Old Bond Street, w1 (629-6176). Highly important French, Italian and Flemish oil paintings and drawings, and surprisingly, some things that are not very expensive. (See also under Nineteenth and early twentieth century, page 240.)

Colnaghi's, 14 Old Bond Street, w1 (493-1943). Old master paintings and drawings of the highest quality.

Hazlitt, Gooden and Fox, 38 Bury Street, w1 (930-6422). Sixteenth- to eighteenth-century Italian pictures. (See also under Nineteenth and early twentieth century, page 240.)

Heim, 59 Jermyn Street, sw1 (493-0688), specialize in French and Italian sculptures and pictures, particularly the Baroque.

Brian Koetser, 38 Duke Street, sw1 (930-6309). Six-teenth- and seventeenth-century Dutch and Flemish pictures of fine quality but not necessarily by big names.

Leonard Koetser, 13 Duke Street, sw1 (930-9348). Top-quality Dutch, Flemish and Italian pictures of the sixteenth and seventeenth centuries. (Mr Koetser is the father of Brian Koetser listed above.)

Leggatt, 30 St James's Street, sw1 (930-3772). Finest English pictures, sixteenth to nineteenth centuries.

Sabin, 4 Cork Street, w1 (734-6186). Eighteenth-century English paintings and drawings.

Temple Gallery, 4 Yeoman's Row, sw3 (589-6622), specialize in early Greek, Russian and Byzantine icons.

Terry-Engell, 8 Bury Street, sw1 (839-2606), specialize in seventeenth-century Dutch and Flemish paintings.

Wildenstein, 147 New Bond Street, w1 (629-0602), is known equally well in Paris, New York and London for important paintings and drawings.

Nineteenth and early twentieth century

Agnew's, 43 Old Bond Street, w1 (629-6176). English watercolours and some French and English drawings from the nineteenth and early twentieth centuries.

Browse and Darby, 19 Cork Street, w1 (734-7984). Nineteenth- and twentieth-century paintings, drawings and sculpture of quality.

Crane, 321 King's Road, sw3 (352-5857). Nineteenth-century primitives, mostly English. Some earlier, a few later.

D'Offay, 9 Dering Street, w1 (629-1578). Twentieth-century English paintings and drawings. The gallery are agents for Bloomsbury painters Vanessa Bell and Duncan Grant. (See also Contemporary art, page 241.)

Fine Art Society, 148 New Bond Street, w1 (629-5116). Primarily English and Scottish paintings and watercolours.

Lefevre, 30 Bruton Street, w1 (629-2250). Top French Impressionists.

Maas, 15A Clifford Street, W1 (734-2302), specialize in Pre-Raphaelite paintings and watercolours.

Gerald Norman, 8 Duke Street, SW1 (839-7595). English watercolours by known and unknown artists.

Terry-Engell, 8 Bury Street, SW1 (839-2606), exhibit nineteenth-century French landscapes (see also Old masters, page 240).

Tryon, 41 Dover Street, W1 (493-5161). Specialists in sporting and natural history paintings and graphics, 1800 to the present. (See also the Moorland Gallery, page 243.)

Waddington and Tooth, 2 and 34 Cork Street, W1 (439-1866). French Impressionists and other European paintings can be seen here; also Barbizon school. (See also Contemporary art, page 244.)

Wildenstein, 147 New Bond Street, W1 (629-0602). French firm with an international reputation for Impressionist pictures.

Contemporary art

Brook Street Gallery, 24 Brook Street, W1 (493-1550). Paintings, drawings and sculpture by twentieth-century masters.

Browse and Darby, 19 Cork Street, W1 (734-7984) are an established gallery exhibiting nineteenth- and twentieth-century works. Phillip Sutton and Keith Grant are two artists whose work can be seen here.

Cartoon Originals, 5A Gloucester Road, SW7 (584-2001). Framed original drawings by leading cartoonists: *Punch* and *Private Eye*, Osbert Lancaster, Ffolkes, Larry. Prices average around £30.

Crane Kalman, 178 Brompton Road, SW3 (584-7566). English and continental pictures by artists like Matthew Smith, Mondrian, Ben Nicholson, Graham Sutherland – and also work by contemporary traditional artists.

D'Offay, 9 Dering Street, W1 (629-1578). Although noted for Bloomsbury and other early twentieth-century works and styles, D'Offay also show Lucien Freud, Clive Barker and a few other contemporary painters.

Drian, 7 Porchester Place, w2 (723-9473), has given a lot of young artists their start over the past twenty years and represents some 300 artists from all over the world.

Fischer Fine Art, 30 King Street, sw1 (839-3942), exhibit German expressionists and Russian constructivists plus top artists like Henry Moore, and younger ones like Michael Leonard, D. H. Smith, Ben Jonson and John Ridgewell.

Angela Flowers, 3 Portland Mews, w1 (734-0240), is a place to spot new talent doing different things. Some of her 'finds' are Boyd and Evans, David Hepher, Derek Hirst, and Patrick Hughes.

Gimpel Fils, 30 Davies Street, w1 (493-2488). A well-established gallery exhibiting pictures by such artists as Alan Davie, Robert Adams, Yves Klein, Pierre Soulages, Georges Mathieu; also Eskimo sculpture and painting.

Nigel Greenwood, 41 Sloane Gardens, sw3 (730-8824), is an *avant-garde* gallery focusing on young artists, mostly British. The gallery entrance looks like a private residence, but ring the bell, Artists include Gilbert and George, John Walker, Keith Milow.

Anneley Juda, 11 Tottenham Mews, w1 (580-7593), displays twentieth-century geometric and constructivist artists; also *avant-garde* artists such as Christo.

Lefevre, 30 Bruton Street, w1 (629-2250). exhibit Lowry and Burra. (See also under Nineteenth and early twentieth century, page 240.)

Leicester, 22A Cork Street, w1 (437-8995). No longer the leading contemporary gallery in London, the Leicester Gallery is still good for straightforward modern pictures.

Lisson, 68 Bell Street, nw1 (262-1539), have highly-adventurous paintings and three dimensional art by the likes of Robert Ryman and Richard Long.

Marlborough Fine Art, 39 Old Bond Street, w1 (493-7302), show the work of some of the most important – and expensive – contemporary artists alive and dead: Jackson Pollock, Mark Rothko, Franz Kline, Francis Bacon, Barbara Hepworth, Sidney Nolan, John Piper.

Mayor, 14 South Molton Street, w1 (629-0917), is *avant-garde*, and features a number of American artists: Roy Lichtenstein, Dennis Oppenheim, Andy Warhol.

Moorland, 23 Cork Street, w1 (734-6961). Sporting and natural history pictures, prints and bronzes by both nineteenth-century and contemporary artists. (See also the Tryon Gallery, page 241. It has the same owner.)

New Art Centre, 41 Sloane Street, sw1 (235-5844), normally has two one-man exhibits showing simultaneously. The Centre represents John Hubbard, Albert Irvin, Mary Potter and others.

Obelisk, 15 Crawford Street, w1 (486-9821). Specializes in surreal and abstract paintings, and has a reputation for 'finds'. Among those whose work is represented are Vasarely and Bellmer.

Marjorie Parr, 285 King's Road, sw3 (352-0768). Paintings, sculpture and pottery, including works by John Hitchin, Douglas Portway, Enzo Plazzotta, Denis Mitchell and Bernard Leach.

Piccadilly, 16A Cork Street, w1 (629-2875). Highly reputable gallery with an emphasis on symbolist artists such as Khnopff, Klimt, and Georges Minne.

Portal Gallery, 16A Grafton Street, w1 (493-0706). Naïve primitive and fantasy paintings by both contemporary and earlier artists. Portal pride themselves on comparatively reasonable prices. The artists exhibited include James Lloyd and John Allen.

Redfern, 20 Cork Street, w1 (734-1732), have paintings, drawings, sculpture and graphics by established artists like Sutherland, Dubuffet, Matta and Henry Moore or 'comers' like Patrick Proctor and Bryan Kneale.

Robert Self, 9 Cork Street, w1 (437-5836), show nineteenth- and twentieth-century fine photography and some modern paintings. Exhibitions change at the gallery each month.

Rowan, 31A Bruton Place, W1 (493-3727), are a very reputable gallery showing British artists like Philip King, Bridget Riley, Jeremy Moon, and Barry Flanagan.

Felicity Samuel, 16 Savile Row, W1 (734-8557). *Avant-garde* works by both British and American artists, especially Californians, can be seen here: Ivor Abrahams, Joe Goode, Nigel Hall and Tom Holland.

Francis Kyle, 9 Maddox Street, W1 (499-6870). Promising new gallery showing drawings, watercolours, small paintings, prints. Representative artists are Valerio Adami, Paul Neagu, Ian Gardner, Glynn Boyd Harte. The gallery has regular discussions and talks relating to new areas in the visual arts.

Nicholas Treadwell, 36 Chiltern Street, W1 (486-1414). Fantasy, realism, erotica, humour – all describe this gallery, and Mr Treadwell believes it is also the friendliest in London. Representative artists are Robert Knight, John Holmes Mike Gorman.

Trafford, 119 Mount Street, W1 (499-2021). A good place for straightforward, moneyed modern tastes. Lots of *trompe-l'œil*.

Waddington and Tooth, 2 and 34 Cork Street, W1 (439-1866). The merger of these two distinguished galleries has produced one of the finest lists of exhibiting artists in Britain. These include Dubuffet, Picasso, Kenneth Nolan and English painters Elizabeth Frink, Ivon Hitchens, Ben Nicholson, Allen Jones, Matthew Smith and Augustus John. (See also under Nineteenth and early twentieth century, page 240.)

Prints and maps

Since interest in prints falls into the subject-oriented and the artist-oriented, this section is divided accordingly. That is to say, the first part deals with prints with a topographical, historical, military, natural history, etc. bias, and the second with old and new master prints in which the artist and his conception are more important to buyers than the subject which he portrays. A third section is included for photo-mechanical reproductions. (Buyers are warned that it is possible to find 'reproductions' in original print galleries too. These have usually been signed by the artist to increase their value.)

A note to novices: many people are confused about what the difference between an *original print* and a *reproduction* is. Unfortunately, there is no legal definition and this makes misunderstanding and misleading possible. Among reputable dealers, an 'original print' means that the *master image* has been made by the artist himself. The actual *printing* may have been done by someone else. The artist's signature indicates that he has approved the print. There are four ways, generally speaking, that prints are made and none of these involve photo-mechanics which 'reproduce' rather than 'print'.

Lithography, invented in the eighteenth century, involves drawing an image on a stone or plate with a greasy material and then moistening it. When an inked roller is applied to the stone the ink sticks to the greasy surface only and the image can thus be transferred by pressing paper to the stone.

Screenprinting or serigraphy works like stencilling. The parts of the paper or printing surface not intended to receive colour are masked out. Ink is then forced through a stretched gauze on to the paper.

Woodcut or wood engraving is a relief process. The background is carved out in a block so that the image stands out and can be stamped.

Etching is the opposite of the above. The design is incised, burned into a plate with acid, for example. The rest of the plate is then varnished to protect it and the plate is inked and wiped, leaving ink on the incised surface only. The print is made by pressing the plate on to dampened paper.

Aquatint, soft ground mezzotint and drypoint all involve this basic engraving technique.

Most contemporary artists print in limited editions. This means that each print is numbered both with its own number and that of the size of the edition, for instance 4/70 is the fourth print made in an edition of seventy. When the agreed edition has been reached the master image is defaced to prevent more being made.

Antique prints, on the other hand, whether 'subject' or 'artist', are not often the work of the artist himself. In fact the engraver's name often appears as well as that of the artist who painted the picture or drew the original design. Dürer's famous woodcuts, for example, were cut by a master woodcarver, not by the artist. But Dürer did engrave his own copper engravings.

Given the historical flexibility of artist-printer involvement and possibility of new techniques in printmaking – probably of a photo-mechanical nature, yet superior to present techniques – the ambiguity of words like 'original' print is bound to continue until language and law become precise. Meanwhile there is plenty of opportunity to sell the unsuspecting public items that are not quite what they are supposed to be, so do not hesitate to ask dealers questions about processes and degree of artist involvement. The ruder their response, the more likely that they have something to hide. Finally, when buying a print, remember that (in addition to the fact that you like it) the closer the artist has been involved, the more likely it is to keep its value in the long term.

'Subject' prints and maps

Baynton-Williams, 18 Lowndes Street, SW1 (235-6595), are specialists in prints and maps over 100 years old. The shop's 12,000 items are equally divided between maps and prints. There are subjects like sports, ballooning, shipping, and views. Maps are by Speed, Saxton and also carto-graphers of other countries. [££+]

Parker Gallery, 2 Albemarle Street, w1 (499-5906), London's oldest print dealers, are noted for their military and naval subjects. Antique prints cost from £10. [££+]

Arthur Reader, 71 Charing Cross Road, wc2 (437-2653). Old engravings on topographical, naval, mili-tary and other subjects from £2. Musty, old-fashioned atmosphere. [££]

Finbar MacDonnell, 17 Camden Passage, n1 (226-0537). Inexpensive prints and maps, primarily topo-graphical, with a good stock of English views. [£]

Pigeonhole Picture Shop, 13 Langton Street, sw10 (352-2677). Decorative antique prints, all attractively mounted. Emphasis on colour. [££]

Weinreb and Douwma, 93 Great Russell Street, wc1 (636-4895), are antiquarian print and map sellers. They have a good general stock, above average quality. Carica-tures and Piranesis are specialities, but classical, ethno-graphical, topographical and fashion are some of the other areas well-represented. [££+]

Richard Green, 4 New Bond Street, w1 (499-5553), has important English eighteenth- and nineteenth-century prints on all subjects. Prices are from £100. [£££]

Andrew Edmunds, 44 Lexington Street, w1 (437-8594). Small general stock of decorative and topographical prints, and prints by English artists before 1830. Speciality (and a very large stock) of caricatures. From a few pounds. [££+]

Francis Edwards, 83 Marylebone High Street, w1 (935-9221), has the largest selection of antique maps in London (over 200,000) and some of the most important. Mr Tooley, who heads the map room, has been in the busi-ness for fifty years and publishes his own journal on map-collecting. Stock dates from the fifteenth century and covers all the countries of the world. Whether you want a sixteenth-century woodcut map of America, an eighteenth-century map of remote Easter Island or a Speed map of an English county, you can find it here. [££+]

Mapsellers, 37 Southampton Street, wc2 (836-8444), are an off-shoot of distinguished philatelists, Stanley Gibbons. Mapsellers stock printed maps ranging in cost from £5 to £5,000 and in period from the fifteenth century to 1850. Valuation and framing services available. Catalogue and price lists. [££+]

Edward Stanford, 12 Long Acre, wc2 (836-1321), is the world's largest *modern* map shop, with ordnance surveys of Britain, Europe and many other countries; topographical, geographical, military and road maps. Stanford maps are useful rather than decorative or of historical interest. [£+]

Map House, 54 Beauchamp Place, sw3 (589-4325), carries mostly antique maps of countries (1650–1850). Also some modern maps for everyday use. [££]

Note: there are several print sellers in the Portobello Market and their prices tend to be very reasonable. A good place to look round.

'Artist' prints

Christopher Mendez, 51 Lexington Street, w1 (734-2385). Fine old master prints of all schools but with special interest in early English prints. Mendez have graphics by Dürer, Rembrandt, Breughel and Constable but are equally proud of their stock of engravings by lesser-known masters. [££+]

William Weston Gallery, 7 Royal Arcade, w1 (493-0722). Important nineteenth- and twentieth-century prints by Picasso, Henry Moore, the Impressionists, the Norwich school and others. Stock from £20. [£££]

Lumley Cazalet, 24 Davies Street, w1 (629-4493). Original prints by *Belle Époque* and twentieth-century artists, but Matisse is the household name. These fetch some £3,000 on average. Other works start at £6. [£££]

Colnaghi's, 14 Old Bond Street, w1 (493-1943), have two print departments: one deals with old masters (pre-1850) and the other handles modern masters. The gallery holds three print exhibitions a year but stock can be seen in the files any time. [£££]

Christopher Drake (629-5571, by appointment only), sells old and modern masters, Dürer to Picasso, plus a large stock of nineteenth- and twentieth-century English prints. Average prices are £10 to £50. [££+]

Marlborough Graphics, 17 Old Bond Street, w1 (629-5161), publish and sell prints by artists whose works are sold at Marlborough Fine Art: John Piper, Victor Pasmore, Sidney Nolan. Editions are normally limited to seventy or so. [£££]

Craddock and Barnard, 32 Museum Street, wc1 (636-3937), have old master engravings from the fifteenth to the seventeenth century, and a serious atmosphere. Prices are from a few pounds . [££+]

Christie's Contemporary Art, 11 Albemarle Street, w1 (409-1307), is the auction rooms' bid to get in on the print boom. Christie's publish prints and although they keep a small gallery at the above address, most of the business is by mail order. They send free illustrated catalogues out quarterly, advertising works by leading artists in limited editions of 150–250. Average cost is £30 . [££+]

Zella 9, 2 Park Walk, Fulham Road, sw10 (351-0588), is many people's favourite print gallery; pleasant, helpful and lots to see by good English artists who are not necessarily 'names'. Zella has the work of art students on occasion. Contemporary posters too. Richard Beer, Julia Matcham, Valerie Daniel, Valerie Thornton and many others. [££]

DM Gallery, 72 Fulham Road, sw3 (589-8208), is a smart contemporary gallery holding about ten exhibitions a year. DM do not handle entire editions. They sell selected prints by 'name' artists like Hockney and Dine whose prints can fetch £1,000. DM are also noted for prints by American realists like John Clem Clarke. Items not in current exhibition can be seen in the basement of the gallery. Prices start at £10. [££+, £££]

Curwen, 1 Colville Place, Whitfield Street, W1 (636-1459). An irreproachable name in printing, Curwen produce and sell prints by well- and lesser-known artists and run a Print Club to which a life membership costs only £5. Members get 20 per cent reductions on all new editions. Graphics by Henry Moore, Albany Wiseman, David Gentleman, and potter Bernard Leach. [££]

Lords Gallery, 26 Wellington Road, NW8 (722-4444). Incredibly fine selection of original posters including well-known names like Toulouse-Lautrec and Mucha and many equally fascinating examples by more obscure artists. [££+]

Jordan, Camden Lock, Chalk Farm Road, NW1 (267-2437). Friendly gallery in a fascinating location that makes it worth a visit for the site alone. Jordan stock runs the gamut of contemporary graphics from young unknowns to Hockney and, of course, Picasso. From £5. A new exhibition every three weeks. [££, ££+]

Patrick Seale Prints, 2 Motcomb Street, SW1 (235-0934). Complete editions of prints by established artists are for sale at the gallery or by mail order. The mail-order side of the business is called *Observer Art* and advertises in the *Observer* colour supplement. Editions are large: on average numbering about 150 but going to 1,000 in a case like Dali. This keeps the price of *each* print down. Patrick Seale also has a print hire service for offices. Subscribers get ten new colour reproductions (which fit the same frames) every six months. [££, ££+]

Waddington and Tooth Graphics, 31 Cork Street, W1 (439-1866), are an offshoot of the fine art gallery and publish and sell prints by artists whose paintings they exhibit, like Caulfield, Frink and Hoyland. They also sell a lot of American graphics by 'name' artists like Rauschenberg and Oldenburg and some modern masters – Braque, Miro, etc. [££+, £££]

The Workshop, 83 Lamb's Conduit Street, WC1

(242-5335). Graphics by young artists and some original cartoons. [££]

John Campbell, 164 Walton Street, sw3 (584-9268), and 68 Rosslyn Hill, nw3 (794-5482). Original posters from 1890 to the 1940s; Lautrec, Beardsley, Mucha, Cassandra, and Newbold. Catalogue 30p. [££+]

Reproductions

Pallas Gallery, 28 Shelton Street, wc2 (836-1977), have the biggest collection of fine art reproductions in the country. They act as publishers and agents for the New York Graphic Society. All schools of painting, cave to contemporary. Prices vary from about 65p to £10 depending on size, quality of paper and type of process, and there is a huge selection of fine art postcards.

Athena Reproductions, 133 Oxford Street, w1 (734-3383), and six other London branches publish inexpensive reproductions of famous paintings and posters. Prices are about £1 for 'poster quality' reproductions and double that for 'soft print' quality, which means better-quality paper. Pictures can also be bought mounted on board or framed. 600 titles. Free catalogue. These are mass-produced prints, and colours tend to be inferior, but they are decorative.

Ganymede Press, 10 Great Turnstile Street, wc1 (405-9836), publish and sell quality reproductions by artists of all periods. There are about seventy-five titles including several Lowrys. Average price is around £3. Illustrated catalogue is not free.

Advertising Agency Poster Bureau, 42 Kingsway, wc2 (831-7211), can provide you with a free poster from almost any current ad campaign. Many of these are very imaginative and make enterprising solutions to budget decorating. There is no proper gallery on the premises so you have to know what poster you want in advance.

London Transport Posters, 280 Old Marylebone Road, NW1 (262-3444). These are inexpensive posters advertising London events and sights and created by established artists. Samples are on display in the poster shop and the cost is around 75p. Worth a visit.

Most London museums have a selection of reproductions from their collections on sale.

Services

Restoration

Drescher Ltd, 17 Alverstone Road, NW2 (459-5543). Expert paper restoration. Drescher mend tears, remove foxing, match missing pieces and clean fine prints, drawings and maps.

William Lowe, 75 Randolph Avenue, W9 (286-5018), specialize in the restoration of icons.

Bourlet, Patrickson, 249 Fulham Road, SW3 (351-3292), are picture agents providing a complete service for pictures valued at millions or only a few pounds. They do restoration, framing, packing and shipping.

Morrill's, 68 Golden House, Great Pulteney Street, W1 (437-4031), clean, re-line and restore pictures of all qualities. Sotheby's is a client.

William Drown, 110 New Bond Street, W1 (629-1949), restore important pictures but are reluctant to take on new clients unless, presumably, your picture presents a special challenge or is unusually valuable.

Framing

Upbrook Studios, 37 Craven Road, w2 (723-1948), make wooden frames of the finest quality for old and new paintings. Most are gilded. The studio have a collection of antique carved frames but are reluctant to part with them. [£££]

H. Spiller, 37 Beak Street, w1 (437-4661), sell antique carved frames which they will alter to fit a particular picture. A very small one costs £50. (Spillers also hire pictures to film companies and offices but not to individuals.) [£££]

F. Pollak, 20 Blue Bell Yard, St James's Street, sw1 (493-1434), make fine hand-carved frames to order. Pollak also clean and restore frames. [£££]

Blackman Harvey, 29 Earlham Street, wc2 (836-1904), will frame a picture in only forty-eight hours provided you are willing to pay a third extra. The normal service takes a fortnight. There is a large selection of mouldings, and a workshop on the premises. [££]

Framery, 39 Blandford Street, w1 (935-4838), have a system called Artlager in which a glass front is clipped on to a hardboard backing, thus dispensing with a conventional 'frame'. It cuts costs in half and is suitable for many contemporary graphics, photos and documents. Framery also sell aluminium frames. [£+]

Rowley, 115 Kensington Church Street, w8 (727-6495), do very good work but take a long time. A two month wait is not unusual. Rowley have a large selection of mouldings and about the biggest range of mats in London. [££+]

Robert Sielle, 21 St Albans Grove, w8 (937-4957), are framing consultants for all types of pictures and prints. Any kind of mat and mounting can be made to order. They do carved frames for icons or perspex for contemporary prints, pedestals for sculpture, and can also repair old silver frames. [££+]

Zella 9, 2 Park Walk, Fulham Road, sw10 (351-0588), is a print gallery with a seven-day framing service in brass, aluminium and perspex. [££]

253

Winsor and Newton, 51 Rathbone Place, w1 (636-4231), sell self-assemble framing kits in wood or aluminium in many sizes. Wood kits are already mitred. You glue, stain or paint to suit yourself. (Glass must be cut elsewhere, see index.) Aluminium kits have perspex 'glass' included. [£]

Note: do-it-yourself framers can buy mouldings from timber merchants and have glass cut to size. You also need a mitre box to cut corners. See index under Timber, Glass and Carpentry respectively.

Instruction

Centre for the Study of Modern Art, 59 West Heath Road, nw3 (458-5577), runs a three-month diploma course covering painting, graphics, sculpture and architecture from the mid-nineteenth century to the present day. Also short two-week courses on Modern British Art, Modern American Art, Collecting Modern Graphics and other topics. All are intensive daily courses and lecturers are well-known members of galleries, the Courtauld Institute or artists themselves. The courses are held at the Institute of Contemporary Art in the Mall.

Inner London Education Authority, County Hall, se1 (633-3441), hold classes in art history. For details, ring them or purchase their magazine *Floodlight* at your local newsagent.

CHAPTER 16

Records and tapes

All new British recordings of classical music and general release L.P.s of jazz, nostalgia, film music, etc. are reviewed monthly in the *Gramophone* and in *Records and Recording*. The *Gramophone* also advertises hard-to-find oldies. Rock 'n' roll and top-of-the-pops enthusiasts can find out about new releases from *Let It Rock*, a glossy monthly specializing in this field, or can write to Charlie Gillett, c/o London Radio, for his free news-sheet, the *Honky Tonk Guide for Record Collectors*. This tells where to find all sorts of hand-printed magazines and bulletins dealing with the rock sub-stratum. Finally, there is the *Penguin Stereo Record Guide* which lists some 3,500 stereo recordings and grades them on technical quality and aesthetics: exceptional recordings receive a rosette. The Guide is updated at regular intervals.

An estimated 50 per cent of the record business in London is mail-order but the reason why foreigners buy records here varies depending on where they live. For continentals the reason is simple. Records cost less in Britain. In America, however, the cost is about the same as in Britain but the pressings are often not as good as they are here and on the Continent. Then too, people from English-speaking countries who order continental labels tend to order them from English dealers to avoid language problems, so London dealers stock a broader selection than they might ordinarily.

HMV, 363 Oxford Street, W1 (629-1240), is the biggest record shop in Europe with three floors of records and one of tapes (cassettes and 8-track). This is a good place to buy general L.P.s – film music, dance music and popular vocal and instrumental music from all countries. They have a notable collection of popular Indian music. In fact, you can get most things at HMV and the only reason many people don't is the impersonal, deparment-store atmosphere in so vast a place. (The floor devoted to rock and pop has made some effort to overcome this with a go-go decor.) Special export department. Seven smaller London branches.

Henry Stave, 11 Great Marlborough Street, W1 (437-4153), specialize in classical recordings and are unique in publishing their own extensive mail-order catalogue. This also lists plays, poems, foreign languages and other spoken word recordings. Record stacks in the shop are conveniently arranged alphabetically by composer within each category of classical music. Many American imports. Bound volumes of the *Gramophone* magazine and other publications are on the counter for customers' perusal. There are some second-hands and some cassettes. Stave's will often take part-exchange on old classical L.P.s and will purchase mono collections. A distinct effort is made to make customers' visits agreeable.

Gramophone Exchange, 80 Wardour Street, W1 (437-5313), probably have the largest classical record stock in London. This includes a big secondhand department with many 78s. Imports from all over the world. There are two booths for hearing secondhand stock but new recordings cannot be played before purchase. The Exchange, as the name suggests, takes part exchange on old records and buys old collections too. The staff are knowledgeable and helpful.

Thomas Heinitz, 35 Moscow Road, W2 (229-2077). Mr Heinitz's main reputation is for fine stereo equipment but he also sells classical records, and customers who buy his equipment get 20 per cent off any subsequent record purchases up to the price of the equipment. Every Saturday afternoon from 2 p.m. to 4.30 p.m. Mr Heinitz gives a free record recital of new releases played on the finest stereo equipment. The first Saturday in the month is devoted to symphonies and concertos, the second to miscellaneous orchestral music, the third to instrumental and chamber music and the fourth to vocal. This is the best deal in town for listening to newly-recorded classical music for free.

Collector's Corner, 62 New Oxford Street, WC1 (580-6155), and 63 Monmouth Street, WC2 (836-5614), are classical specialists with an emphasis on operatic and other vocal recordings. This firm has been around a long time and some people feel it isn't keeping up with modern competition, but it is still good in its area. A few 'nostalgia' records too.

Templar, 86 High Holborn, WC1 (242-8669), and branches, sell discount classical records and some cassettes. They take at least 10 per cent off the recommended price of every record and sometimes a lot more, and do boxed sets at big discounts. All records are guaranteed without flaw or your money back.

Discurio, 9 Shepherd Street, W1 (493-6939), has an excellent reputation for service, advice and stock. Discurio is 60 per cent classical music and the rest is foreign popular, (modern Greek, Indian, French and German vocal and instrumental but not 'pop' or rock and roll) and music of the twenties, thirties and forties. They also have spoken word recordings. One floor is all deletions (new records that have been dropped from the publisher's catalogue) and special purchases at discount prices. You may hear a record on their open system before you buy it but they put it on, not you.

Farringdon Records, 42 Cheapside, EC2 (248-2816), is *the* place to go for classical deletions.

Collet's Record Shop, 180 Shaftesbury Avenue, WC2 (640-3969), is a jazz and folk music shop selling old and new recordings: Bluegrass, Eskimo, Indian ragas, Dixieland, Charlie Mingus etc. It's a jazz and folk buffs' hangout: bulletin board with relevant notices, books, magazines, sheet music and listening booth. Folk is upstairs and jazz, appropriately, is in the cellar.

Dobell's Folk Record Shop, 75 Charing Cross Road, WC2 (437-5746), believe they have the largest collection of blues in the country, if not the world. American and English folk is their speciality but some international folk music is stocked too. Also pre-war 78s. There are listening facilities and Dobell's will take part-exchange on old records.

Dobell's Jazz Record Shop, 77 Charing Cross Road, WC2 (437-4197), next door to the folk shop listed above, sell every kind of jazz: Dixieland, Be-Bop, Big Bands, Swing, and *avant-garde*. They have continental and American imports, some cassettes, a secondhand basement, and two listening booths.

Virgin, 130 Notting Hill Gate, W11 (221-6177). Big tuned-in pop shop, with all the latest L.P.s and singles. Headsets for listening, and cushions to do so in comfort. Branches at Marble Arch and New Oxford Street.

Your Best Buys, 9 St Martin's Court, WC2 (836-8514), claim to have Europe's largest collection of cassettes. All are at less than recommended retail price. There is something for everyone: pop, classical, instrumental, children's stories and blank tapes.

Harlequin, 201 Oxford Street, W1 (437-2476), and fifty London branches, sell all kinds of music, but are recommended for pop. Harlequin have American pop imports and sell cassettes and cartridges. Listening facilities.

Stern's West African Record Shop, 126 Tottenham Court Road, W1 (387-1539), stocks records from Nigeria, Ghana, Congo and some other parts of Africa.

Moondogs, 400 High Street North, E12 (552-0809), specializes in old recordings of rock and roll, rhythm and blues, in 78s, 45s, and L.P.s. Take the tube to Manor Park or get a 25 bus.

Record Corner, 27 Bedford Hill, Balham, SW12 (673-6130), sells Soul and Jamaican reggae in singles and L.P.s.

Dial a Disc to hear a recording from one of the week's

top-of-the-charts, ring 160 between 6 p.m. and 8 a.m. (7 p.m. during Test Matches.)

Music Discount Centre, 61 and 67 Park Road, NW1 (723-9375), is a discount store specializing in classical records and tapes: all record sets are sold 25 per cent below list price and cassettes are discounted at 20 per cent. There is an export department which will send records all over the world and all mail-order purchases are 25 per cent off. Not surprisingly, many customers keep charge accounts.

Charing Cross Library, 4 Charing Cross Road, WC2 (930-3274). Most branches of the public library have some records on loan but the largest selection is to be found at the City of Westminster branch. This is at the disposal of anyone who lives or works in Westminster. The collection is mostly classical and records can be kept for three weeks.

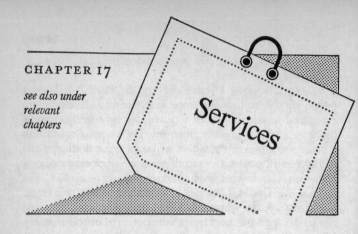

Ancestors

Society of Genealogists, 37 Harrington Gardens, sw 7 (373-7054), will trace your ancestors if they are English or Welsh or put you on to similar experts in Scotland and Ireland. The Society has a comprehensive reference library where for a small fee you can do research yourself.

College of Arms, Queen Victoria Street, ec4 (248-2762). If your search for a coat-of-arms proves futile, you may apply to the College of Arms to grant one. Upon acceptance, a coat-of-arms will be designed for you by the heralds and kept on register at the College. The cost is about £400 for an individual and rather more for a company. Applicants do not have to be British citizens. Applications should be made in writing to the College at the above address.

Mullins, 9 New Bond Street, w 1 (493-5767), heraldic specialists, will engrave crests on rings, cuff-links and the like or paint family trees or arms on almost any surface.

Heraldry Today, 10 Beauchamp Place, sw 3 (584-1656), is a bookshop of heraldry and genealogy. They undertake searches for books relating to any family name.

Domestic services

Problem Ltd, 179 Vauxhall Bridge Road, sw1 (828-8181), is a membership 'help' agency performing a multiplicity of services for the home. A fee of £10 entitles members to plumbers and electricians on the double, part-time cooks, cleaners, painters, secretaries, clock repairers, baby-sitters, seamstresses and dog walkers – almost any home service at moderate fees, performed by capable people. Problem operates twenty-four hours a day. Members can join B.U.P.A. at a reduction and there are several free services as well: you can leave messages on Problem's phone or ask them to take messages for you. In case of a TV, fridge or oven breakdown they will give you a free temporary replacement. You just pay transport. Many members have been subscribers for years.

London Domestics, 313 Brompton Road, sw3 (584-0161), offer temporary help for housewives on a daily or periodic basis. This is an efficient and extremely helpful organization. The staff they provide are mostly young people from all walks of life – out-of-work actors, housewives earning extra money – whose references have been carefully checked and who will clean your home, wait at table or wash up after a party. The fees are reasonable, there is a three-hour minimum, and you pay any travelling costs. (See also Babysitters Unlimited, page 263.)

Doorsteps Ltd, 26 Eaton Terrace, sw1 (730-9244), provide male cleaners exclusively. Doorsteps' special Spring Cleaning Service (any time of year) includes wall washing, rug shampooing, curtain cleaning – all the basic, heavy stuff. They do ordinary daily cleaning too but this is more expensive than hiring women cleaners. You can also get window cleaning, painting and decorating done. Four-hour minimum.

Lumley, 17 Walton Street, sw3 (581-2241). Temporary cooks are what Lumley's is noted for and this is the only agency that Cordon Bleu recommends. Lumley cooks will shop, cook and clean up for a meal of any size and they can be employed for the weekend, holidays and for short stints in the country. Lumley's also supply bottlewashers, temporary secretaries and flower arrangers.

Solve Your Problem, 25A Kensington Church Street, w8 (937-0906), specialize in solving domestic help problems at short notice. They will provide temporary child-minders but are best known for their party help: cooks, barmen, waitresses. Very reliable but there is a stiff agency fee on top of wages.

We People, 92 Tavistock Road, w11 (727-1228), do van removals, carpentry, electrical repairs and odd jobs, and can provide plumbers, painters, baby-sitters, and dressmakers. This is not an agency but a cooperative of willing, if informal, young people who work for reasonable wages and will come and hang a mirror or move a heavy chest as well as take on more complex jobs. Especially recommended for jobs other firms won't bother with.

Gentle Ghosts, 33 Norland Road, w1 (603-2871), operate very much like We People (see above). They are a non-profit group whose premises are available to community activities. Gentle Ghost do a lot of charity jobs as well as odd jobs and repairs, building and carpentry. They clean flats, mind babies, put up shelves, type, dressmake, garden and give tuition in cooking and yoga. This is a new breed replacing the professional craftsman of yesteryear and casualness, kindliness and 'doing one's thing' are keynotes.

Brompton Bureau, 10 Beauchamp Place, sw3 (584-6242), are a top domestic staff agency which can still find a 'Jeeves' or a lady's maid. They can provide cooks, chauffeurs and housekeeping couples. Top references required on both sides. Placements locally and abroad. Some temporary appointments.

Au Pair Bureau, 87 Regent Street, w1 (930-4757), will find an au pair to suit your needs. They supply details and photos of girls from all over the world. You contact the one you like best and if you reach an agreement then the au pair comes to you at her own expense. You pay an introduction fee to the agency, then there is a twelve-day trial period during which either party can cancel out. If this happens the agency will get you another girl. Wages for au pairs vary from £5 to £35 a week depending on how much work and how many hours are required.

Knightsbridge Nannies, 5 Beauchamp Place, SW3 (584-9323). Qualified nannies, governesses and mothers' helps on a permanent or temporary basis. The British nannie, once the bastion of the Empire, is nearly extinct, says Mrs Walters, who runs this agency, and most modern nannies want to work on a daily or temporary basis. Mrs Walter's nannies have the nursery governesses examination board certificate (N.N.E.B.) and she sends them all over the world – when she can get them. Demands on nannies and by nannies have changed considerably over the years and today's nannie is usually expected to be a car driver and to be prepared to do a bit of cooking now and then, if only for her charges. For their part, nannies insist on their own bedrooms, and at least twenty-four hours in each week and one weekend in four off. Getting time off is the *bête noire* of the modern nannie, explains Mrs Walters, and prospective employers should bear in mind that this point is of equal importance to salary – sometimes more so.

Universal Aunts, 36 Walpole Street, SW3 (730-9834), are famous for helping out in any number of emergency situations. They will buy you a yacht, organize your parties, or get you an au pair or a house in the country, but they are best-known as child escorts, baby-sitters and proxy parents. Try any kind of problem on them, however.

Babysitters Unlimited, 313 Brompton Road, SW3 (730-7777). There is a membership fee for this service of £3 a year. Eighty per cent of the sitters are registered nurses, the rest are carefully vetted mothers and nannies, and twenty-four hours notice is required. You pay travelling costs; this means a taxi at least one way. (Part of London Domestics, see page 261.)

Babyminders, Oldbury Place, W1 (935-3515), and

Childminders, 67A Marylebone High Street, W1 (935-4386), are both owned by the same company but are operated separately. The main difference seems to be that Babyminders, the oldest service of its kind in London, tends to have the more old-fashioned type of nannie. Both services require a small membership fee.

Visitors Welcome, 17 Radley Mews, W8 (937-9755), a children's escort service, will meet a child or take it to a boat, plane or train. Patronized mostly by families who live abroad and send their children to school in England, the agency will arrange overnight accommodation for children and even get a foster family for a short period if necessary.

Hospital services for home care

International Medical Personnel, 11 Hinde Street, W1 (486-3096), provide nurses for the care of patients at home. The agency has both S.R.N.s and Enrolled nurses (two years of training), and will provide day and night nurses, residential or non-residential. They also place nurses in the country.

Cory Bros., 166 High Road, N2 (444-9966), rent wheelchairs, commodes and sun lamps by the week.

John Bell and Croyden, 50 Wigmore Street, W1 (935-5555), are the biggest general medical suppliers in central London. Bedpans, syringes, trusses, crutches, drugs for sale. Wheelchairs and suction machines for rent. Free delivery.

Egerton Hospital Equipment, Tower Hill, Horsham, Sussex (0403-3800), hire electrically-operated hospital beds by the week (four-week minimum). They have four models specially designed to be comfortable for the patient, and to help any nurse who has to tend the patient without additional hospital assistance. London deliveries.

British Red Cross, 6 Grosvenor Crescent, SW1 (235-7131), often have equipment for rent at their neighbourhood sections around London but what you get depends on what is on hand in your particular area. Ring the head office for further details.

Disabled Living Foundation, 346 Kensington High Street, w14 (602-2491), is an information service for the disabled and will give advice on benefits, insurance, rehabilitation. They will help locate special apparatus and other requirements.

Boots Chemists, Criterion Building, Piccadilly, w1 (930-4761), is *always* open.

Medic Alert, 9 Hanover Street, w1 (499-2261), issues bracelets or necklaces with engraved notification of any hidden health problems – asthma, diabetes, allergies or a rare blood group. In case of accident, additional background information can be obtained by doctors from the organization files in a few minutes. Medic Alert is a registered charity and an international organization.

Information services

Recorded information

The following services give information by telephone and are provided by the Post Office, often in conjunction with another organization.

Correct Time, dial 123.

Local Weather Forecast, dial 246-8091. For greater detail phone the Meteorological office, 836-4311.

Road Conditions, 246-8021. Information on traffic and road conditions within fifty miles of London.

***Financial Times* Index and Business News Summary**, 246-8026. Latest share index (updated four times a day) plus a brief summary of business news. After 10 p.m. there is a stock market report, company news and the next day's business diary. Reviews of the past week on the stock exchange and other related topics are recorded at the weekend.

Test Match Scores, dial 160. During Test Matches in England, the scores are available at this number between 8 a.m. and 7 p.m. Monday to Saturday.

Teletourist, 246-8041 gives the main events of the day in London. In French 246-8043, German 246-8045, Italian 246-8049 and Spanish 246-8047.

Miscellaneous

Daily Telegraph **Information Service**, 135 Fleet Street, EC4 (353-4242), answer news and general knowledge questions. If you want to know how to address a letter to a duke, when the battle of Crécy was fought or who was Chancellor of the Exchequer in 1910, the *Daily Telegraph* can tell you.

London Council of Social Service, 68 Chalton Street, NW1 (388-0241), run 100 *Citizens' Advice Bureaux* in greater London. These are independent, impartial services that treat all cases and queries confidentially. The service is free. Housing problems, consumer difficulties, marital, child and employment problems, social security benefits and legal rights are all areas they can help with. For the nearest Bureau ring the head office above or look in the telephone directory under Citizens' Advice Bureau.

Consumers' Association, 14 Buckingham Street, WC2 (839-1222), is a non-profit organization totally free from government or industrial grants whose purpose is to help the public by giving pre-buying information and advice. The Association publishes *Which* magazine, available through subscription or your local library. The magazine reports on tests of all kinds of consumer goods and recommends the best buy and value for money. They also publish quarterly supplements, *Money Which*, *Motoring Which*, *Handyman's Which* and *Holiday Which*. The Consumers' Association is responsible for the establishment in greater London of eight Consumer Advice Centres which are run by the local boroughs. Ring them for an address near you.

Greater London Information Service, 928-0303, is

part of the G.L.C. and answers queries about local borough and Council matters.

British Tourist Authority, 64 St James's Street, SW1 (629-9191). Callers at the Tourist Information office can get free pamphlets on most aspects of travel and entertainment in Britain: walking tours, hotels, farmhouse accommodation, camping sites, pony trekking, fishing, concerts and theatrical events. There are special complaint forms should any place prove sub-standard.

London Tourist Board, 4 Grosvenor Gardens, SW1 (730-0791), and Platform 15, Victoria Mainline Station, gives information on London events, hotels, and other needs such as medical and transport. A student advice and inexpensive accommodation centre is located at 8 Buckingham Palace Road, SW1. Other accommodation information is available from the Victoria Station branch.

City of London Information Centre, St Paul's Churchyard, EC4 (606-3030), provided by the Guildhall, supplies information about events and places of interest in the square mile of the City of London.

BIT, 146 Great Western Road, W11 (229-8219), is a twenty-four hour help and advice service on personal and other problems. BIT acts as a referral service and even operates a cash pad for the needy.

Messenger services

Post Office Express Messengers. Ring 606-9876 for the number to dial in your area. Express messengers will collect a letter or parcel and deliver it to its destination. The fee is 50p per mile plus the cost of travel.

Inter-City Couriers, 37 Soho Square, W1 (439-0761), do deliveries by motorbike anywhere, at reasonable charges. They normally collect within half an hour.

Office-at-home services

Peter Coxson Typing Service, c/o Mary Kay Bureau, 31 Delmerend House, Ixworth Place, sw3 (584-0198). Expert typing of manuscripts, reports, plays, etc., by highly-qualified typists working at home.

Five to Nine, 17 Wigmore Street, w1 (493-3512), is a twenty-four-hour typing service for all kinds of work including legal and accounting. Work brought in at 5 p.m. is ready at 9 a.m. next morning.

Freelance Services, 37A Maida Vale, w9 (286-0115), provide qualified people to do any type of research, data processing, editing or accountancy plus boring jobs like envelope-addressing and stamp-licking.

Writers' and Speakers' Research, 56 Brunswick Gardens, w8 (727-2289), is a highly-reputable and long-established service which does research for books, articles and speeches – long- and short-term.

London Visitors and Interpreters Service, 175 Piccadilly, w1 (493-2757), provide interpreters, guides and written translations in virtually any language.

Metyclean, 92 Victoria Street, sw1 (828-2511), and 137 Strand, wc2 (240-2321), hire typewriters and adding machines by the week or year. You can get a small portable or a professional I.B.M. 'golfball' model. Collection and delivery service; Metyclean also repair typewriters and adding machines.

Air Call, 176 Vauxhall Bridge Road, sw1 (834-9000), is a telephone answering service that will pick up your phone and take messages when you're not home and, for an additional fee, 'beep' you by transmitter wherever you are to let you know there is a message waiting. Air Call have a radio telephone service for automobiles.

Ansa Consultants, 4 Sydenham Road, se26 (778-2331), rent telephone answering tape-recording machines by the year (Shipton Autophone brand). The 'Interrogator' model allows you to phone your own number and get any messages on the tape played to you over the phone.

British Monomarks, BM Box 1, WC1 (404-5011). You can conduct your business or private affairs from home or presumably even from jail using facilities available at British Monomarks. They provide private post boxes, a telephone answering service, telex service and registered office facilities in central London.

Party services (see also under Domestic services,
   page 261 and Transport hire, page 273)

This section is divided into children's parties and adult parties but by the very nature of the subject there is considerable overlap.

Children's parties

Partymad, 67 Gloucester Avenue, NW1 (586-0169). Invitations, paper and plastic tableware, streamers, balloons of all sizes, cake decorations, pastry cutters, carnival hats and games. Lots of American imports.

Kensington Carnival, 123 Ifield Road, SW10 (370-4358). Children's party equipment: chairs, benches, tables, tableware, see-saws, slides, and roundabouts. They can also supply party games, gifts, and entertainers from their agency.

Barnum's, 67 Hammersmith Road, W14 (602-1211), are probably the biggest suppliers for children's parties and have an illustrated catalogue to save you a trip. They stock costume hats, balloons, paper lanterns, false noses, moustaches, wigs, papier mâché heads and masks, and can provide party equipment like marquees, platforms, tickets, decorations and gifts.

Theatre Zoo, 28 New Row, WC2 (836-3150), hire animal costumes and masks for kids 3 foot 9 inches tall and over. They also have a number of masks and theatrical costume gear for adults – beards, wigs, party and costume hats.

Gerrards, 85 Royal College Street, NW1 (387-2765),

hire every kind of stuffed animal; also costume two-person horses and cows.

Davenport's, 51 Great Russell Street, WC1 (405-8524), specialize in conjuring tricks, puzzles and jokes.

A. Tomasso, 4A The Broadway, Southgate, N14 (886-4198), rents barrel organs.

BB Film Services, 8 The Rutts, Bushey Heath, Herts. (950-2775), are a friendly and efficient firm who specialize in showing 16 mm children's films – cartoons or full-length features. They bring the film and projector, set it up and run it. They will also hire and show 16 mm feature films to adults.

Norman Meyers, 13 Pennine Drive, NW2 (452-5055). Top children's entertainer and presumably court jester, since he keeps Royal children amused. Mr Meyers will organize the fun and games as well as perform, and can lay on the catering if necessary. Expensive.

Reg Webb, 73 Wimborne Avenue, Hayes, Middlesex (573-1895). A magician and children's entertainer, Mr Webb organizes the games and competitions at parties, then performs in a magic show or with puppets or balloon animals. Dependable and children apparently love him.

Percy Press, 73 Morshead Mansions, Morshead Road, W9 (286-3603), is Britain's outstanding Punch and Judy puppeteer. Mr Press's two sons have joined him in the business and recently the family took Punch and Judy to Japan, and toured where the puppeteer's art is an ancient tradition.

Grown-up parties

Party Planners, 56 Ladbroke Grove, W11 (229-9666), will put together any kind of party, whether it be tea for two or a ball for 2,000. They will come up with ideas about food, drink, entertainment, hire all the necessaries and even address the invitations. Fees are by the hour, not on percentage of money spent.

London At Home, 2A Milner Street, SW3 (584-5650), provide elegant residences in Mayfair and Belgravia for cocktail parties and receptions. The agency will handle the catering if required.

John Edgington, 52 Neate Street, SE5 (703-7055), hires marquees of all types: utilitarian canvas covers or candy-striped, fully-lined tents with floors, carpet and chandeliers.

Hire Service Shops, 192 Campden Hill Road, w8 (727-0897) and branches, hire china, stainless steel and silver cutlery, glassware, serving dishes, large-size kitchen equipment, coffee-jugs and teapots, linen, chairs, tables, coat hangers and coat-racks, hot plates, warming cupboards, cocktail bars, awnings and marquees, chemical toilets, coloured lighting, and barbecues. Collection and delivery service. Free illustrated catalogue.

Searcy's, 136 Brompton Road, sw3 (584-3344), rent elegant locations for parties, plus all catering facilities if needed. They also hire silver, china, glass and temporary staff. Brochures available.

Polar Bear Ice Cubes, 12 Abingdon Road, w8 (937-8998, or at night 352-4054). 24-hour service supplying ice in bags from $2\frac{1}{2}$ to 50 lbs. Delivery within two hours. A bag will sit for about four hours without deterioration.

Nathaniel Berry, 14 City Road, EC1 (606-1784), hire upright or grand pianos. An upright costs about £20 for an evening, including delivery and collection.

Wigmore Hall Studios, 38 Wigmore Street, w1 (935-2265). Bösendorfer grand pianos for concerts at home.

Soutter Electronics, 82 Clapham Park Road, sw4 (622-2843), hire juke boxes. The unobtrusive cabinet model contains 100 45s, while the classic push-button style holds fifty recordings. Discs are programmed according to the style of party: rock, soul, nostalgia, etc.

Juliana's, 7 Kensington Church Court, w8 (937-1555), supply travelling discotheques with two operators: one boy and one girl. Music from the twenties to the latest. The fee is for the length of the party as long as it doesn't last more than one day, and the basic price is around £90. This can come to more with lighting, etc., and considerably more with a 'happening' stmosphere of flashing lights, etc.

Dateline, 23 Abingdon Road, w8 (937-0102). If the party guest list is too short you might try this computer dating service. You fill out a form about yourself, and the computer selects six people of the opposite sex that it knows about and thinks you are most likely to get along with. (Six people will get your name also.) You get in touch and find out if this scientific method can really chart body chemistry. Half-price fees for girls under twenty-six (guess why).

Kenneth Turner, 8 Avery Row, w1 (499-4952). London's leading party florist, whose fanciful arrangements of fresh and/or dried flowers transform dull marquees into stately pleasure domes. [£££]

Pawnbrokers

T. M. Sutton, 156 Victoria Street, sw1 (834-0310). Leading pawnbrokers, specializing in jewellery and silver. Loans are between 35 and 50 per cent of retail value and the interest on loans is 20 per cent per annum. Tickets are valid for six months but clients are notified before loans fall due. Failure to pay up results in confiscation of the goods pawned.

Bosher, 464 Edgware Road, w2 (723-1482), are pawnbrokers who also take furs.

Tattooists

Jock's Tattoo Studio, 287 Pentonville Road, n1 (837-0805), have 3,000 designs on the wall to choose from or you can suggest your own. It takes at least fifteen minutes to get one tattoo and an estimated sixty hours to get your whole body done. Jock says the most common design requested is 'Mom and Dad' in a small heart. Is it painful? That, he says, depends on the condition you're in when you come to get it. The cost is upwards of £1·50.

Tickets

Obtainables, Panton House, 25 Haymarket, SW1 (839-5363), locate hard-to-get tickets for opera and theatre and for football and other sporting events. Expensive

Keith Prowse, Mayfair Hotel, Berkeley Street, W1 (493-4236), and branches,

Abbey Box Office, 27 Victoria Street, SW1 (222-2061), (222-3357 for sports). Both agencies handle most London theatrical and sporting events. Fees are on a sliding scale.

Ibbs and Tillett, 124 Wigmore Street, W1 (486-4021), specialize in musical events. They handle bookings for Glyndebourne, for example.

Transport hire

The following lists the more off-beat forms of transport hire. For car-hire see the Yellow Pages of the telephone directory.

Saviles, 99 Battersea Rise, SW11 (228-4279), is the best place to hire a standard-size three-speed bike. Service and maintenance are first-class. Saviles also sell bikes of all types.

Bicycle Revival, 28 North End Parade, North End Road, W14 (602-4499), and 17 Elizabeth Street, SW1 (730-6716), rent ten-speed touring bikes and small- and large-wheel bikes.

London Transport Private Hire, 11 Grosvenor Place, SW1 (235-5432), will rent you a double-decker bus.

Chelsea Scooters, 504 King's Road, SW10 (351-1679), hire mopeds. Despite the name they no longer hire scooters because of the insurance and licence problems.

Knightsbridge Riding School, 11 Elvaston Mews, SW7 (584-8474), will hire a horse or a landau with one or two horse-power. (See also Riding, page 283.)

Thames Motor Boat, Westminster Pier, SW1 (930-1661), hire launches. The *Princess Frieda* holds sixty to eighty and the *Greenwich Belle* about 250 for a ride or 150 for dancing. April to October.

Jason's Trip, Argonaut Gallery, *opposite* 60 Blomfield Road, w2 (286-3428), hire canopied canal narrow boats in the evenings for trips along the Regent's Canal. They supply catering if required.

London Air Taxi Centre, 18 Eldon Street, EC2 (588-3578), do not own any planes but act as an agency. Tell them where you want to go, how many seats you require and when you have to be there and they will find the best deal.

Rent-A-Copter, 2 Lowndes Street, SW1 (235-6477). Helicopter hire is always expensive.

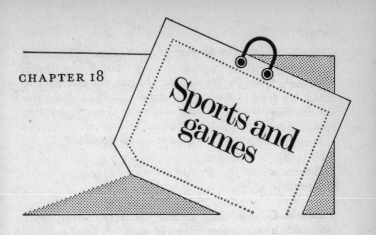

CHAPTER 18

Sports and games

This chapter is divided into sections according to subject. If, however, you wish to browse in a general sports shop, then go to either Lillywhites, Piccadilly Circus, W1 (930-3181) or Harrods 'Olympic Way', fourth floor of the Knightsbridge store (730-1234).

Archery

Note to beginners: archery lessons are available at I.L.E.A. classes and they will provide the necessary equipment. Beginners are strongly advised not to purchase equipment without the advice of an instructor since, to be effective, bows must be fitted according to individual size and ability.

The Archery Centre, 290 High Street, Croydon, Surrey (686-1686), stocks all equipment for archers at any level of experience and the staff are archers themselves and therefore particularly helpful.

D. J. Quick, 11A Stakes Road, Waterlooville, Portsmouth (701-4541), are perhaps the finest archery equipment company in Britain. Though not a London firm they have an excellent mail-order catalogue with sizes carefully detailed for mail order. They make all their own supplies.

County of London Archery Association, 33 Bramwell House, Churchill Gardens, SW1 (405-1720). Lynn Underwood, who runs the Association, will give you the name of your local archery club. For a small membership fee you can use their shooting ground and enter club competitions and other activities. Miss Underwood will answer any queries about archery if you write to her at the above address.

Billiards

Thurston and Co., 1 Sharples Hall Street, NW1 (586-0088), make billiard tables in traditional and contemporary designs. A full-size table with cues and balls costs between £1,700 and £1,800. Snooker balls are extra, and so are erection and delivery. The average delivery time for a new table is six weeks.

John Bennett, 157 Old Kent Road, SE1 (237-4411), sell reconditioned billiard tables and accessories. The cost is about £1,000, and Bennett will also repair tables in London or in the country.

Jeffreys Bros., 291 City Road, EC1 (253-4688), provide reconditioned billiard tables to order. Allow two to three months for completion.

Board games

Just Games, 1 Lower James Street, W1 (734-6124), are specialists in adult games. They present a variety of ways to satisfy the competitive instinct within the confines of the drawing room or stimulate the non-combatant brains in a number of single-minded intrigues. There are chess, backgammon, Japanese Go, Diplomacy and several sophisticated war games that take about sixteen hours to play. Mathematical puzzles and jigsaws of 250 pieces (fine art jigsaws are a speciality) present solemn single challenges. Also Mahjong, tarot cards, collectors' playing cards and ordinary playing cards, miscellaneous board games and some thirty books on games. Broadsheet available on request.

Chess Centre, 3 Harcourt Street, w1 (402-5393). While chess sets can now be bought in most departmental stores, the Centre specializes in them. Traditional and unusual designs in a variety of materials from 50p to £350.

Harrods, Knightsbridge, sw1 (730-1234), have a good range of chess sets, backgammon, card games, etc.

ABP, 68 Lambeth Street, e1 (283-1848), sell casino supplies. These are of a professional standard, and a roulette wheel costs around £400. Baccarat too.

Hamleys, 200 Regent Street, w1 (734-3161), carry most children's games and puzzles. (See also under Toys, Chapter 20.)

Baumkotter, 63A Kensington Church Street, w8 (937-5171), repair quality chess pieces.

Boxing

Lonsdale Sports Equipment, 21 Beak Street, w1 (437-1526). The best source of boxing equipment whether you are a child or professional boxer. (Mohammed Ali and Ken Norton are customers.) Lonsdale stock boxing gloves, sparring gloves and bag gloves (for punching bags) and bags to punch; shorts, dressing gowns, singlets, and punching balls for kids. They also hire and put up rings. Illustrated catalogue.

Camping and climbing

Blacks of Greenock, 53 Rathbone Place, w1 (636-6645), 22 Gray's Inn Road, wc1 (405-4426), and 146 The Grove, Stratford, e15 (534-6547), are *the* people for camping equipment whether you want the comforts of home or the rudiments for roughing it. Blacks' tents range from elaborate trailer models with three bedrooms to simple fly-

sheets and specialist alpine and arctic survival tents. Blacks
sell chemical toilets, sleeping bags, camp furniture, canteens
and mess kits, primus stoves and camping gaz. They have
anoraks for all climates, vinyl storm suits, Bergen and Karri-
mor rucksacks and frames, Bowie knives and Victorinox
pocket knives with seven blades plus tweezers and tooth-
pick: also compasses and insect repellent. Blacks rent tents,
baggage trailers, roof racks, boats and camping accessories
on a daily basis. They make all their tents and sleeping bags.
Fully illustrated catalogue and price list.

Robert Lawrie, 54 Seymour Street, w1 (723-5252). Behind the rather forbidding residential door in Seymour
Street, is one of the friendliest amd most helpful specialty
shops in London. It has an international reputation. Robert
Lawrie is the son of a shoemaker and in his youth learned
the craft himself. His interest in climbing caused him to design proper boots for himself, then for his friends and so on.
Since 1933 he has shod and equipped every Everest expe-
dition, including Hillary's. He even has a glacier named
after him. While Lawrie is an Alpine specialist, he is famous
for boots for all serious walkers and climbers. Boots are
ready-to-wear or made to individual order. Lawrie sells ice
axes, picks, goggles, rucksacks, waterproof wear, crampons,
chocs on wire, pitons – all the things you need to get to the
top. There are books on climbing, and rambling guides to
most areas of the world. Advice is free and any enthusiastic
walker or climber will undoubtedly benefit from a visit to
Mr Lawrie.

Milletts Western, 445 Oxford Street, w1 (491-7381). Inexpensive camping gear: tents, bedrolls, fell boots, sailing
and climbing anoraks and accessories. There are many
branches but the above address has the largest stock of
camping equipment.

Rentatent, Rossendale Street, Upper Clapton, e5
(806-7707), hire camping equipment and sell slightly-used
equipment.

West London Camping Supplies, 84b Lillie Road,
sw6 (385-9922), cater to the needs of tourists travelling by

car or with backpacks: roof racks, rucksacks, lightweight Japanese sleeping bags.

E. Stanford, 12 Long Acre, WC2 (836-1321), the world's largest map shop, has walking scale-maps of Britain and many other countries.

Cricket

En-Tout-Cas, 56 Hamm Moor Lane, Addlestone, Surrey (Weybridge 41129). Although not a London firm, En-Tout-Cas have an excellent mail-order catalogue and stock everything for the cricket ground: scoreboxes and boards, practice netting, sight screens, wicket covers and reflex trainers. They also supply several kinds of artificial cricket surface. Write c/o En-Tout-Cas Ltd, Syston, Leicester for catalogue.

Jack Hobbs, 11A Islington High Street, N1 (837-8611), are well known to cricket enthusiasts for their equipment and clothes. Gray-Nicolls bats. Free catalogue. Football gear when cricket is out of season.

Croquet

Lillywhites, Piccadilly Circus, SW1 (930-3181), and
Harrods, Knightsbridge, SW1 (730-1234), stock a variety of boxed sets, including Jacques, for Association or garden croquet.

Cycling (see also Transport hire, page 273)

Shopertunities, 37 High Holborn, WC1 (242-8961) and 164 Uxbridge Road, W12 (749-1431). Probably the best place in London to buy small-wheel, one-gear bikes. There is a brake for each wheel and the bike folds into a suitcase size. Unbeatable price. Mail order from Uxbridge branch.

Saviles, 99 Battersea Rise, SW11 (228-4279). Excellent

selection of bikes, both standard and small-wheel types. Bicycle attachments such as baskets, lights and locks. Complete servicing.

Bell Street Bikes, Basement, 95 Bell Street, NW1, sell and hire bikes and do bicycle repairs.

Tandem Centre, 281 Old Kent Road, SE1 (231-1641), specialize in the sale and hire of tandem bicycles, but they also sell other bikes, both English and imported models. Repairs and spare parts available.

Fencing

Leon Paul, 14 New North Street, WC1 (405-3832), are the only manufacturers of fencing equipment in Great Britain. They sell their own foils, masks, jackets, gloves and special German-made fencing shoes at the above address and are happy to advise beginners.

Amateur Fencing Association, 83 Perham Road, W14 (385-7442), will give you the name of the fencing club nearest you. Fencing lessons are available through the I.L.E.A.

Fishing

Hardy, 61 Pall Mall, SW1 (930-7577), are known the world over for fishing tackle. Their reputation, supreme in game fishing, has now extended to sea fishing and coarse fishing. Hardy's make all their own equipment and visiting Americans are usually surprised to find that it is not all that expensive. Most rods are fibreglass but split bamboo can be ordered if you are prepared to wait. There has been some difficulty getting cane recently. Segmented rods now have special carbon fibre reinforced ferrules for additional strength. There are spinning and sea fishing tackle, lures, flies, gaffs, nets, etc. Hardy reckon there is almost no area in the world which they can't advise you about, and provide you with the best equipment for. Like all the really first-class places, they are polite, helpful and know their stuff. Complete, illustrated catalogue on request. [££+]

Farlow, 5B Pall Mall, SW1 (839-2423), sell their own line of high-quality fishing tackle and also A.B.U. equipment. Their impregnated split cane salmon rods are more expensive than Hardy's but there is a range of more moderately priced goods as well. Farlow carry a complete line of tackle and silks and feathers for tying flies. They also sell fish smokers and fishing clothes. Complete catalogue. [££+]

Woolworth's, 311 Oxford Street, W1 (629-8611), and branches everywhere. If you want a rod for a child or just something adequate to catch a fish on, Hardy's recommend Woolworth's low-priced rod and reel kit. [£]

Gerry's of Wimbledon, 170 The Broadway, SW19 (542-7792), is one of the biggest tackle shops in Britain and stocks all grades of equipment for all kinds of fishing. (Coarse fishing is the biggest category.) Live bait, a big catalogue. [££]

London Anglers Association, 183 Hoe Street, Walthamstow, E17 (520-7477). There are over 600 clubs affiliated with this association and members of them are entitled to use, for no additional fee, the 250 miles of water the Association owns. This is almost entirely coarse fishing. You can join the Association on an individual basis as well as through a club.

The Field, 8 Stratton Street, W1 (499-7881), publish a book called *Where to Fish* which lists all the rivers and major lakes in Britain and Ireland, giving details of fishing, including costs, accommodation, how to reserve and when the season is.

Football

Sport Drobny, 33 Thurloe Place, SW7 (581-2934). Balls for rugby and soccer, and football shoes and clothes.

En-Tout-Cas, 56 Hamm Moor Lane, Addlestone, Surrey

(Weybridge 41129). Equipment for Association, Junior and Five-a-side football: goal posts, nets, corner poles and flags. Illustrated catalogue 25p from En-Tout-Cas Ltd, Syston, Leicester.

Golf

Lillywhites, Piccadilly Circus, sw1 (930-3181). Excellent stock of golfing equipment and clothes including Spalding, MacGregor and Dunlop clubs. Golf shoes, golf umbrellas, shooting sticks, golf bags and Slazenger golfing clothes.

Harrods, Knightsbridge, sw1 (730-1234), have a good golf shop with staff who can advise you.

Leslie King Golf School, 47 Lowndes Square, sw1 (235-2468). Golf instruction at all levels.

Simpsons, 203 Piccadilly, w1 (734-2002), have a golf shop in the basement with clubs priced from about £100 to the American 'Ping' set at three times that price. All accessories.

Golf Gear, 40 Wellington Street, wc2 (836-6514), is a new shop specializing entirely in golf equipment and golf wear. Clubs by most leading manufacturers are in stock including hard-to-get ladies' left-handed clubs. Price list on request.

Hunting (see Riding, page 283)

Net games

En-Tout-Cas, 56 Hamm Moor Lane, Addlestone, Surrey (Weybridge 41129). It is not a London firm, but En-Tout-Cas has one of the most prolific mail-order sporting catalogues (25p). They are the world's largest builders of hard tennis courts and sell all tennis equipment. They have a 'tennis trainer' machine and a 'coacher', and their own make of rackets and balls. They also have badminton courts and equipment for basketball, netball, and volleyball. Write to En-Tous-Cas Ltd, Syston, Leicester for catalogue.

Lillywhites, Piccadilly Circus, sw 1 (930-3180), carry several makes of tennis rackets: Wilson, Dunlop, Slazenger, Donnay, etc. They have an expert on duty in the shop and run a twenty-four-hour re-stringing service with seven different qualities of string. Lillywhites will have your favourite racket copied or a special racket made for you by a leading manufacturer. Tennis clothes for men, women and children, and equipment for other net games including badminton and volleyball; also squash.

Sport Drobny, 33 Thurloe Place, sw 7 (581-2934). Tennis clothes and shoes for men and women and 'Alligator' shirts. Also ping-pong tables and squash and tennis rackets. (Drobny won at Wimbledon in 1954.)

Lowes, 173 Sloane Street, sw 1 (235-8484), is another good place for tennis clothes and equipment.

Riding

Gidden's, 15D Clifford Street, w 1 (734-2788), is a favourite of many of the horsey set including, presumably, the Queen since they hold the Royal Warrant for saddles. Gidden's have their own workshops and make most of their tack themselves. They can copy an item, make a special size or do a custom design. They recently equipped the personal household cavalry of an oil sheikh but if you just want a halter adjusted, they'll do that too. Gidden's off-the-peg riding wear is not particularly expensive and they stock a French moulded rubber boot that is almost indistinguishable from leather and costs only £15. Mail-order catalogue sent on request: you pay the postage and if you make a purchase the catalogue postage is deducted. [££+]

Moss Bros., Bedford Street, wc 2 (240-4567), have the most comprehensive stock of riding wear for men, women and children: jodphurs, breeches, hacking jackets and the usual gear plus pink coats and pink tailcoats, tattersall waistcoats, hunt shirts, stocks and polo necks, riding boots and a small supply of secondhand wear. They stock all the basic tack, and will hire riding clothes but point out that the chance of tear in wear makes it expensive. [££, ££+]

Austin Reed, 103 Regent Street, w1 (734-6789), have a large department of Harry Hall riding wear for men, women and children, some tack, and a good selection of hacking jackets, ready-made boots, hunting caps, etc. [££, ££+]

Huntsman, 11 Savile Row, w1 (734-7441), are the world's premier makers of bespoke riding clothes for men and women. Huntsman have been breeches makers since the eighteenth century, and are the only people left who can clean pink coats properly. (For more details see Men's clothes, page 99.) [£££]

Maxwell's, 177 New Bond Street, w1 (493-1097), make the world's finest riding boots. They are all hand-made and hand-lasted and take at least a year to get. The cost of a pair of boots with trees is in the region of £200. Maxwell's were spurriers in the eighteenth century and still stock a variety of spurs. (Not inappropriately, Huntsman and Maxwell now have joint ownership.) [£££]

Swaine, Adeney, Brigg and Sons, 185 Piccadilly, w1 (734-4277), whipmakers to the Queen, sell riding crops and whips, hunting and coach horns, spurs, bits, riding wear and tack; also sundries like curry combs, blankets, and neat's-foot oil. Catalogue on request. [££+]

George Parker, 12 Upper St Martin's Lane, wc2 (836-1164). Lodged in narrow, rickety showrooms smelling of leather and saddlesoap, Parker's sell everything for horses but are famous for saddles and polo sticks (they took over Holbrows). Nearly all saddles are their own make and many are custom-made. There is a twelve-month waiting list for their most famous model, the Toptani (from £120). They also carry the Barnsby saddle. Parker's will make saddles in any style: side saddles, army, Western, etc. They also stock secondhand saddles and have boots and caps on sale or to order. A hand-made ready-to-wear boot made on Maxwell lasts costs around £55. Free catalogue. [££+]

Bathurst Riding Stables, 63 Bathurst Mews, w2 (723-2813), hire horses for riding in Hyde Park and give lessons in both riding, and stable management. The horses are working hunter types and all rides are accompanied. Bathurst lend out boots if you aren't equipped and can get into what they have. They also sell secondhand riding clothes when they can get them.

Knightsbridge Riding School, 11 Elvaston Mews, sw7 (584-8474), hire horses for hacking in the park and board horses when they have room.

J. A. Allen, 1 Lower Grosvenor Place, sw1 (834-5606), is a bookshop specializing exclusively in the subject of horses. Allen's publish a good many of the books themselves, notably *Bailey's Hunting Directory* which lists all the hunts in Britain and France – fox, stag, beagling, etc. – and gives names of masters and hunt secretaries, subscription fees, and other details. It costs about £6.

Shooting

Purdey, 57 South Audley Street, w1 (499-1801). There is not much to see if you wander into Purdey's, and they look a bit surprised to see you if you do. Two giant water buffalo and one sable head adorn the walls and there is a display case containing one finished gun and examples of it in all stages of construction. Purdey's make about 100 of these guns a year. They are, and have been for over a century, the quintessential name in sporting shotguns. All their models are entirely handcrafted; the stocks are cut from carefully-selected French walnut and each gun is made to fit the size and specifications of its owner. The present waiting period for a Purdey gun is about three and a half years and looks like getting longer. The price for a pair of side-by-side shotguns is £11,000 and up. Over-and-unders cost £6,000 each. A secondhand Purdey sells for even more at auction because it can not only be delivered at once, but also, being one of a kind, is a collector's item. [£££]

Holland and Holland, 13 Bruton Street, w1 (499-4411), are gunmakers of the same stature as Purdey (above). In fact, among the top three or four gunsmiths in London the only real difference is one of personal preference. Quality and workmanship are equally fine. Holland and Holland make double barrel (side-by-side) shotguns and rifles. They also make trap guns, mostly for Americans. Holland and Holland turn out less than 100 guns a year and there is a five-year waiting period for new orders. This means they cannot tell you what the gun will cost by the time it's finished. You pay a £1,000 deposit when you place your order. Then, in about three years when they get round to starting on it they will let you know what they estimate it's going to cost. You can decide to go ahead or to get your deposit back. Holland and Holland have a few secondhand guns of their own make and other quality English makes which they will re-fit to a new owner; but don't expect them to be any less expensive. The firm have their own shooting grounds outside London where clients arrive, they say, by helicopter, Bentley and (once) a motorcycle, to practise or learn. [£££]

Churchill, Atkin, Grant and Lang, 61 Pall Mall, sw1 (839-5515), make only fifty guns a year but they have a good supply, comparatively speaking, of their own and other top-quality secondhand shotguns and rifles. There is a waiting period of between six months and three years for a new gun. The cost of a twelve-bore shotgun is roughly between £1,000 and £5,000. Churchill also sell gun boots, jackets, heavy socks, etc. The staff are helpful and polite, and wear white dusters. (At Purdey they wear ordinary suits and at Holland and Holland, striped trousers, which, no doubt, says something.) [£££]

Boss, 13 Cork Street, w1 (493-0711), make top-quality shotguns. Like most London gunsmiths about 60 per cent of their business is overseas. At Boss there is a three-year waiting period and prices are currently running around

£5,000 each for a side-by-side twelve-bore shotgun. (They don't make rifles any more.) [£££]

John Rigby, 13 Pall Mall, sw1 (734-7611), are famous for stalking and big game rifles. Some models are in stock, others take up to a year to get. Prices start around £450 but Rigby's ·416 calibre big game rifle is around £1,600. [££+]

Cogswell and Harrison, 168 Piccadilly, w1 (493-4746), sell shooting supplies of all types and qualities. Shotguns cost from £100. They have automatic pistols, revolvers, air guns, even sub-machine guns for sale to governments only(?); plus gun oil, whistles, decoys and the usual accessories. Cogswell and Harrison also do repairs. To buy a pistol you must have a licence. This means getting an application from the police, shooting regularly with a club for at least six months, getting them to endorse the application and then returning the form to the police who do a security check and decide whether to issue a licence. Each weapon you possess must be registered on the licence. [££, ££+]

British Field Sports Society, 26 Caxton Street, sw1 (222-5407), is a sort of lobby for the prevention of cruelty to sportsmen. They preserve and protect field sports and therefore they can also tell you what shooting is available to rent but are reluctant to do so since they don't want a lot of outsiders or foreigners shooting up the game or, worse, driving up the cost of it. Pretend you haven't been able to get your usual moor this year.

Strutt and Parker, 13 Hill Street, w1 (629-7282), are agents for sporting estates, largely in Scotland, which can be leased by the week, season or for longer. Pheasant and grouse shooting, stalking, and salmon and trout fishing with or without accommodation. The rights are normally let several months in advance, for instance, August grouse shooting at Christmas. Write for details, giving some idea of what you want and when.

West London Shooting Grounds, West End Road, Northolt, Middlesex (845-1377). This is primarily a shotgun practice and training ground. Lessons are available and they will lend you a gun for them if you don't have one.

Tropiccadilly, Airey and Wheeler, 44 Piccadilly, w 1 (734-8616). Safari wear has changed a great deal in the past few years but traditional bush jackets, walking shorts, desert boots, and khakis made-to-measure or off-the-peg, are still available at Tropiccadilly. Latest drip-dry items too. (See also *Alkit* under Men's clothes, page 109.)

Rowland Ward, Crawley Road, Wood Green, N22 (889-6433), are taxidermists with an international reputation for big game trophies. They have a branch in Nairobi but all skins are sent to London for preparation. They also stuff fish, fox masks and other game. No pets.

Skiing

Pindisports, 14 Holborn, EC1 (242-3278), 13 Brompton Arcade, sw3 (584-2464), and other branches, have been official suppliers to every Olympic ski team since 1962 but they are equally reputable as family outfitters. Anoraks, salopettes and ski trousers, boots for all grades of skiiers, and French, American and Austrian skiis. Illustrated catalogue. [££+]

The Ski Shop, 158 Notting Hill Gate, w11 (229-8228), a particularly helpful shop with everything for skiing, stocks inexpensive Scandinavian ski wear and more pricey French and Italian clothes The equipment department is run by ex-racers and instructors who are able to give reliable advice. The shop favours French skis and Italian boots. All boots are preheated inside before being tried on in an attempt to simulate body heat generated while skiing. There is a ski reconditioning and checking service. Other notables are grass skis for summer skiing and all-in-one outfits for children. [££, ££+]

Ski Mart, 227 Ebury Street, sw1 (730-2322), part of the Weekend Ski Club, sells secondhand skis, bindings and sticks at considerable reductions [£+]

Alpine Sports, 309 Brompton Road, sw3 (584-2543), are reliable specialists in skiwear and ski equipment. They produce an illustrated catalogue and carry, among other things, Head ski clothes. [£, ££]

Lillywhites, Piccadilly, sw1 (930-3181), have a good winter ski shop and a water ski shop with wetsuits, snorkels, masks and fins, surfboards and under-water gear. Advice is available in both departments. [££]

Trophies

Len Fowler, 78B Neal Street, wc2 (836-6120), sell sporting prizes and presentation trophies for any kind of event: plaques or standing trophies in silver or chrome or made from your own drawings.

Water sports

Thames Water Sports, 179 Fulham Palace Road, w6 (381-0558), is *the* place for diving gear on an amateur or professional level – everything from compressed air to decompression chambers. Thames Water Sports sell wetsuits, under-water-fishing equipment and several makes of tanks, but La Spirotechnique is the predominant brand. They also make wetsuits to measure and repair gear.

British Sub Aqua Club, 70 Brompton Road, sw3 (584-7163). If you want to dive with tanks you should learn at the Sub Aqua Club's classes. In order to hire equipment in most places, particularly abroad, you must produce your Sub Aqua membership card and log book. You begin classes in a swimming pool with snorkel, mask and fins which you must provide. When you get to the tank stage the club will often lend you equipment, but most people have their own by this time. Write to the above address for the location of the club nearest to you.

Sportsways, 185 Fulham Palace Road, w6 (385-4874), sell under-water cameras and watches, life jackets, diving apparel, diving equipment and spear guns.

Lillywhites, Piccadilly, sw1 (930-3181). Water-skis by several manufacturers, also swimming rings and armbands for children.

Yachting

Captain O. M. Watts, 48 Albemarle Street, w1 (493-4633). Captain Watts is the favourite yachting establishment of many sailing enthusiasts. The premises are chock-a-block with compasses, sextants, rope, ship's bells, pulleys, bilge pumps and a vast array of miscellaneous ship chandlery, sailing handbooks, sailing lore and sailing charts. In the basement are life jackets and sailing wear for men, women and children. Watts also act as a yacht agency. Catalogues.

Arthur Beale, 194 Shaftesbury Avenue, wc2 (836-9043), started as rope makers on the Fleet river 400 years ago. The Fleet river still flows (beneath what is now Fleet Street), and Beale's still make rope, but nowadays they sell other chandlery supplies too: marine paints, deck varnish, stainless steel and brass nuts and bolts, copper nails, oil lamps, and spare glass chimneys. They are one of the few London stockists of wire rope and have a wire splicing and rigging service. Upstairs are charts of British coastal and inland waterways, international code flags, Union Jacks and some sailing wear.

Jack Holt, The Embankment, Putney, sw15 (788-9255), make sails, spars, dinghys and riders. They are designers, builders and chandlers but stock some sailing wear including sailing wetsuits. Comprehensive catalogue.

Russell and Chapple, 23 Monmouth Street, wc2 (836-7521), specialize in fitted canvas boat covers. These are made to order and take about six weeks.

London Yacht Centre, 13 Artillery Lane, e1 (247-0521), by Liverpool Street Station, sells everything for sailing yachts except sails. Catalogue available.

London Dinghy Centre, 232 Hithergreen Lane, se13 (318-1848). Sailing dinghys from eight to seventeen feet long for family entertainment or racing. Most are fibreglass, some wood, some composite. The Centre stock Enterprise, Wayfarer, Pacer, Gull and other makes, and have a sail trainer – a device which hooks the boat to a computer – enabling them to give lessons *in situ* up to Royal Yacht Association level.

Churchill Motor Cruiser School, 71 Oxford Street, W1 (734-2717), operate a weekend and a five-day course in boat-handling, navigation and seamanship. The course begins at Chichester and pupils live on the boat and cruise along the south coast. At the end of a five-day course they say a beginner ought to be able to pass the R.Y.A.'s tests grade one and two and be able to take a boat to France.

Boat Showrooms of London, 286 Kensington High Street, W14 (602-0123), sell mainly motor boats, from twelve-foot ski-boats to twenty-five-foot weekend cruisers. They stock engines by Mercury, Johnson, Evinrude and Volvo Penta. Boat repairs are done from their workshops in Pimlico Wharf. They are also general stockists of chandlery and some sub aqua gear.

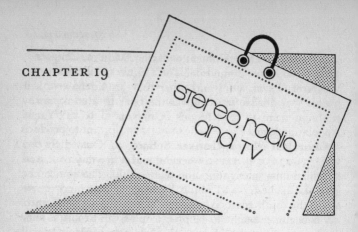

CHAPTER 19

Discounted goods are a well-known feature of the world of sound, but while they are undoubtedly money-saving you have to go to the trouble of finding both the item you want and the best price you can get it for. This can be time-consuming. You must also be prepared for drawbacks regarding servicing, for even though you get a year's guarantee on any item no matter where you buy it, discount house servicing facilities can be agonizingly slow and frustrating, and if new merchandise is faulty you may have to wait a long time before it is replaced. Furthermore, you often have to get further repairs done on your own after the guarantee has expired. For reasons such as these many people prefer to buy from firms where good, fast service is assured and, in the case of television, to rent sets because the rental normally includes a same-day repair service.

All the discount houses listed in Chapter 10 sell radio, television and hi fi equipment, and potential buyers are also advised to read the chapter's introduction to buying by discount. For browsing and shopping for sound equipment and television, discount or otherwise, try the Oxford Street end of Tottenham Court Road, and the Marble Arch end of the Edgware Road. These are London's electronics kingdoms and they have numerous shops selling hi fi equipment, radios and televisions.

For used and secondhand goods, see Auctions, Chapter 2, particularly Harrods and Bonham's Chelsea Galleries.

Thomas Heinitz, 32 Moscow Road, w2 (229-2077), is the doyen of hi fi music. His is an owner-operated company and Mr Heinitz stresses that it is not geared to 'hi fi for hi fi's sake', but seeks to provide the best equipment to produce the sound of music in whatever price range customers can afford. Heinitz is not snobby about lavish equipment and recommends units from £100. (A good, general purpose unit, says Mr Heinitz, is the Yamaha 'Music Centre', to which a variety of good speakers can be attached.) Heinitz services and installs all equipment and if your room is very large or presents special acoustic problems, Mr Heinitz will visit you and recommend a solution. The firm has a big stock of classical recordings, and customers who buy equipment get 20 per cent off on all record purchases up to the cost of the equipment they buy. Heinitz also has stereo recitals every Saturday afternoon (see page 256 for details). [££, £££]

Imhof's, 112 New Oxford Street, wc1 (636-7878). Like Heinitz, Imhof's concentrate on quality and service. They have a very large range of equipment on three floors, including demonstration facilities. Imhof's do a big export business and have installed equipment as far afield as the kingdom of Nepal, but normally service and installation are within a thirty-five-mile radius of London. Complete units with speakers are available for under £100 or you can pay £800 for a unit with a built-in tape deck. [££, £££]

Laskys, 481 Oxford Street, w1 (493-8641), and branches, sell most well-known brands of hi fi, radio and television equipment and many are considerably discounted. Year's guarantee on parts and service and they have their own servicing department. If Laskys have the equipment you want then you will probably get it there for less than you would elsewhere. [££]

Henry's Radio, 404 Edgware Road, w2 (723-1008), and other addresses. Recommended for do-it-yourself hi fi and radio equipment and for other electronic components such as bird warblers and radio control equipment. Henry's sell parts and published designs. Mail-order catalogue. [££]

Chelsea Car Stereo Centre, 559 King's Road, sw6 (736-8351), sell, install and repair radios and stereo cassettes or 8-track players for automobiles. Quadraphonic sound, too. Prices from about £50. [££]

Zarach, 183 Sloane Street, sw1 (235-6146), stock a small range of televisions elegantly housed in perspex globes with chrome or brass bases. Models are by Grundig or Sony but have been completely stripped down and reassembled in specially-designed casings. 12-inch to 26-inch screen sizes in black and white or colour. Remote control models available, one of which comes down through the ceiling and costs about £1,400. [£££]

Television rental and repair

If you rent a television you are supposed to buy a licence from the Post Office just as if you had bought a set. All rentals are, by law, reported to the Post Office by the lessor. This presents a special difficulty with short-term rentals because licences are issued on a yearly basis only and the result is that short-term licences are usually ignored by all parties concerned.

Several companies rent black and white and colour televisions (colour licences cost a lot more), and the shortlist of firms below provides a wide range of brands and screen sizes. Minimum rental is generally for one year. All have quick servicing facilities.

British Relay TV, at Selfridges, Oxford Street, w1 (629-1234), and several branches in and around London.

Granada TV Rental, 39 Camden High Street, nw1 (387-2358), and

Redfern, 798 Holloway Road, n19 (272-2183), and, for servicing, (272-7551).

Colour Centre, 64 Edgware Road, w2 (723-4036), specialize in short-term television rentals. Minimum is one week. Wide range of colour models and a 14-inch portable black and white model. Same-day repairs except on Sunday. Long-term rentals, too.

South Kensington Radio and TV Service, 30 Thurloe Street, sw7 (589-0377), will repair most brands of televisions and radios, but you must bring them to the shop. There is no delivery or collection service. Two or three days is normal repair time unless special parts have to be ordered.

CHAPTER 20

*see also under
Clothes, Chapter 4;
Crafts, Chapter 5
and Sports and
games,
Chapter 18*

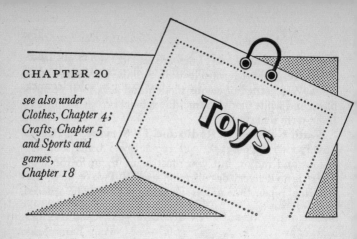

Hamleys, 200 Regent Street, W 1 (734-3161). Six floors and an annexe stuffed full of games, toys, sporting equipment and child distractors of all sorts. There are costume dolls, models, cricket bats, stuffed toys, go-cars, craft kits, and chemistry sets – enough to give anyone who has to buy a gift for a child plenty of ideas. Catalogue. [££, ££+]

Pollock's Toy Museum, 1 Scala Street, W 1 (636-3452), is both a museum and a toy shop. Housed in a rickety building that is like a doll's house itself are exhibitions of dolls and toys of several nations. In the basement is a mock-up of the workshop of the late Mr Pollock, last of the toy theatre publishers. His paper cut-outs, black and white or hand-coloured, were the original of the familiar phrase 'penny plain, twopence coloured'. Toy theatres and plays are still the things Pollock's are famous for but there are other nostalgic toys that will catch the hearts of parents as much as children: jumping jacks, marbles, peg doll kits, kaleidoscopes, paper dolls, rag puppets to make, wooden yoyos and tops, flower presses and reproduction wooden dolls. You don't need a child in tow to enjoy Pollock's. [£+]

Tridias, 44 Monmouth Street, WC2 (240-2369), is the favourite toyshop of many grown ups and, presumably, their offspring. Tridias occupies premises once used by Pollock's (above) and the cosy atmosphere is reminiscent of

Pollock's. The majority of toys on the two floors are traditional in character: wooden hobby horses, Raggedy Ann
and Andy, unpainted doll's houses of considerable elegance,
doll's house furniture, and appealing soft toys. There is a
room of games and puzzles. Another speciality are Sasha
dolls with huge wardrobes. [££+]

James Galt, 30 Great Marlborough Street, w1
(734-0829), on the corner of Carnaby Street, are educational
toy specialists who manufacture their own toys. Galt toys
are fun as well as 'educational' and are distinguished for
the simplicity of their design. They include things for jumping, climbing and swinging on, building blocks and bricks,
inexpensive doll's houses, child-sized string hammocks,
paints in big economy sizes and buckets of modelling clay,
an excellent tool kit, cut-out models of famous buildings,
stuffed animals with definite personalities and lots of things
to make. [££]

Abbatt, 74 Wigmore Street, w1 (487-4382). Abbatt's
own brand of educational toys – unpainted wooden toys,
interlocking letters and jigsaws – are much sought after.
The store concentrates on children eight years and under,
and their sand trays, climbing frames and building blocks
make learning fun. [££]

Julip Model Horses, 18 Beauchamp Place, sw3
(589-0867), is a useful channel for youthful horse passions.
Julip sell hand-made model horses and ponies of solid
moulded rubber. There are twenty-five breeds with individual markings, but that is only the beginning: these horses
are meant to be played with (like dolls) in mimicry of the
real thing. There are stables, blankets, leather tack, even
oats to feed them. You can collect a racing stable, a string
of polo ponies or a pet animal. Models are about £2·50
each but the accessories can add up. [££]

Collet's Chinese Gallery, 40 Great Russell Street, wc1
(580-7538), sell Chinese kites in a variety of bird shapes.
Most are paper, a few are silk. Catalogue on request.
[£+]

Homebound Craftsmen, 25A Holland Street, w8

(937-3924). Soft toys for infants made by the old and disabled and sold at reasonable prices. [£+]

Davenports, 51 Great Russell Street, WC1 (405-8524), is a practical jokers' paradise. Davenports specialize in all sorts of 'jokes', puzzles and conjuring tricks. [£+]

Laffeaty's, 345 King's Road, SW3 (352-2705), is a good, general toyshop for boys and girls. [££]

The Doll's House, 4 Broadley Street, NW8 (723-1418), is more a place for collectors than children. It sells antique and reproduction doll's houses ranging in price from £8 to £300 and hand-made reproduction furniture. There are *petit point* cushions of 1,000 stitches the size of a postage stamp, and miniature dolls too. Most of Mrs Hunt's stock is too nice to turn children loose on. [£££]

Anabel Bartlett, 46 Brondesbury Road, NW6 (328-6218), is a craftswoman who makes miniature furniture of her own design. It is expensive and designed to be played with by grown-ups rather than children. [£££]

170 Children can dial this number after 6 p.m. and hear a bedtime story.

Index

accessories, fashion, 81, 89, 91–2, 137

accommodation, information on, 266–7

advice services, 197–8, 266–7

Africa: antiquities, 28; art, 37; books, 73; music, 258

air transport, hire of, 274

alligators, 225

aluminium, 189; casting, 129; frames, 253–4

amber, 42

ancestors, tracing of, 260

animals: boarding, 228; funerals, 229; hire, 228; medical care, 229–30; photography, 229; portraits, 229; stuffed, 228, 288; training, 228–9; *see also specific types*

antiques, 21–50; auctions, 60–66; packing and shipping, 59; repairs, 51–9; *see also specific countries, materials, types*

aquaria, 226

archery, 275–6

architectural decorations, 27–8, 185–90; repairs, 51, 54

architecture, books on, 72

arms and armour, 29, 45, 123; auctions, 62–3, 65; books, 123–4

art: auctions, 62–6; books, 71–2; classes, 254; reproductions, 251–2; talks and discussions, 244; *see also* drawings, paintings, *etc., and specific areas and countries*

art deco, 26, 29–30, 43, 188; auctions, 63

artists' materials, 116–17

art nouveau, 26, 29–30, 41, 43, 49, 188; auctions, 63

Asia: books, 71–3; music, 256–7; paint brushes, 117; silk, 133;

see also carpets, costumes, furniture, Oriental art

auctions, 50, 60–66

au pair services, 262–3

autographs, 30

baby equipment, 112–13, 220; hire, 113; *see also* nappies

babysitting and childminding services, 261–4

backgammon, 276–7

ballet, 172–3

balsa wood, 123

bamboo furniture, 40, 212

barometers, 35; repairs, 53

barrel organs, hire of, 270

baskets, 209–10, 215; materials for weaving, 117

bathrooms: design service, 201; fixtures, 193, 199–201; *see also* linen

baths, *see* sauna, Turkish

batik, 119

beads, 120, 136

beauty treatments, 168–71, 173; *see also* facials

bedrooms, planning service for, 210

beds, 40, 198, 202–3, 210–11; advice, 203; brass, repairs, 54, 56; *see also* linen

bees, 227; books, 227

bicycles, 273, 279–80; hire, 273, 280; repairs, 280

billiards, 276

birds, 225–6

blinds, 134, 192

boats, 290–91; books, 290; classes, 291; covers, 290; hire, 273–4, 290; yachts, 290–91

bonsai, 141, 146

More about Penguins and Pelicans

The Penguin Guide to London

F. R. Banks

A reliable and comprehensive guide to the first city of
Europe.

Completely revised and up to date, *The Penguin Guide to
London* gives full information about transport,
accommodation, entertainments, sport, and shopping,
with full details of all places of interest, from Buckingham
Palace, St Paul's Cathedral, Westminster Abbey, the
Houses of Parliament and the British Museum to
Hampstead, Soho and the Zoo.

A Cockney Camera

Gordon Winter

'Vividly reflects the different facets of London society'
– *Sunday Telegraph*

Following the tradition of *A Country Camera* (see below), Gordon Winter has compiled this magnificent collection of photographs to illustrate the life of London in Victorian and Edwardian times. The result is a spectacular record of the life of the city, from the grace and elegance of Holland Park and Wimbledon to the grime and penury of the East End. Since these photographs were taken, parts of London have changed beyond recognition and this collection shows how all-embracing the changes of the last seventy years have been.

'Here are street traders, a Sunday school procession, the last herd of cows in Putney, the Clapham omnibus, pubs, Derby day and slums, accurately and perceptively captioned' – *Economist*

A Country Camera

Gordon Winter

One hundred and fifty photographs depict, as no written record could, what life in the English countryside was really like between 1844 and 1914.

The result is a piece of social history, a portrait gallery of the sturdy countrymen and countrywomen who made their lives in the villages and market-towns of rural England.

'Mr Winter is never sentimental, but wittily and endearingly conjures up life in the country in that era which ended with the First World War' – Cecil Beaton in *Punch*